Assessing Children with Specific Learning Difficulties

This comprehensive book provides all the information that practitioners need to know about assessment in relation to their pupils with Specific Learning Difficulties. The why, how and what of assessment is addressed, whilst the link between assessment and intervention is also a key focus.

Looking at the full range of Specific Learning Difficulties, this book provides practical guidance on implementing strategies that are tried and tested for use in any classroom, whilst also acknowledging that assessment is a process involving other professionals and parents. Addressing issues and topics common in inclusive classrooms around the world, key topics covered include:

- Specific Learning Difficulties in context
- Teacher Assessment in literacy, numeracy and movement
- Motor development and co-ordination
- Attention factors in learning
- The key issues on learning differences
- Self-esteem and emotional literacy
- How to enhance skills and the self-sufficiency of teachers.

Assessing Children with Specific Learning Difficulties will be an invaluable guide for classroom teachers, learning support departments, psychologists and other professionals.

Gavin Reid is a fully registered Psychologist with the Health and Care Professions Council (HCPC) in the UK and the College of Psychologists in British Columbia, Canada.

Gad Elbeheri is the Dean of the Australian College of Kuwait; a university providing internationally recognized and accredited tertiary education to the Business and Engineering sectors.

John Everatt is a Professor of Education at the University of Canterbury, New Zealand.

nasen is a professional membership association that supports all those who work with or care for children and young people with special and additional educational needs. Members include teachers, teaching assistants, support workers, other educationalists, students and parents.

nasen supports its members through policy documents, journals, its magazine Special!, publications, professional development courses, regional networks and newsletters. Its website contains more current information such as responses to government consultations. **nasen's** published documents are held in very high regard both in the UK and internationally.

Other titles published in association with the National Association for Special Educational Needs (nasen):

Language for Learning in the Secondary School: A practical guide for supporting students with speech, language and communication needs
Sue Hayden and Emma Jordan
2012/pb: 978-0-415-61975-2

Using Playful Practice to Communicate with Special Children
Margaret Corke
2012/pb: 978-0-415-68767-6

The Equality Act for Educational Professionals: A simple guide to disability and inclusion in schools
Geraldine Hills
2012/pb: 978-0-415-68768-3

More Trouble with Maths: A teacher's complete guide to identifying and diagnosing mathematical difficulties
Steve Chinn
2012/pb: 978-0-415-67013-5

Dyslexia and Inclusion: Classroom Approaches for Assessment, Teaching and Learning, 2ed
Gavin Reid
2012/pb: 978-0-415-60758-2

Promoting and Delivering School-to-School Support for Special Educational Needs: A practical guide for SENCOs
Rita Cheminais
2013/pb 978-0-415-63370-3

Time to Talk: Implementing outstanding practice in speech, language and communication
Jean Gross
2013/pb: 978-0-415-63334-5

Curricula for Teaching Children and Young People with Severe or Profound and Multiple Learning Difficulties: Practical strategies for educational professionals
Peter Imray and Viv Hinchcliffe
2013/pb: 978-0-415-83847-4

Successfully Managing ADHD: A handbook for SENCOs and teachers
Fintan O'Regan
2014/pb: 978-0-415-59770-8

Brilliant Ideas for Using ICT in the Inclusive Classroom, 2ed
Sally McKeown and Angela McGlashon
2015/pb: 978-1-138-80902-4

Boosting Learning in the Primary Classroom: Occupational therapy strategies that really work with pupils
Sheilagh Blyth
2015/pb: 978-1-13-882678-6

Beating Bureaucracy in Special Educational Needs, 3ed
Jean Gross
2015/pb: 978-1-138-89171-5

Transforming Reading Skills in the Secondary School: Simple strategies for improving literacy
Pat Guy
2015/pb: 978-1-138-89272-9

Supporting Children with Speech and Language Difficulties, 2ed
Cathy Allenby, Judith Fearon-Wilson, Sally Merrison and Elizabeth Morling
2015/pb: 978-1-138-85511-3

Supporting Children with Dyspraxia and Motor Co-ordination Difficulties, 2ed
Susan Coulter, Lesley Kynman, Elizabeth Morling, Rob Grayson and Jill Wing
2015/pb: 978-1-138-85507-6

Developing Memory Skills in the Primary Classroom: A complete programme for all
Gill Davies
2015/pb: 978-1-138-89262-0

Language for Learning in the Primary School: A practical guide for supporting pupils with language and communication difficulties across the curriculum, 2ed
Sue Hayden and Emma Jordan
2015/pb: 978-1-138-89862-2

Supporting Children with Autistic Spectrum Disorders, 2ed
Elizabeth Morling and Colleen O'Connell
2016/pb: 978-1-138-85514-4

Understanding and Supporting Pupils with Moderate Learning Difficulties in the Secondary School: A practical guide
Rachael Hayes and Pippa Whittaker
2016/pb: 978-1-138-01910-2

Assessing Children with Specific Learning Difficulties: A teacher's practical guide
Gavin Reid, Gad Elbeheri and John Everatt
2016/pb: 978-0-415-67027-2

Supporting Children with Down's Syndrome, 2ed
Lisa Bentley, Ruth Dance and Elizabeth Morling
2016/pb: 978-1-138-91485-8

Provision Mapping and the SEND Code of Practice: Making it work in primary, secondary and special schools, 2ed
Anne Massey
2016/pb: 978-1-138-90707-2

Supporting Children with Medical Conditions, 2ed
Rob Grayson, Elizabeth Morling and Jill Wing
2016/pb: 978-1-13-891491-9

Achieving Outstanding Classroom Support in Your Secondary School: Tried and tested strategies for teachers and SENCOs
Jill Morgan, Cheryl Jones, Sioned Booth-Coates
2016/pb: 978-1-138-83373-9

Assessing Children with Specific Learning Difficulties

A teacher's practical guide

Gavin Reid, Gad Elbeheri
and John Everatt

Routledge
Taylor & Francis Group

Helping Everyone Achieve

LONDON AND NEW YORK

First published 2016
by Routledge
2 Park Square, Milton Park, Abingdon, Oxon OX14 4RN

and by Routledge
711 Third Avenue, New York, NY 10017

Routledge is an imprint of the Taylor & Francis Group, an informa business

© 2016 Gavin Reid, Gad Elbeheri and John Everatt

The right of Gavin Reid, Gad Elbeheri and John Everatt to be identified as author of this work has been asserted by them in accordance with sections 77 and 78 of the Copyright, Designs and Patents Act 1988.

British Library Cataloguing in Publication Data
A catalogue record for this book is available from the British Library

Library of Congress Cataloging in Publication Data
Reid, Gavin, 1950-
Assessing children with specific learning difficulties : a teacher's practical guide / Gavin Reid, Gad Elbeheri and John Everatt.
pages cm
Includes bibliographical references.
ISBN 978-0-415-59759-3 (hardback) – ISBN 978-0-415-67027-2 (pbk.) – ISBN 978-1-315-69387-3 (ebook) 1. Learning disabled children–Evaluation. 2. Learning disabled children–Education. I. Elbeheri, Gad. II. Everatt, John. III. Title.
LC4704.R445 2016
371.9–dc23
2015004084

ISBN: 978-0-415-59759-3 (hbk)
ISBN: 978-0-415-67027-2 (pbk)
ISBN: 978-1-315-69387-3 (ebk)

Typeset in Bembo
by Cenveo Publisher Services
Printed by Ashford Colour Press Ltd.

Contents

List of figures and tables ix
About the authors xi
Introduction xiii

1 SpLD in context: pointers for practice 1

2 The assessment process 16

3 Teacher assessment: literacy 40

4 Numeracy: mathematics learning difficulties 54

5 Teacher assessment: movement 65

6 Behavioural problems: attention deficit hyperactivity
 disorder and emotional and behavioural disorders 78

7 Assessment and the role of the educational psychologist 94

8 Recognising and dealing with self-esteem, motivation
 and emotional needs 107

9 Identifying and utilising learning preferences
 and styles 117

10 Higher education and the workplace 127

11 Developing an assessment framework   137

12 Sources and resources for assessment   149

    References   163
    Index   185

List of figures and tables

Figure

3.1   Some academic and literacy difficulties experienced
      by people with dyslexia   42

Tables

1.1   Phonics and maths   5
1.2   The overlap   9
2.1   A holistic view of the barriers to learning   26

About the authors

Gavin Reid

Dr Gavin Reid is a fully registered psychologist with the Health and Care Professionals (HCPC) in the UK and the College of Psychologists in British Columbia, Canada.

He has over 25 years' experience as an educational psychologist and also ten years' experience as a classroom teacher. He is an international seminar presenter on specific learning difficulties and an award-winning author of books on a range of topics relating to dyslexia, dyspraxia, ADHD, autistic spectrum disorders (ASD), effective learning and motivation.

He has authored and edited 28 books and has been involved in a wide range of research projects. His books have been translated into French, Italian, Croatian, Polish and Arabic. He has also co-authored the assessment instrument Special Needs Assessment Profile (SNAP), which is widely used in schools in many countries.

Dr Reid currently undertakes full assessments using a range of up-to-date tests and procedures from around age four to adults. He can assess for dyslexia, dyspraxia, dyscalculia, dysgraphia, ADHD, ASD and any of the other related difficulties. He provides a full contextualised report which contains recommendations and ideas to develop the child/adult's learning skills.

He has been visiting Professor at the University of British Columbia, in Vancouver, on two occasions and was previously senior lecturer at the University of Edinburgh in the UK. He is a popular international seminar presenter and has presented in over 75 countries.

His website is www.drgavinreid.com Email gavinreid66@gmail.com

Gad Elbeheri

Dr Gad Elbeheri is the Dean of the Australian College of Kuwait, a university providing internationally recognised and accredited tertiary education to the business and engineering sectors. He is also an expert for the Centre for Child Evaluation and Teaching, a leading NGO that combines research and practice on specific learning disabilities.

An applied linguist who obtained his PhD from the University of Durham, UK, Dr Elbeheri has a keen interest in cross-linguistic studies of specific learning difficulties and inclusive education. He is a director-at-large of the International Dyslexia Association and an Editorial Board Member of *Dyslexia: An International Journal of Research and Practice*.

Dr Elbeheri has made over 30 conference and seminar presentations around the world. He has published over seven books in both English and Arabic in the field of dyslexia, and over ten peer-reviewed journal articles on dyslexia and its manifestations in Arabic. He has participated in producing nationally standardised tests and computer-based screening programs in Arabic.

John Everatt

John Everatt is a professor of Education at the University of Canterbury, New Zealand. Prior to this, he was a lecturer in psychology and research methods at the universities of Surrey and Wales in the UK. He received a PhD from the University of Nottingham and has lectured on education and psychology programmes, as well as giving guest lectures on topics related to learning difficulties, across Asia, Europe and North America.

John Everatt's work focuses on literacy learning problems and related developmental learning difficulties, though he also conducts research on literacy acquisition, additional language learning and cross-language/orthography comparisons. The main perspective used in this research has been a focus on factors that lead to differences in skills levels across individuals, both among children and adult learners. Although initial work looked at English-language populations, further research has investigated the relationship between literacy learning and language by considering common skills across the two areas and by assessing the characteristics of different scripts and how these might lead to different manifestations of reading/writing problems. This has led to collaboration in countries in Europe, South-East Asia, Africa, Arabia, India and China, looking at language/literacy skills in monolingual, bilingual and second-language populations.

Introduction

We feel that there is a need for this book. One of the major changes in the field of specific learning difficulties (SpLDs) over recent years has been in the area of teacher training. In the UK this has certainly 'taken off' and the development of regulatory and quality assurance bodies in specialist teacher training such as the British Dyslexia Association Teacher Training Accrediation Board, PATOSS and the Helen Arkell Dyslexia Centre have done a great deal to ensure that training is robust, avaliable and relevant.

As a result there is now a great number of specialist teachers in the UK conducting assessments for dyslexia and other SpLDs. This is perhaps a unique situation internationally. Many countries do have specialist teachers who are qualified to assesss, but the regulatory and certification role of these top UK orgainsations have ensured a degree of quality assurance, uniformity and public confidence. There is now confidence that well-conducted specialist teacher assessments carried out by appropriately trained professionals are a welcome and useful addition to the range of options in diagnosis and evaluation of children who are at risk of or have an SpLD.

In this book we have decided to use the term 'specific learning difficulties'. This is a broad term and we have deliberately gone for this as it incorporates literacy, movement and numeracy as well as issues with attention. These areas are reflected in different chapters in the book.

We have also included some general chapters to look at key factors that may be helpful to assessors and to teachers when conducting an assessment. We have made the point that assessment is a process and not a 'one stop shop'! Ideally it should involve a number of professionals as well as parents, but the key to a successful assessment is communication. It is important that information is transferred between those involved in the assessment. This may include: teacher, learning support teacher, psychologist, speech and language therapist, occupational therapist, optomitrist and parents.

We have decided to devote one chapter to the role of the psychologist because, traditionally, psychologists have been involved in diagnosis. It can be noted, however, in that chapter that this traditional role is no longer as clearly defined as it once was. The publication of the British Psychological Society (BPS) working party report on dyslexia and assessment in 1999 (BPS, 1999) certainly helped psychologists a great deal and provided a clearer pathway to follow, but the majority of psychologists are working under the auspices of the education authority and this, to a great extent, has had an impact on their working practices.

We have indicated quite strongly in this book that assessment is more than carrying out a test. Without doubt testing is crucial, but an assessment also needs to gather information and incorporate aspects relating to the curriculum and classroom practices.

We are also very aware of the individual preferences of learners and his/her needs. We have therefore devoted chapters to individual learning preferences, self-esteem and emotional needs. The research does indicate that there is a high correlation between learning difficulties and learned helplessness and this has an impact on self-esteem. It might, in fact, be argued that self-esteeem is the most crucial element in successful learning. It is therefore a point of interest that the results of the assessment can actually help to boost the child's self-esteem. This can be done through informed and considerate feedback and, if possible, the child should be included in this process.

We have made the point in the book that assessment should have a clear link with practice and through this linkage it should be possible to include recommendations for interventions. These should help the child access the curriculum, but also increase his/her self-esteem.

We are aware that many countries now have legislation that has in some way had an impact on assessment and diagnosis. This is the case in the UK with the recent Special Education legislation (the Special Educational Needs and Disability Regulations 2014, which came into force in September 2014). Additionally, we have to consider regulations from examination centres and the Joint Qualifications Council (JQC) regarding the type and quality of information they need in order to authorise examinations accommodations.

We have tried to do this while also sticking to the aims and purpose of this book, which is not only to provide guidance for teachers, but also to help them become aware of the key issues and the notion that there are different ways of doing an assessment. It is important, therefore, to consider the local context and, very importantly, the individual child. We have decided, however, not to devote chapters to legislation and prescriptive guidance (which is often in any case available in the web), but to help teachers and readers of the book reflect on their own practices and to justify why they do things a certain way. For that reason we have included some theory, although the main purpose is to provide a practically focused book. But we have tried to link theory and practice; this can be particularly noted in the literacy and movement chapters, but, in fact, is a feature of the whole book.

Although the authors are colleagues and have collobrated in a great number of projects over many years, it is interesting to note that they have recent international experiences from different countries – Gavin Reid from Canada and Scotland, Gad Elebheri from Kuwait and the USA and John Everatt from New Zealand, as well as the UK. Each of us have worked in many countries and we agree that this has enriched our views and helped to shape our ideas and indeed this book.

We hope you will obtain some fresh insights and be able to embrace the ideas and strategies within the pages of this book. We have always indicated that communication is the key to successful assessment and intervention and we hope that this book paves a way for us to communicate with you to assist in the development of ideas and strategies that you can utilise in your professional work.

Dr Gavin Reid, Edinburgh, UK
Dr Gad Elbehei, Kuwait
Dr John Everatt, Christchurch, New Zealand
January 2015

Chapter 1

SpLD in context

Pointers for practice

Specific Learning Difficulties (SpLD)

The term 'specific learning difficulties' refers to children who experience a range of challenges in one or more of the following areas: literacy, numeracy, writing, movement and attention. It can also include other aspects of learning that may prevent them from reaching their potential. In some children these challenges can be very significant and provide a real barrier for learners, thus preventing them from effectively accessing the curriculum. The difficulties range from mild to severe.

There is a range of labels that can be used to describe individual aspects of SpLD and many of these labels can show overlapping characteristics. This is referred to as co-morbidity or co-occurrence. The most popular of these labels include dyslexia, dyspraxia, dyscalculia, dysgraphia and attention deficit hyperactivity disorder (ADHD). There is a growing body of evidence to suggest that co-morbidity may be highly prevalent (Bishop and Snowling, 2004) and, in fact, the norm rather than the exception.

The overlap and continuum

As indicated above, SpLDs can be seen within a continuum and there is likely to be some overlap between several of these. It is not unusual for dyslexia, dyspraxia and, to a certain extent, ADHD to share some of common factors. Before discussing the value or otherwise of the term 'co-morbidity' it will be beneficial to briefly describe the individual labels within 'specific learning difficulties' which are in popular use.

Dyslexia

A definition of dyslexia is shown below.

> Dyslexia is a processing difference experienced by people of all ages, often characterized by difficulties in literacy, it can affect other cognitive areas such as memory, speed of processing, time management, co-ordination and

directional aspects. There may be visual and phonological difficulties and there is usually some discrepancy in performances in different areas of learning. It is important that the individual differences and learning styles are acknowledged since these will impact on the outcome of learning and assessment. It is also important to consider the learning and work context as the nature of the difficulties associated with dyslexia may well be more pronounced in some learning situations. (Reid, 2009)

This is a broad definition and in view of the range of challenges that can be associated with dyslexia this is one of the appeals of this definition. Some specific early indicators of dyslexia are shown below:

- working memory difficulties (forgetfulness)
- language and speech difficulty
- difficulty forming letters
- difficulty remembering letters of the alphabet and the sequence
- history of dyslexia in the family
- co-ordination difficulties e.g. bumping into tables and chairs (can also be a sign of dyspraxia)
- difficulty with tasks which require fine motor skills such as tying shoelaces (can also be sign of dyspraxia)
- reluctance to concentrate on a task for a reasonable period of time (can also be a sign of attention difficulties)
- confusing words which sound similar
- reluctance to go to school
- signs of not enjoying school
- reluctance to read
- difficulty learning words and letters
- difficulty with phonics (sounds)
- general co-ordination difficulties (can also be sign of dyspraxia)
- losing items
- difficulty forming letters
- difficulty copying
- difficulty colouring
- poor organisation of materials.

Dyspraxia

Dyspraxia is a motor/co-ordination difficulty. It can be seen within a continuum from mild to severe and can affect fine motor activities such as pencil grip and gross motor activities such as movement and balance. Portwood (1999) describes dyspraxia as 'motor difficulties caused by perceptual problems, especially visual-motor and kinesthetic motor difficulties'.

The definition of dyspraxia provided by the Dyspraxia Trust in England is an 'impairment or immaturity in the organisation of movement which leads to associated problems with language, perception and thought' (Dyspraxia Trust, 2001).

Children with dyspraxia can have difficulties with:

- gross motor skills – balance, co-ordination
- co-ordination
- judging force in ball throwing
- balance/posture
- running, hopping and jumping
- fastening buttons and tying laces
- kinaesthetic memory
- using two hands simultaneously
- spatial awareness and directional awareness.

In secondary school they may also experience difficulties with:

- copying and reading diagrams
- recalling detailed instructions
- reading and writing
- copying from board
- using classroom equipment e.g. rulers, compass, scissors
- following timetables
- finding way round school and also in some subjects such as physical education.

Children with dyspraxia can also have difficulties with:

- speech and language
- social skills
- attention/concentration.

Some children with dyspraxia may also show signs of dysgraphia, although dysgraphia can exist on its own. Some of the characteristics of dysgraphia include:

- letter inconsistencies
- mixture of upper and lower case
- irregular letter size and shapes
- unfinished letters
- often a reluctant writer
- poor visual perception
- poor fine motor skills.

With dysgraphia, therefore, it is important to consider the following:

- hand dominance
- pencil grip
- posture
- paper position
- pressure on paper
- wrist movement
- letter formation
- left-to-right orientation
- reversals of letters
- spacing
- letter size, formation consistency
- style – joins in letters
- speed
- fatigue factors.

Some of the difficulties described above relate to skills that are necessary for a range of everyday learning tasks and these difficulties can affect attention, memory and reading development. This means that although dyspraxia may be the primary difficulty in some cases there can be secondary indicators of dyslexia or attention difficulties.

Dyscalculia

Dyscalculia is a condition that affects the ability to acquire arithmetical skills. Dyscalculic learners will usually have difficulty understanding simple number concepts, lack an intuitive grasp of numbers and have problems learning number facts and procedures. Even if they produce a correct answer or use a correct method, they may do so mechanically and without confidence (DfES, 2001).

Dr Steve Chinn, a prolific author and recognised expert in dyscalculia, suggests in relation to identifying dyscalculia as a basic indicator that the child will be performing below expectations. The difficulties that can be noted include:

- problems understanding the value of numbers
- problems understanding the relationship between numbers, e.g. nine is one less than ten
- being able to rapidly recall basic number facts
- may recall mathematical facts but with no real understanding.

Henderson, Came and Brough (2003) indicate that the factors that need to be considered in developing and assessment protocol for dyscalculia include:

- the literacy challenges in maths
- organisation and presentation of work

- speed of working
- memory and sequencing
- anxiety and fear of maths
- learning basic facts
- directional confusion and sequencing difficulties
- thinking and learning styles (inchworms and grasshoppers, Chinn, 2009).

It seems that the language of maths is an important factor; if this is not clearly explained to the child then they will fail in the maths task and soon maths demoralisation will occur and learned helplessness. This is when the fear of maths sets in.

Henderson, Came and Brough (2003) suggest a phonic approach is useful, as in Table 1.1.

Wardrop (2014, personal communication) also adopts this approach and utilises the principles and the practices of the Orton–Gillingham approach.

A similar planning strategy as shown in the example above can be applied to memory in maths – that is, what to look for and how to help. This also provides a good example of the link between assessment and teaching which has been a central point in this chapter.

Table 1.1 Phonics and maths

What to look out for	How to help
Pronunciation and spelling of complex maths words such as 'isosceles triangle' can cause problems.	Teach spelling of the maths words in a multi-sensory way, e.g. trace, colour significant parts of the word or similar letter patterns. Take care to articulate the maths words clearly, e.g. the difference between 40 and 14.
Poor visual recognition of the word and poor recognition of the correct spellings.	Learn the tricky words visually. Recognise the shape of the word and draw the outline of a word.
Complex mathematical vocabulary within a topic is often difficult to read.	Teach decoding of long mathematical words through syllable work. Make a word wall of difficult topic words.
Mathematical words are often difficult to spell, e.g. horizontal, perpendicular, *eight* or ate.	Teach words in groups or chunks working on the syllables or similar letter patterns in word families.
Slow in writing common words and confusion with little words.	Allow more time for recording work, copying from the board etc. Clearly display common little words.
When doing an investigation the pupil may have sequencing difficulties, which affect the way they record a calculation. The pupil will often forget the first step of the method.	Talk through the method and encourage them to note down each step as they work through their investigation.

Attention deficit disorders (ADD and ADHD)

There has been considerable debate regarding the concept of attention disorders. A number of perspectives can be noted ranging from the medical and educational to the social.

The most widely accepted guidance on ADHD can be seen in the American Psychiatric Association's *Diagnostic and Statistical Manual of Mental Disorders* (*DSM-V*, 2013[1]). This indicates that: 'ADHD is characterized by a pattern of behavior, present in multiple settings (e.g., school and home), that can result in performance issues in social, educational, or work settings.'

As in its predecessor, *DSM-IV*, symptoms are divided into two categories of inattention, and hyperactivity and impulsivity that include behaviours like failure to pay close attention to details, difficulty organising tasks and activities, excessive talking, fidgeting, or an inability to remain seated in appropriate situations.

Children must have at least six symptoms from either (or both) the inattention group of criteria and the hyperactivity and impulsivity criteria, while older adolescents and adults (over age 17 years) must present with five.

The nine inattentive symptoms are:

- often fails to give close attention to details or makes careless mistakes in schoolwork, work, or during other activities (e.g. overlooks or misses details, work is inaccurate);
- often has difficulty sustaining attention in tasks or play activities (e.g. has difficulty remaining focused during lectures, conversations, or lengthy reading);
- often does not seem to listen when spoken to directly (e.g. mind seems elsewhere, even in the absence of any obvious distraction);
- often does not follow through on instructions and fails to finish school work, chores, or duties in the workplace (e.g. starts tasks but quickly loses focus and is easily sidetracked);
- often has difficulty organising tasks and activities (e.g. difficulty managing sequential tasks; difficulty keeping materials and belongings in order; messy, disorganised work; has poor time management; fails to meet deadlines);
- often avoids or is reluctant to engage in tasks that require sustained mental effort (e.g. schoolwork or homework; for older adolescents and adults, preparing reports, completing forms, reviewing lengthy papers);
- often loses things necessary for tasks or activities (e.g. school materials, pencils, books, tools, wallets, keys, paperwork, eyeglasses and mobile telephones);
- is often easily distracted by extraneous stimuli (e.g. for older adolescents and adults this may include unrelated thoughts).

Additionally, the person can be forgetful in daily activities (e.g. doing chores, running errands; for older adolescents and adults, returning calls, paying bills, keeping appointments).

The nine hyperactive-impulsive symptoms are:

- often fidgets with or taps hands or squirms in seat;
- often leaves seat in situations when remaining seated is expected (e.g. leaves his or her place in the classroom, in the office or other workplace, or in other situations that require remaining in place);
- often runs about or climbs in situations where it is inappropriate (in adolescents or adults this may be limited to feeling restless);
- often unable to play or engage in leisure activities quietly;
- is often 'on the go' acting as if 'driven by a motor' (e.g. is unable to be or uncomfortable being still for extended time, as in restaurants, meetings; may be experienced by others as being restless or difficult to keep up with);
- often talks excessively;
- often blurts out answers before questions have been completed (e.g. completes people's sentences; cannot wait for turn in conversation);
- often has difficulty awaiting turn (e.g. while waiting in line);
- often interrupts or intrudes on others (e.g. butts into conversations, games, or activities; may start using other people's things without asking or receiving permission; for adolescents and adults, may intrude into or take over what others are doing).

In *DSM-IV*, the age of onset criteria was 'some hyperactive-impulsive or inattentive symptoms that caused impairment were present before age 7 years'. This reflected the view that ADHD emerged relatively early in development and interfered with a child's functioning at a relatively young age. In *DSM-V* this has been revised to 'several inattentive or hyperactive-impulsive symptoms were present prior to 12 years'. Thus, symptoms can now appear up to five years later. And, there is no longer the requirement that the symptoms create impairment by age 12, just that they are present. *DSM-V* has changed this to 'several inattentive or hyperactive-impulsive symptoms are present in two or more settings'. Thus, symptoms must only be evident in more than one context but don't have to impair an individual's functioning in multiple contexts. This is also more lenient than *DSM-IV* (adapted from Rabiner, 2013).

Although there has been considerable amount of literature on ADHD, there is still controversy regarding the unitary model of ADHD as a discrete syndrome. There is also some debate on the nature of the syndrome and particularly its primary causes. For example, Barkley (2006) suggests that it is a unitary condition and that the primary impairment relates to behaviour inhibition and this has a cascading effect on other cognitive functions. This view is, however, countered by Rutter (1995), who suggests that a cognitive deficit specific to ADHD has still to be determined and even if the majority have cognitive impairments the trait is not common to all children with ADHD. It is perhaps useful at this point to attempt to place the symptoms and characteristics of ADHD into some form of framework to help understand the different strands and various characteristics which can contribute to ADHD.

Co-morbidity and ADHD

It is not surprising that there is a strong view that an overlap exists between ADHD and dyslexia. Many of the cognitive attention processing mechanisms which children with ADHD seem to have difficulty with, such as short-term memory, sustained attention, processing speed and accuracy in copying, can also be noted in children with dyslexia. Willcutt and Pennington (2000) noted in a large-scale study that individuals with reading disabilities were more likely than individuals without reading disabilities to meet the criteria for ADHD and that the association was stronger for inattention than for hyperactivity.

But this notion of co-morbidity has been criticised and the value of the term questioned (Kaplan *et al.*, 2001). It is suggested that the term 'co-morbidity' assumes that the etiologies of the different specific difficulties are independent. Yet in practice, according to Kaplan *et al.*, it is very rare to see discrete conditions existing in isolation. In a research study involving 179 children the researchers, in order to investigate the notion of co-morbidity, used criteria to assess for seven disorders – reading disability, attention deficit hyperactivity disorder (ADHD), developmental co-ordination disorder, oppositional defiant disorder, conduct disorder, depression and anxiety. It was found that at least 50 per cent of the sample tested met the criteria for at least two diagnoses and the children with ADHD were at the highest risk of having a second disorder. The question presented by Kaplan *et al.* is whether children are actually displaying several co-morbid disorders or, in fact, are displaying manifestations of one underlying disorder. This, of course, raises questions regarding the assessment procedures and was the rationale behind the 'special needs assessment procedures' (SNAP) (Weedon and Reid, 2003, 2005, 2009). This indicates that is likely that children will show indicators of other conditions and the accumulation of descriptive information on the presenting difficulties can be useful for the class teacher. It is important, however, that information is not based solely on clinical assessment or clinical judgement; information should also be gathered from professionals and parents about how the child performs in different situations.

The implication stemming from the notion of co-morbidity lies in the description of the presenting characteristics, which may or may not lead to a label – these can be informative and beneficial in terms of intervention.

The overlap

Table 1.2 below highlights the overlap between the SpLDs; this can have significant implications for assessment and teaching. It is therefore beneficial to work out priorities based on the presenting difficulties rather than the label. This means that the aim of the assessment is not necessarily to obtain a label but to identify the presenting challenges and difficulties that are preventing the child from accessing the curriculum.

Table 1.2 The overlap

Difficulty	Dyslexia	Dyspraxia	ADHD	Dyscalculia
Working memory difficulties	Yes	Yes	Yes	Yes
Forgetfulness (long-term memory)	Yes	Yes	Yes	Yes
Speech difficulty	Yes	Yes	No	No
Reversal of letters	Yes	Yes	No	Yes
Difficulty remembering letters and sequence of alphabet	Yes	Yes	Yes	Yes
Confusing words which sound similar	Yes	Yes	Possibly	Possibly
Difficulty with phonics	Yes	Yes	Possibly	Possibly
Difficulty forming letters, colouring and copying	Yes	Yes	Possibly	Possibly
Family history important	Yes	Yes	Yes	Yes
Co-ordination difficulties e.g. bumping into tables and chairs	Possibly	Yes	Possibly	Possibly
Tasks which require fine motor skills such as tying shoelaces	Yes	Yes	Possibly	Possibly
Slow at reacting to some tasks	Yes	Yes	Possibly	Possibly
Difficulty focusing on longer tasks	Yes	Yes	Yes	Yes
Reluctance to go to school	Possibly	Possibly	Possibly	Possibly
Signs of not enjoying school	Yes	Yes	Possibly	Yes
Reluctance to read	Yes	Yes	Possibly	Possibly
Poor organisation	Yes	Yes	Possibly	Possibly

Implications for assessment

Barriers to learning

It can be concluded from Table 1.2 above that in view of the potential overlap it may be useful to view SpLD in terms of the barriers to learning rather than focusing on the actual label, meaning that the presenting difficulties will be the focus, which will have implications for assessment. This is important as there will be a wide variation of needs even within those children who have the same label, which this will have implications for intervention – for example, not all children with dyslexia will respond to the same type of intervention (Reid, 2008). Intervention needs to be individualised and this has implications for identifying needs and the assessment process in general.

Holistic perspective in assessment

When identifying the barriers to learning it is important to look at students' holistic needs. This would include: cognitive (learning skills), environmental (learning experience) and progress in basic attainments (literacy acquisition). These highlight a number of key factors relating to the learner, the task and the learning experience, emphasising the need not to solely focus on the child and what he or she can or cannot do, but to look at the task that is being presented, the expectations being placed on the learner and the learner's readiness for the task. From that premise, the first step is to identify those factors – cognitive, educational, environmental and social/emotional – that can present barriers to the learner and prevent him/her from acquiring competent literacy and other skills.

It is important that learners with SpLD obtain some success as this will help them develop a positive self-esteem. This is crucial for effective learning. Success can usually be acquired if the learner achieves, so it is important to ensure the task is achievable. If it is not achievable then it needs to be broken down into smaller and more manageable units.

Factors to consider

Planning

- *Knowledge of the child's strengths and difficulties*: this is essential, particularly since not all children with any of the SpLDs such as dyslexia will display the same profile, although they may share the same core difficulties. This is therefore the best starting point as often strengths can be used to help deal with the weaknesses. For example, dyslexic children often have a preference for visual and kinaesthetic learning and a difficulty with auditory learning. So phonic instruction, which relies heavily on sounds, and therefore the auditory modality, needs to be introduced together with visual and experiential forms of learning. The tactile modality involving touch and feeling the shape of letters that make specific sounds should also be utilised, as well as the visual symbol of these letters and letter/sound combinations.
- *Consultation*: the responsibility for dealing with children with specific learning difficulties within the classroom should not solely rest with the class teacher. Ideally it should be seen as a whole-school responsibility. This means that consultation with school management and other colleagues is important, and equally it is important that time is allocated for this.
- *Information from previous teachers, support staff, school management and parents*: this is important and such joint liaison can help to ensure the necessary collaboration to provide support for the class teacher. Importantly, this should be built into the school procedures and the assessment process and not be a reaction to a problem that has occurred – such collaboration can therefore be seen as preventative and proactive.
- *Current level of literacy/numeracy acquisition*: an accurate and full assessment of the child's current level of attainments is necessary in order to effectively plan a programme of learning. The assessment should include comprehension, as well as reading accuracy and fluency and number work. In the case of dyslexia, listening/reading comprehension can often be a more accurate guide to the abilities and understanding of dyslexic children than reading and spelling accuracy. Indeed, it is often the discrepancy between listening

or reading comprehension and reading accuracy that can be a key factor in identifying dyslexia. Information on the level of attainments will be an instrumental factor in planning for learning.

* *Cultural factors*: these are important as these can influence the selection of books and teaching materials and whether some of the concepts in the text need to be singled out for additional and differentiated explanation. Cultural values are an important factor. It has been suggested that the 'big dip' in performance noted in some bilingual children in later primary school may be explained by a failure of professionals to understand and appreciate the cultural values and the actual level of competence of the bilingual child, particularly in relation to conceptual development and competence in thinking skills. In order for a teaching approach with bilingual students to be fully effective it has to be comprehensive, which means that it needs to incorporate the views of parents and the community. This requires considerable preparation and pre-planning, as well as consultation with parents and community organisations.

Assessment and intervention: the link

It is essential to consider this at the outset. It should not be an add-on but, in fact, one of the main purposes of the assessment. Some of the general points that can be considered are highlighted below using dyslexia as an example.

Understanding

Often the learner with dyslexia, or indeed any of the other SpLDs, may not actually understand the task. This can, in fact, offer a reason why they can answer a seemingly different question to the one intended. Understanding the task therefore can be a barrier that confronts student with SpLD in most subjects. It is not because they do not have the necessary cognitive skills to understand the task but it is because the task is presented in a manner that makes it very challenging for the student.

Identifying the key points

Many students with SpLD may have difficulty in recognising what the task, or the text, is suggesting because they have not been able to identify the key issues. They may pick up some tangential issues that sidetrack them onto a different path and this can lead to a different type of response from that intended. It is crucial to highlight the key points rather than expect learners with dyslexia to identify these themselves.

Processing information

Two of the key components that need to be considered in relation to identifying and dealing with the barriers for learners with dyslexia relate to the distinction between processing and reasoning. Often the child with dyslexia will have good reasoning ability – given that the barriers have been removed they will be able to access thinking skills and show good comprehension. The processing of information, however, may be more problematic. This can often be noted during the assessment.

Processing involves:

- *Comprehending the task*: that means the learner has to be able to access the vocabulary and the purpose of the task – for some learners this can be demanding. This highlights the importance of pre-task discussion. During that time the teacher would discuss the task, the vocabulary, the concepts and the purpose of the task with the learner. This is essential to ensure that the learner has an appropriate schema for the task as this will assist in the access and utilisation of background knowledge and existing skills. This indicates that one of the key issues is not the 'what' question but the 'how' question – that is, how do I do this, what information do I need and what do I do first? This means that the learner with dyslexia needs support in the actual learning process. This will be time well spent as it has been indicated that often learners with dyslexia can have low metacognitive awareness (Tunmer and Chapman, 1996), indicating the they find the process of learning challenging; once they receive support in this area they can usually deal with the task more competently. This, therefore, can have implications for assessment as it is important that the child has understood the actual question.
- *Implementation of the task*: that is, being able to use the information provided to assist in the answer to the question. This would have implications for being able to identify the key points and focusing on the actual task. It is possible for learners with SpLD to be sidetracked and look at issues that may well be important but may not directly relate to the task.
- *Autonomous learning*: it is often the case that students with SpLD become dependent on a teacher or support teacher when they are tackling questions. This means they are leaning towards a dependency culture and becoming too dependent on another person. This, in the short term, may be exactly what they need but it has dangers. One danger inherent in this can be gleaned from 'Attribution Theory'. This would imply that if learners' become dependent on support they will attribute their success to the presence of the teacher. It is important that this attribution is shifted in order that they attribute success to their own efforts. This is the first and essential step to becoming an independent learner.
- *Reporting on the task*: this is an important factor as this is the final component of learning that is often seen as a measure of competence. Yet learners with SpLD can often have competence in learning but not be able to display that in written form or indeed orally. This can be frustrating so it is

important that support is available to help with organising, sequencing and structuring the key points to assist in the reporting process. This can have particular implications for children with dyslexia and dysgraphia.

Proactive assessment

Anticipating and dealing with the barriers

Some key points:

- *Planning*: meeting the needs and dealing with the barriers the child experiences should be considered at the planning stage. This is crucial and knowledge of the child is an important factor. Planning should not take place in isolation but needs to be contextualised to the learning environment, the anticipated learning experience and the actual learner. It is important therefore to have pre-knowledge of the individual learner when engaged in planning. This can also be achieved through developing an observation schedule or framework that can help to inform both planning and teaching. It is also crucial to obtain information from the parents at this point.
- *Differentiation*: this is really about good teaching and advanced planning. If the curriculum is effectively differentiated to take account of the task, the input, output and the resources that are to be used then it is likely that all students will be catered for in some way. Differentiation is about supporting the learner and guiding him/her from where they are now to where they should be. In other words, it is about helping to make all curricular materials accessible. It is also important to look at the assessment materials as these may have to be differentiated for learners with dyslexia. Differentiation therefore needs to consider the learner, the task and the outcome, as well as the resources.
- *Learner awareness/learning style*: it is worthwhile spending time with the learner so that he/she will be aware of their own learning preferences. It will be useful to help them understand that there are advantages and disadvantages to every learning style and help them to identify their own particular style of learning and how they can use that style effectively.
- *Acknowledging creativity (thinking outside the box)*: this can have implications for assessment as the child may give an unorthodox response to a conventional situation or question. As Tom West suggested in his book *In the Mind's Eye* (1997), 'for dyslexic learners the hard is easy and the easy is hard'! There has been a great deal written on creativity and dyslexia (ibid.). While a number of students with dyslexia will have natural creative abilities, this will not apply to all. At the same time it is important that every student is given opportunities and support to develop and utilise creativity and individual ways of using information.

Some self-talk tactics are described below:

- Acknowledging
    - That's a new idea
    - I see
    - Interesting point

- Restating
    - You want to know ...?
    - Does that mean ...?
    - Are you saying ...?
    - So you are disagreeing with ...?
    - You think ...?

- Clarifying
    - Why do you say that?
    - I don't quite understand what you mean
    - What are we really discussing here?
    - That seems to relate to ...

- Disagreeing
    - You make an interesting point, have you considered ...?
    - Is it possible that ...?
    - Here's another thought ...

- Challenging thinking
    - I wonder how we know ...?
    - Can you give some reasons for ...?

- Redirecting
    - How does that relate to ...?
    - Good point, but have we finished discussing ...

- Expanding
    - I wonder what else this could relate to?

Concluding comments

This chapter has focused on the background to the various SpLDs and particularly the implications and the link between assessment and teaching. This has been deliberate as it is important at the outset to establish this nature of this link. This is a significant consideration in the development of an assessment protocol and the link with practice should be borne in mind at the planning stage in the selection of assessment tools and in the follow-through from the assessment.

It is crucial, therefore, to consider – irrespective of which tools are being used and the nature of the child's challenges – that, whatever is obtained through assessment, there must be a link to intervention. This, above all, is the purpose of assessment – to inform intervention. For that reason this chapter has provided a clear focus on the factors that can be considered in planning the assessment. The assessment–intervention process should be reciprocal, each informing the other.

Note

1 *DSM* is the manual used by clinicians and researchers to diagnose and classify mental disorders. The American Psychiatric Association (APA) published DSM-V in 2013, the culmination of a 14-year revision process.

Chapter 2

The assessment process

This chapter will look at the process that can be used when conducting an assessment for any of the specific learning difficulties (SpLDs). There will also be reference to linking assessment with intervention, as this should be a central tenant of the assessment process.

It is important to appreciate that SpLDs should not *only* be identified through the use of a test; assessment should be a process and that process involves much more than the administration of a test. The assessment needs to consider classroom and curriculum factors, as well as the specific difficulties and strengths shown by the child. These principles apply to all the SpLDs and these will be looked at in more detail later in the book.

The assessment process: some general points

Some general principles to consider are shown below.

- It is important that the lack of availability of a test does not prevent a child's difficulties from being recognised – assessment is more than using a test.
- Many of the characteristics that can contribute to a diagnosis can be noted in the classroom situation. It is therefore important that the class teacher's comments and views are taken into account.
- It is important that teachers have an understanding of the range of SpLDs in order that these characteristics can be recognised in the classroom.
- It is also important that appropriate materials and teaching programmes need to be developed from the results of the assessment; as indicated in the previous chapter, assessment must link to intervention!

When identifying any of the SpLDs it is important that a rationale and a strategy for the assessment are developed. Often a suspicion of the presence of difficulties can be identified through observation, or through the results of routine baseline or screening assessments. This information needs to be put into context so that an overall picture of the child's profile can be seen and evidence of an SpLD. It is helpful if this is done in relation to the curriculum and the barriers to learning are identified. This is necessary, as one of the purposes of assessment is to identify the most appropriate teaching and learning approaches. Some general aspects relating to the purpose of an assessment are related below.

The purpose of an assessment

An assessment should provide:

- an indication of the learner's strengths and weaknesses
- an indication of the learner's current level of performance in attainments
- an explanation for the learner's lack of progress
- identification of aspects of the learner's performance in reading, writing and spelling, which may typify a 'pattern of errors'
- identification of specific areas of competence
- understanding of the student's learning style
- indication of aspects of the curriculum that may interest and motivate the learner
- specific aspects of the curriculum that are challenging for the child
- the child's emotional needs and social skills, as well as the level of self-esteem.

(See Chapter 11 on resources for a list of tests that can be used for dyslexia, dyspraxia, dyscalculia and attention difficulties). Some of the specific characteristics for dyslexia that can be noted include the following.

- **Memory:**
  - poor short-term memory, which means probable difficulty remembering lists
  - may also be due to confusion or lack of understanding and poor organisational strategies.

- **Organisation:**
  - poor organisational strategies in general
  - poor organisation of timetable, materials and equipment
  - difficulty in remembering homework and organising homework notebook.

- **Movement:**
  - may have difficulty with co-ordination and tasks such as tying shoelaces
  - bumping into furniture in the classroom, tripping and frequently falling.

- **Speech development:**
  - confusing similar sounds
  - poor articulation

- o   difficulty blending sounds into words
- o   poor awareness of rhyme
- o   poor syntactic structure
- o   naming difficulties.

It is important to recognise that many of the factors above can be seen in a continuum of difficulties from mild to severe, and the extent and severity of these difficulties will have an impact on the assessment results and the subsequent recommendations for support. Although these are focused on dyslexia they can also be found in dyspraxia and other SpLDs, such as dyscalculia and attention difficulties.

Assessment considerations and strategies: dyslexia

Dyslexia should not only be identified through the use of a test. Assessment for dyslexia is a process and that process involves much more than the administration of a test. The assessment needs to consider classroom and curriculum factors, as well as the specific difficulties and strengths shown by the child.

Specifically, assessment should consider three aspects – difficulties/strengths, discrepancies and differences – and these should relate to the classroom environment and the curriculum.

The central difficulty is usually related to the decoding, or the encoding, of print and this may be the result of different contributory factors. For example, some difficulties may include phonological processing, memory problems, organisational and sequencing difficulties, movement and co-ordination, language problems, or visual–perceptual/auditory–perceptual difficulties.

The discrepancies may be apparent in comparing decoding and reading/listening comprehension, between oral and written responses and in performances within the different subject areas of the curriculum.

It is also important to acknowledge **the differences** between individual children with dyslexia. The identification process should, therefore, also consider learning styles and cognitive styles. An appreciation of this can help to effectively link assessment and teaching.

Challenges

The main challenges usually relate to decoding, or encoding of print. This can be due to difficulties with:

- acquiring phonological awareness
- memory problems
- organisational and sequencing difficulties
- movement and co-ordination
- language problems
- visual–perceptual/auditory–perceptual difficulties.

Discrepancies

The discrepancies may be apparent

- in comparing decoding skills with reading/listening comprehension
- between oral and written skills
- in performances within the different subject areas of the curriculum.

Differences

It is also important to acknowledge the differences between individual children with dyslexia. The identification process should therefore also consider:

- learning styles
- environmental preferences for learning
- learning strategies.

Environment

Factors that need to be considered include:

- classroom layout
- school ethos
- social groupings
- peer relations within class.

Formative assessment

Formative assessment can be complementary to the use of more formal tests. It is usually informal, though not always, but there is scope for the use of more informal measures in informal assessment, which can provide teachers with opportunities to:

- notice what is happening during learning activities
- recognise where the learning of individuals and groups of students is going
- see how they can help to take that learning further.

This provides opportunities for teachers to become 'reflective practitioners'. It is generally accepted that reflective practitioners can notice what is different or unusual about patterns of progress in student learning. They think carefully and deeply about what assessment information is telling them about student understanding, and also more particularly about their own teaching and what they should or can do differently to connect to and respond to the thinking of each student. It is then possible to provide a different kind of feedback to the student.

For example the feedback can:

- focus on the tasks and the associated learning, not necessarily the student difficulties
- confirm that he or she is on the right track
- includes suggestions that help the student (i.e. that scaffold their learning)
- is frequent and given when there is opportunity for the student to take action
- is in the context of a dialogue about the learning.

Feedback that connects directly to specific and challenging goals related to students' prior knowledge and experience helps those students to focus more productively on new goals and next learning steps.

Formal assessment: strategies and materials

Phonological assessment

To a great extent this can be carried out by the teacher from teacher-adapted materials or, indeed, through observation of the child's reading pattern. It covers the following areas:

- non-word reading
- sound recognition
- syllable segmentation
- recognising prefixes, suffixes and syllables
- rhyme recognition and production
- phoneme segmentation such as blending, recognition of initial and final phonemes.

Screening/baseline assessment

There are some issues that can be raised in relation to screening and baseline assessment. These include:

- What is the most desirable age (or ages) for children to be screened?
- Which skills, abilities and attainments in performances should children be screened for?
- How should the results of any screening procedures be used?

It is important that the results of screening and baseline assessments are used diagnostically and not to prematurely label children. There are some screening tests that have been developed specifically to identify the possibility of dyslexia. These can yield very useful information but should be used in conjunction with other data obtained from observations made by the teacher of the child's work and progress in class and in different areas of the curriculum.

Informal checklists

This form of assessment can provide some general data on the broad areas of difficulty experienced by the child. For example, the teacher may decide the child has a pronounced difficulty in the use of contextual cues, but this does not provide information as to why this difficulty persists and the kind of difficulties the pupil experiences with contextual cues. Does the child use contextual cues on some occasions, and under certain conditions? The teacher would be required to carry out investigations to obtain some further explanations of the difficulty.

Discrepancies

An approach to assessment that can be readily carried out by the teacher can involve the noting of discrepancies between different components of reading. These can include the following:

- decoding test (non-words reading test)
- word reading test
- phonological awareness test
- listening comprehension test
- reading comprehension test.

The information gleaned from this type of assessment strategy can be compared and any obvious discrepancies can be noted. For example, a child with dyslexia may have a low score on a decoding test and particularly one that involves non-words while in the listening comprehension test he/she may score considerably higher.

The differences

It is important to obtain information on the differences as well as the difficulties and the discrepancies. The interactive observational style index shown here can provide some pointers on the kind of information that can be useful.

This type of information can help to inform teaching and can be used before embarking on developing differentiated materials. It should be recognised that not all learners with dyslexia will have the same learning behaviours. It therefore follows that the type of intervention and the presentation of materials will differ; as much information as possible should be obtained on the learner's preferences.

It is important, therefore, to note in observational assessment the preferred mode of learning. Many children will, of course, show preferences and skills

Interactive observational style index

Emotional

- Motivation

    ○   What topics, tasks and activities interest the child?
    ○   About what topics does the child speak confidently?
    ○   What kinds of prompting and cueing are necessary to increase motivation?
    ○   What type incentives motivate the child: leadership opportunities, working with others, gold star, free time, physical activity and so forth?
    ○   Does the child seem to work because of interest in learning or to please others – parents, teachers, friends?

- Persistence

    ○   Does the child stick with a task until completion without breaks?
    ○   Are frequent breaks necessary when working on difficult tasks?
    ○   What is the quality of the child's work with and without breaks?

- Responsibility

    ○   To what extent does the child take responsibility for his own learning?
    ○   Does the child attribute his/her successes and failures to self or others?
    ○   Does the child grasp the relationship between effort expended and results achieved?
    ○   Does the child conform to classroom routines or consistently respond with nonconformity?

- Structure

    ○   Are the child's personal effects (desk, clothing, materials) well organised or cluttered?
    ○   How does the child respond to someone imposing organisational structure on him or her?
    ○   When provided specific, detailed guidelines for task completion, does the child faithfully follow them or work around them?

Social

- Interaction
    ○   Is there a noticeable difference between the child's positive spirit and interactions when working alone, one-to-one, in a small group, or with the whole class?

- o   When is the child's best work accomplished – when working alone, with one other or in a small group?
- o   Does the child ask for approval or to have work checked frequently?

- Communication

  - o   Is the child's language spontaneous or is prompting needed?
  - o   Does the child like to tell stories with considerable detail?
  - o   Does the child give the main events and gloss over details?
  - o   Does the child listen to others when they talk or is he/she constantly interrupting?

Cognitive

- Modality preference

  - o   What type instructions – written, oral, visual – does the child most easily understand?
  - o   Does the child respond more quickly and easily to questions about stories heard or read?
  - o   Does the child's oral communication include appropriate variations in pitch, intonation and volume?
  - o   In his spare time, does the child draw, build things, write, play sports, or listen to music?
  - o   When working on the computer for pleasure, does the child play games, search for information, or practice academic skill development?
  - o   Does the child take notes, write a word to recall how it is spelt, or draw maps when giving directions?
  - o   Given an array of options and asked to demonstrate his/her knowledge of a topic by drawing, writing, giving an oral report, or demonstrating/acting, what would he/she choose?
  - o   Under what specific types of learning (reading, maths, sports, etc.) is tension evident such as nail biting, misbehaviour, distressed facial expressions, limited eye contact and so forth?

- Sequential or simultaneous learning

  - o   Does the child begin with step one and proceed in an orderly fashion or have difficulty following sequential information?
  - o   Does the child jump from one task to another and back again or stay focused on one topic?
  - o   Is there a logical sequence to the child's explanations or do his/her thoughts 'bounce around' from one idea to another?

- When telling a story, does the child begin at the beginning and give a blow-by-blow sequence of events or does he/she skip around, share the highlights, or speak mostly in how the movie *felt*?
- When asked to write a report, does the child seek detailed directions or want only the topic?
- What type tasks are likely to be tackled with confidence?

- Impulsive versus reflective

  - Are the child's responses rapid and spontaneous or delayed and reflective?
  - Does the child return to a topic or behaviour long after others have ceased talking about it?
  - Does the child seem to consider past events before taking action?
  - Does the child respond motorically before obtaining adequate detail for the task?

Physical

- Mobility

  - Does the child move around the class frequently or fidget when seated?
  - Does the child like to stand or walk while learning something new?
  - Does the child slump or sit up when working?
  - Does the child jiggle his/her foot extensively?
  - Does the child become entangled in his/her chair when working quietly?

- Food intake

  - Does the child snack, chew on a pencil or bite on a finger when studying?
  - Does the child seek water frequently when studying?
  - Does the child chew on his/her hair, collar or button while working?

- Time of day

  - During which time of day is the child most alert?
  - Is there a noticeable difference between morning work completed versus afternoon work?

Reflection

- Sound

  - Under what conditions – sound or quiet – is the child relaxed but alert when learning?
  - Does the child seek out places to work that are particularly quiet?

- Light

  - Does the child squint in 'normal' lighting?
  - Is there a tendency for the child to put his/her head down in brightly lit classrooms?
  - Does the child like to work in dimly lit areas or say that the light is too bright?

- Temperature

  - Does the child leave on his/her coat when others seem warm?
  - Does the child appear comfortable in rooms below 68° Fahrenheit?

- Furniture design

  - When given a choice, does the child sit on the floor, lie down, or sit in a straight chair to read?
  - When given free time, does the child choose an activity requiring formal or informal posture?

- Metacognition

  - Is the child aware of his or her learning style strengths?
  - Does the child analyse the environment in regard to his/her learning with questions such as:

    - Is the light level right for me?
    - Am I able to focus with this level of sound?
    - Is the furniture comfortable for me?
    - Am I comfortable with the temperature?

  - Does the child demonstrate internal assessment of self by asking questions such as:

    - Have I done this before?
    - How did I tackle it?
    - What did I find easy?
    - What was difficult?
    - Why did I find it easy or difficult?
    - What did I learn?
    - What do I have to do to accomplish this task?
    - How should I tackle it?
    - Should I tackle it the same way as before?

- Prediction

  - Does the child make plans and work towards goals or let things happen as they will?
  - Is the child willing to take academic risks or does he/she play it safe by responding only when called upon?
  - Does the child demonstrate enthusiasm about gaining new knowledge and skills or does he/she hesitate?
  - Is there a relationship between the child's 'misbehaviour' and difficult tasks?

- Feedback

  - How does the child respond to different types of feedback: non-verbal (smile), check mark, oral praise, a detailed explanation, pat on the shoulder, comparison of scores with previous scores earnt, comparison of scores with classmates' performance and so forth?
  - How much external prompting is needed before the child can access previous knowledge?

(Adapted from Given and Reid, 1999)

Table 2.1   A holistic view of the barriers to learning

Cognitive	Emotional
Differences in information processing: visual–orthographic processing phonological processing limited capacity working memory poor sequencing weak spatial awareness lacking co-ordination/dexterity	Reading, spelling, writing Proofreading Numeracy Organisation, planning, time keeping Inappropriate labelling Social communication On-task behaviour
Social/emotional factors can account for:	**Environmental factors** that are a mis-match with learning needs:
lack of confidence low self-esteem isolation anxiety stress lack of understanding from peers and adults lack of hope due to history of failure	literacy demands lack of visiual aids/prompts undue time pressures peer and social expectations limited access to technology noise levels formal learning situations create discomfort, stress, poor concentration

in a number of modes of learning. Multi-sensory teaching, therefore, is crucial in order to accommodate as many modes as possible.

Diagnostic and informal assessment

An example of a diagnostic strategy is shown below.

Miscue analysis during oral reading: background

The strategy known as miscue analysis is based on the 'top-down' approach to reading that was developed from the work of Goodman (1967). Goodman argues that the reader first has to make predictions as to the most likely meaning of the text. Such predictions are based on how the reader perceives the graphic, syntactic and semantic information contained in the text.

Goodman suggests that by using miscue analysis a teacher can listen to a child read and determine whether a mistake or 'miscue' results. These miscues can arise from symbolic, syntactic or semantic errors. Symbolic errors would mean that the child has misread the actual letter(s) and this can be a result of a visual difficulty. Syntactic errors may occur when the child reads the word 'of' instead of 'for'. This would indicate that the child does not have the grammatical structures of sentences but can make a fairly good stab at the symbolic features of the word – even though it is still wrong. The other type of errors – semantic errors – are quite common with children with dyslexia as these kind of errors would indicate the reader is relying heavily on context. An example of a semantic error would be reading the word 'bus' instead of 'car'.

The type of errors often noted in miscue analysis and the significance of these are shown below:

- **Omissions** These may occur if the child is reading for meaning rather than the actual print. He/she may omit small words that do not add anything significant to the meaning of the passage.
- **Additions** These may reflect superficial reading with, perhaps, an over-dependence on context clues.
- **Substitutions** These can be visual or semantic substitutions and they may reflect an over-dependence on context clues.
- **Repetitions** These may indicate poor directional attack, especially if the child reads the same line again. These may also indicate some hesitancy on the part of the child, perhaps being unable to read the next word in the line.
- **Reversals** These may reflect the lack of left–right orientation. Reversals may also indicate some visual difficulty and perhaps a lack of reading for meaning.

- **Hesitations** These can occur when the reader is unsure of the text and perhaps lacking in confidence in reading. For the same reason that repetitions may occur, the reader may also be anticipating a difficult word later in the sentence.
- **Self-corrections** These would occur when the reader becomes more aware of meaning and less dependent on simple word recognition. It is important to recognise the extent of self-corrections as this can indicate that the child does have an understanding of the passage.

Children with dyslexia can show most of the miscues noted above, especially as, often, they read for meaning and, therefore, additions and substitutions can be quite common.

Barriers to learning

It is useful to view early identification and, indeed, the assessment process in terms of overcoming barriers to learning rather than through a child-deficit focus. In reality, however, both information on the child and the curriculum are needed. Essentially, the 'overcoming barriers to learning' approach requires that all children undertake the same curriculum, irrespective of the perceived abilities and difficulties. An example of this can be the way in which curriculum objectives are identified and assessing the extent to which the child has met them and what action may be needed to help him or her meet the objectives more fully. This action can take the form of some assistance for the child, but equally it can be in terms of reassessing the objectives or refining them in some way to make them more accessible.

A key aspect of this is the monitoring process, which must be based on actual curriculum attainments. The process can be extended to include details of the nature of the work within the curriculum that the child is finding challenging; for example, which letters does the child know and not know and which books can the child read fluently and why should this be the case? Such an approach needs to view the child's classwork in a comprehensive and detailed manner, otherwise it can become merely another type of checklist. Additionally, a degree of precision is needed to assist the teacher to see whether the child is achieving the targets. In order to do this, a sample of work is necessary and should be taken from the actual work of the class.

The importance of this type of perspective is that the emphasis is on the barriers that prevent the child from meeting these targets rather than identifying what the child cannot do. This is essentially a whole-staff and therefore a whole-school responsibility as it is important that attitudes relating to progress and curriculum access are consistent throughout the school. There should be a consistent view throughout the school on the understanding of dyslexia and the role of teachers and curriculum planning in making effective learning a reality for all children, including those with dyslexia.

Specialist teachers and whole-school involvement

According to Bell and McLean (2015), the field of training specialist teachers and assessors is evolving, both in terms of our understanding of dyslexia and literacy difficulties and in systems and protocols of teaching and learning for people with special educational needs (SEN) within the school system and beyond. In England, although the network of specialist teachers and assessors is expanding, government policy states clearly that *every* teacher is a teacher of children with special educational needs (DfE/DoH, 2014). The *SEN Code of Practice* covers students aged up to 25 and emphasises the responsibility of schools to assess and support all learners who are not making progress in line with national expectations. This means that schools, colleges, universities and other training providers now need to develop the skills of specialists within their teams. As part of this provision Education and Health and Care Plans are intended for those children or young people with SEN who need education provision. Trained specialist teachers are likely to be key players in the process.

Bell and McLean also argue that it was recognised by Gordon Brown's Labour government (2007–10) that there was a need for a specialist dyslexia teacher in every school and funding for a limited period was allocated to train such teachers, using existing, high-quality training courses (DCSF, 2009). If and when such targets for specialist teachers are achieved, each English school must decide on priorities for the use of their SEN funding in relation to dyslexia and this will depend on the school pupil population and their diverse needs. This has been reinforced by a requirement under the recent *Code of Practice* (DfE/DoH, 2014) for all local authorities in England, to collaborate with schools and other agencies, to publish a 'Local Offer' outlining SEN support. This sets out provision available for children and young people with SEN in the area.

It is the view of many involved in this area that the identification of dyslexia and how to teach dyslexic children are the responsibility of specialists, and such specialists should therefore be identified within schools and undertake the responsibility of recognising and meeting the needs of children with dyslexia. This, however, should not always be the case. Ideally, responsibility should be on a whole-school basis and all teachers should have some knowledge of dyslexia – in particular, the literacy and learning needs of children with dyslexia – and this can complement the role of specialists.

Assessing reading ability and skills (from Came and Reid, 2008)

1   **Background Information:** a summary of the pupil's reading-related information based on scores of standardised achievement tests, criterion referenced tests, and basal end-of-book tests. The current reading status of the pupil is indicated as is any supplementary help he/she is receiving.

2   **Purpose of Referral:** a synopsis of the reasons for the request for diagnostic evaluation. Included are comments of specific reading concerns expressed by classroom teachers, resource personnel, school psychologists, parents, etc.

3   **Testing:** a brief description of the pupil's behaviour and displayed attitude during the testing battery. Also stated are the specific areas of reading that were tested.

4   **Diagnostic Summary:** an explanation of the results of tests administered in each reading skill area:

    a   *Emergent/Readiness Skills* – Checks for: beginning reading skills Deficiency Suggests: difficulty understanding and following directions

    b   *Auditory Skills* – Checks for: hearing and remembering sounds in words
Deficiency Suggests: difficulty understanding and following oral directions, instructions, class discussions, and establishing sound/symbol relationships necessary for phonic instruction

    c   *Visual Skills* – Checks for: seeing and remembering printed or written material
Deficiency Suggests: difficulty remembering letters in words – consequently writing words with letters reversed or jumbled or perceiving words incorrectly for decoding

    d   *Word Recognition Skills* – Checks for: recognising and applying the sounds for the symbols such as phonic generalisations and syllabic principles
Deficiency Suggests: difficulty reading fluently with many mispronunciations

    e   *Language and Vocabulary Development* – Checks for: understanding and expressing adequate language and the concepts of written words
Deficiency Suggests: difficulty understanding written material and understanding classroom instructions

    f   *Oral Reading/Comprehension* – Checks for: decoding ability, fluency, accuracy, and comprehension

    g   *Silent Reading/Comprehension* – Checks for: understanding of vocabulary and comprehension

    h   *Listening Comprehension* – Checks for: processing information presented orally and comparing listening to oral/silent reading ability.

5   **Interpretation of Diagnosis:** the tester's opinion of what might be blocking the pupil's reading growth – the reading weaknesses and the strengths the teacher must take into consideration in adjusting the curriculum to meet the pupil's needs

6   **Learning Goals:** a concise list of goals the tester has devised to improve the pupil's learning to read

7   **Teaching Recommendations:** specific suggestions and methods to aid in providing appropriate instruction in order for the pupil to attain the goals

8   **Learning Activities:** Suggestions are designed to help you understand and assist the pupil in coping.

(Reproduced with permission Learning Works, Came and Reid, 2008)

This emphasises their view that assessment should not be carried out in isolation. It needs a context, a purpose and appropriate linkage with intervention. Similarly, teaching reading should not be carried out in isolation. Assessment therefore is the starting point but it is important that the time allocated to assessment is used appropriately and productively. That is why they suggest that a range of materials be used and that the teacher needs to be empowered to take some responsibility for the assessment process – to observe, to diagnose, to monitor.

Contextualising assessment with a view to intervention

It is important to ensure that the assessment process and results from any tests used are contextualised in relation to the curriculum and the nature of the child's learning situation. Sometimes factors within the classroom and the materials that are being used may account for the difficulties the child is displaying as much as the child's own attributes. Came and Reid (2008) tackle the issue of assessing literacy from the view of identifying concern and empowering the teacher to be in a position to do this. In their publication *Concern, Assess, Provide (CAP) It All!* (ibid.), Came and Reid provide a range of materials that can be used in the classroom context and focus directly on the student's current work. They ask the key question 'What is literacy?' and suggest that the answer to that question will determine selection of information to undertake an assessment. This can mean addressing the functional aspects of literacy (technical) or the purpose of literacy (meaning). One of the important aspects of this is to have efficient and effective monitoring mechanisms in place to ensure that all aspects of the reading process are addressed. Unlike some other tests, they include assessment of children's inferential understanding of text as well as the literal meaning of the passage. Identifying the inferences in texts is an important element for developing higher-order thinking and processing skills and particularly important for children with dyslexia as often their main focus tends to be on mastering the bottom–up sub-skills of reading; the inferential meanings of the text are sometimes lost.

Metacognitive assessment

Metacognition refers to the child's self-knowledge of learning. It examines the quality of the learning process: the structure and organisation of the learner's knowledge base, of mental models (schemata) and efficiency of student self-monitoring. Metacognitive knowledge therefore involves both content and process knowledge. Most traditional forms of assessment look only at the content base, and what the child can and cannot do becomes the product of the assessment. It is important to consider, however, that a preoccupation with identifying the nature of the difficulties should not prevent an assessment of the child's learning processes. This has considerable linkage with appropriate teaching and how materials should be presented.

There are a number of ways of assessing the metacognitive strategies of the learner. Some of these are described below.

Assisted assessment

Brown and Campione (1994), dissatisfied with the limited information that can be obtained from normative procedures, have developed a soundly researched model for assisted or dynamic assessment, focusing on the task and the process of learning. They have also linked this form of assessment with the intervention model known as 'reciprocal teaching' (Palincsar and Klenk, 1992).

The focus of Campione and Brown's work relates to aspects of learning and transfer; the information obtained provides an indication of the nature and amount of help needed by the child, rather than the child's level of attainment or improvement. This can be revealed through 'prompts', memory tasks and help with developing learning strategies.

Campione and Brown argue that there should be a link between assessment and instruction. They argue that traditional tests are intended to be predictive and prescriptive, but fail on both counts. Their argument rests on the assertions that children can be too readily mis-classified and that traditional tests do not really provide a clear indication of what is actually required for instruction. They argue that the context of assessment is important and divide assessment into two aspects.

Static tests

In these the child works unaided on sets of items and is given but a single chance to demonstrate his or her proficiency. Thus no aid is provided; social interaction between the tester and the child is minimised; objective scoring systems can be readily implemented and norms can be available.

Although such tests may fulfil a useful purpose they have considerable short-comings as they say very little about the processes involved in the acquisition of the responses. For example, some children may get the right answer for the wrong reason.

Dynamic tests

Dynamic-type tests emphasise the individual's potential for change. Such tests do not attempt to assess how much improvement has taken place, but rather how much help children need to reach a specified criterion and how much help they will need to transfer this to novel situations. Such tests are therefore metacognitive in that they can provide information on how the child is learning. By noting the cues necessary to facilitate the correct response from the child, the teacher can obtain some information on how the child thinks and learns. Such information can be relayed back to the child to illustrate how he or she managed to obtain the correct response. Thus, assessment is a learning experience, not a testing one.

The role of metacognition in learning is of great importance as this relates to the learner's awareness of thinking and learning. Tunmer and Chapman (1996) have shown how dyslexic children have poor metacognitive awareness and this leads them to adopt inappropriate learning behaviours in reading and spelling.

Essentially, metacognition relates to thinking about thinking, being aware of the learning process and utilising that in new learning. The teacher then has an instrumental role to play in developing metacognitive awareness (Peer and Reid, 2001). This can be done by asking the student some fundamental questions and through observing the learning behaviour of students, such as the example below.

Facilitating metacognitive awareness

When tackling a new task does the child demonstrate self-assessment by asking questions such as:

- Have I done this before?
- How did I tackle it?
- What did I find easy?
- What was difficult?
- Why did I find it easy or difficult?
- What did I learn?
- What do I have to do to accomplish this task?
- How should I tackle it?
- Should I tackle it the same way as before?

Metacognitive strategies

The use of metacognitive strategies can help to develop reading comprehension and expressive writing skills. Some specific metacognitive strategies include:

- Visual imagery – discussing and sketching images from text
- Summary sentences – identifying the main ideas in text
- Webbing – the use of concept maps of the ideas from a text

- Self-interrogation – asking questions about what learners already know about a topic and what they may be expected to learn from the new passage.

The most frequently used approach to assess metacognitive understanding is to ask students directly what they know or what they do while engaging in particular cognitive activities. Verbal reports are typically elicited through structured interviews, such as that originally used by Flavell, or by question-naires that include multiple response options to a series of items.

Most questionnaires are domain-specific (e.g. they focus only on reading or only on maths), but some are intended to be more domain-general. A domain-general inventory might assess an individual's knowledge about cognition and regulation of cognition (including planning, monitoring and self-evaluating their learning). A useful self-report strategy for assessing metacognitive aware-ness is to ask students to think aloud about what they are doing and thinking as they solve a problem or read a text. You would then note the steps they are taking. This is particularly important for children with dyslexia as they may well obtain the correct answer but can be unsure of how they obtained that answer.

All the way through an assessment – whether formal or informal – the assessor should be considering what would be the most appropriate form of interven-tion. The assessor should be looking for clues regarding the most appropriate strategies that the learner can access. Wray, below, highlights some of the skills that can be displayed by good readers and this can give some lead in to some desirable reading strategies.

Skills displayed by good readers (Wray, 1994)

It is important therefore to consider some of the elements identified by Wray (1994) regarding the skills displayed by good readers as these provide a good example of metacognitive awareness in reading.

Good readers usually:

- generate questions while they read
- monitor and resolve comprehension problems
- utilise mental images as they read
- re-read when necessary
- self-correct if an error was made when reading.

Using those factors described by Wray, it is important, therefore, to ensure that the reader has a clear picture of the purpose of reading and an understanding of the text about to be read. There is considerable evidence to suggest that pre-reading discussion can enhance reading fluency and understanding.

Information processing

Children with SpLD, and particularly dyslexia, often experience an information processing difference and it is important that this is recognised as it can lead to effective intervention. Information processing describes the interaction between the learner and the task. Essentially the information processing cycle has three main components. These are:

- **Input** – auditory, visual, tactile, kinaesthetic
- **Cognition** – memory, understanding, organising and making sense of information
- **Output** – reading aloud, talking, discussing, drawing, seeing, experiencing.

Children with SpLD can have difficulty at all three stages of this cycle. It is important, therefore, to draw on diagnostic data that involves these three stages. It can be useful to acknowledge this when identifying the difficulties experienced by the child. For example, one can ask whether the same difficulties are experienced if the material is presented visually as opposed to auditorily. Perhaps the individual can learn more effectively if he/she is able to experience the actual learning through the kinaesthetic modality. Although this is related to teaching approaches, it is crucial that this is acknowledged in the identification and assessment process as it is important that reasons for the difficulty are sought and that a clear link can be forged between assessment and teaching approaches.

Information processing-suggestions for linking assessment with intervention

Input

- Identify the student's preferred learning style, particularly visual, auditory, kinaesthetic or tactile preferences, as these can be crucial in how information is presented. It is important to target new information to the learner's preferred modality.
- Present new information in small steps – this will ensure that the short-term memory does not become overloaded with information before it is fully consolidated.
- New material will need to be repeatedly presented through over learning. This does not mean that the repetition should be in the same form – rather it is important that it should be varied using as wide a range of materials and strategies as possible.
- It is a good idea to present the key points at the initial stage of learning new material. This helps to provide a framework for the new material and can help to relate new information to previous knowledge.

Cognition

- Information should be related to previous knowledge. This ensures that concepts are developed and the information can be placed into a learning framework, or schema, by the learner. Successful learning is often due to efficient organisation of information. It is important, therefore, to group information together and to show the connection between the two. For example, if the topic to be covered was the Harry Potter series of books, then concepts such as witchcraft and magic, and the words associated with these, would need to be explained and some of the related ideas discussed. This should be done prior to reading the text.
- Some specific memory strategies, such as mind mapping and mnemonics, can be used to help the learner remember some of the key words or more challenging ideas. This can be done visually through mind mapping.

Output

- Often children with SpLD have difficulty identifying the key points in new learning or in a text. This can be overcome by providing the child with these key points or words at the beginning stage of learning the new material. Additionally, the learner can acquire skills in this by practising using summaries. Each period of new learning should be summarised by the learner – this, in itself, helps to identify the key points.
- It may also be beneficial to measure progress orally rather than in writing, particularly in-class continuous assessment. It is not unusual for children with dyslexia to be much more proficient orally than in written form. Oral presentation of information can therefore help to instil confidence. By contrast, often a written exercise can be damaging in terms of confidence, unless considerable preparation and planning have helped to ensure that some of the points indicated above are put in to place.

An assessment framework

Below is an example of a framework that may assist in the planning of an assessment.

- Sensory assessment: this involves hearing, vision, etc. This is particularly important for young children.
- Information from parents: this is crucial – parents have a considerable amount of information on their child and it is important that this is shared with the assessor.
- Word recognition test: it is also important that the assessor includes single-word reading. This takes away the use of context so it is a more realistic test of actual reading skills.

- Non-word recognition test: this is a pure test of decoding as the words have to be decoded so the learner has to have some knowledge of how to decode the word and some competence in phonological processing.
- Spelling test: it is always useful to include a spelling test as spelling can be very diagnostic of the difficulties the children may be experiencing in literacy.
- Phonological assessment: this is particularly important for children with dyslexia as a difficulty in phonics is usually the main issue that is causing difficulties in literacy.
- Miscue analysis: this, or something similar, can be used in a diagnostic way to look at the type of errors the child is making.
- Reading/listening comprehension test: it is important to obtain a measure of the child's comprehension and it is a good idea to use both reading comprehension and listening comprehension.
- Free writing: this is always useful and it can be done in timed and untimed conditions. It can give an idea of how the child structures written work, as well as whether he/she is able utilise their oral vocabulary in written work.
- Curriculum information: this helps the assessor contextualise the assessment for the purpose of identifying the learner's needs. This is also important for tracking progress.
- Observational assessment: this should, if at all possible, be included in an assessment protocol. Children can perform differently in the test situation compared to the classroom. It also gives some idea of how the child performs and interacts with his/her peer group.
- Additional relevant information: there can be a number of different professionals involved in an assessment so it is useful to obtain information from those who may have seen the child prior to this, including speech and language therapists, medical professionals, occupational therapist and optometrists.

Linking assessment with intervention

Key issues

Some of the key issues relating to specific learning difficulties are:

- the subject content – ensuring it is accessible
- subject delivery – ensuring that the presentation of the curriculum acknowledges the specific challenges and the learning style as well as the strengths of students with specific learning difficulties and that the planning takes into account the potential difficulties they may experience with learning
- assessment – as far as possible a wide range of assessment strategies should be used so that pointers for intervention can be obtained
- learning styles – it is important to acknowledge that new learning needs to be presented in a manner that can suit the student's learning style.

Pointers for differentiation

It is also important that some of the key aspects for differentiation are considered in presenting the results of the assessment, thus ensuring that the assessment links with intervention.

Factors such as those shown below can be useful:

- knowledge of the readability levels of text and sources of information
- the design of resources, including the layout and the use of diagrams; the latter need to be clearly labelled
- provision of printed materials such as notes to prevent rote note taking
- the provision of key words – this is important as it can help to provide the student with a framework for the topic and prevent any difficulties he/she may display with word retrieval
- specialised vocabulary spelling lists are important as, in some subjects (particularly in secondary school), there may be specialised technical vocabulary
- use of coloured paper – there is some evidence that different colours of background and font can enhance some children's reading and attention
- page layout is very important and should be visual but not overcrowded. Coloured background is also usually preferable. Font size can also be a key factor and this should not be too small. In relation to the actual font itself, it has been suggested that Sasoon font, Comic Sans and Times New Roman are quite accessible.

Summary

There is no golden formula for identifying and addressing the special learning needs of every student who experiences difficulties of a dyslexic nature. Addressing difficulties is a question of problem-solving the inter-relationship and interaction between the characteristics of the individual learner, the requirements of the curriculum and factors related to the learning environment and teachers' pedagogies.

Dyslexia should not *only* be identified through the use of a test. The identification of dyslexia is a process and that 'process' involves much more than the administration of a test or a group of tests. Specifically, identification should consider three aspects in particular – discrepancies, difficulties and differences (including strengths) – and these should relate to the classroom environment and the curriculum as well as the learning preferences of the child. The assessment therefore needs to consider classroom and curriculum factors, the learning preferences of the child and the specific difficulties and strengths. Essentially, it needs to consider the task and the curriculum as well as the learning environment and the learning experience.

Key points

- Assessment of dyslexia and, indeed, the other SpLDs is a process that involves more than using a test.
- The assessment process needs to consider the difficulties, the discrepancies and the differences.
- Teachers can develop diagnostic phonological assessment.
- Assessment of reading and spelling should be diagnostic.
- The difference in learning styles and learning preferences needs to be taken into account.
- Assessment needs to have a clear link to intervention.

Chapter 3

Teacher assessment

Literacy

Introduction

Literacy is a complex set of skills that comprise the inter-related processes of reading and writing required within range of social and cultural contexts. Reading requires decoding, accurate and fluent word recognition and comprehension at the word, phrase, sentence and text levels. Writing requires automatic letter formation and/or keyboarding, accurate and fluent spelling, sentence construction and the ability to compose a variety of different text structures with coherence and cohesion. Sound identification and recall, letter recognition, alphabet recall, instant word recognition and sound–symbol associations are all the 'building blocks' of reading (Wright and Jacobs, 2003). If these skills are not achieved and the milestones not met, it can be challenging for children to achieve any type of success in (as cited in Martin, Martin and Carvalho, 2008).

Recent studies of genetic influences indicate that reading skills can be partially attributed to biological 'wiring' and to life experiences (Moats, 2004). This notion is coupled with the idea that literacy takes 'root', long before schooling begins, with the development of language. Children exposed to books at an early age are believed to receive appropriate modelling of language, with exposure to the alphabet and the audible speech it represents.

In the UK the National Literacy Trust figures optimistically suggest that many more children now reach the expected level for their age in literacy than in 1997. The key indicator, the percentage of pupils reaching level four (the level expected for their age) in national tests for English (reading and writing) at age 11, has increased from 63 per cent to 80 per cent in this time. In the mid-1990s just half of children reached the level expected for their age. These targets apply to all children, of all abilities and social classes, including those who speak English as an additional language.

Curtis (2008), however, draws attention to the fact that in England around 20 per cent of children emerge from their primary school experience without the basic levels of attainment expected of them in literacy. This is in spite of a ten-year intensive focus on literacy teaching by the UK government.

The CBI's 2008 Education and Skills Survey 'Taking Stock' (CBI, 2008) found that 41 per cent of employers surveyed were concerned about employees' basic literacy. For firms with basic skills concerns, the quality of written English – constructing properly spelt sentences with accurate grammar – was the major literacy concern (72 per cent). Additionally, according to the American National Assessment of Educational Progress (Jitendra, Edwards and Starosta, 2004), 40 per cent of fourth-grade students in the USA read below their grade level.

This problem also seems to increase and become more serious in the case of children with SpLDs (dyslexia). 'Dyslexia' is a popular and accepted term in the UK and in many other countries and the British Dyslexia Association (BDA) assert that 10 per cent of the British population are dyslexic, 4 per cent severely so.[1]

In the USA in 2002, the US Department of Education (Manset-Williamson and Nelson, 2005) reported that, of the approximately 2.9 million school-aged children receiving public services for learning difficulties, the majority were identified as having a learning disability because of developmental delays in reading. In the USA, the broad term 'learning disabilities' (LD) is used to describe a wide variety of disorders, including 'disorders in one or more of the basic psychological processes involved in understanding or using spoken or written language' (IDEA, 2004 Section 300.8 (c)(10)) (cited in Reynolds, Johnson and Salzman, 2012).

Factors to consider

Academic problems of students with SpLDs may be evident in listening comprehension, reading, writing or mathematics. Problems in non-academic areas, such as lack of organisation, impulsive decision-making, lack of metacognition and lack of social–emotional control, can and do make academic life even more frustrating (Chang, 1996; Reid, 2009). The BDA website provides some comments on this (in the UK) from individuals themselves (see Fig. 3.1), which gives some insights into the difficulties they experience at both academic and literacy levels.

The number of students classified as having SpLDs has grown dramatically during the past 20 years, which has led to an increase in the amount of research conducted to determine the most effective intervention methods for the development of reading and other skills, such as writing, maths, language and motor development. Children with SpLDs/dyslexia mainly experience difficulty with reading (Swanson, 2008) in comparison with the general student population.

Underdeveloped literacy skills have profound consequences for students, families and society. These effects are academic, social, emotional and economic in nature. Children with dyslexia are often inadequately prepared for the academic challenges presented across the educational continuum in both

'I see things from a different perspective.'

'I can come up with solutions no one else has thought of and I think fast on my feet.'

'When I am reading, occasionally a passage will get all jumbled up, but when it happens I have to read and re-read the passage over again.'

'I know what I want to say, but I can never find the right words.'

'In formal situations, although I know what I want to say, I struggle, lose focus and then my mind goes blank and I panic.'

'I have the right ideas, but I can't get them down on paper.'[2]

Figure 3.1 Some academic and literacy difficulties experienced by people with dyslexia.

primary and secondary settings. Secondary students with dyslexia experience significant deficits in reading and maths when compared to other students at the same year level (Dodds and Lumsden, 2001). Additionally, children and young people with dyslexia (or low literacy levels) are inclined to drop out of school at higher rates than the general population. In the USA only 11 per cent of students with dyslexia, compared to 53 per cent of students in the general education population, have attended a four-year post-secondary programme and Barton (2004) reports that the 25 fastest-growing professions have greater than average literacy demands while the fastest-declining professions have lower than average literacy demands. Students must not only possess proficiency with print, but also with the skills and strategies required by what is an increasingly digital environment. Therefore, it is imperative that intervention for students with dyslexia begins when literacy needs are first identified.

It is known that pre-literacy screening can be very effective and cost effective and can commence before the onset of literacy or beginning school (Fawcett and Nicolson, 1995, 2008).

A good example of this can be seen in the Report of the Task Force on Dyslexia (2001).

The report recommends a phased assessment model specifically for identifying difficulties arising from dyslexia. This includes:

Phase 1 – Initial identification of learning differences (ages three to five), which provides the following indicators of learning differences.

Phase 2 – Identification of a possible learning difficulty arising from dyslexia (age five to seven onwards). This includes monitoring, observation, diagnostic assessment reviews by class teacher and learning support teacher, and consideration of intervention approaches, which can also include home/ school programmes.

Phase 3 – This phase reports on the formal identification of dyslexia and an analysis of needs from ages seven to 12 onwards. This includes a review of the interventions that have been implemented up to that point, including the input from parents as well as teachers. This phase also considers the effects of the child's learning difficulty on his/her self-esteem, as well as the effects of any other related learning difficulty.

Phase 4 – This involves the provision of multi-disciplinary annual reviews from aged 12 onwards. These reviews would ensure the presence of an individual education programme. This phase also alerts the school to the possibility of unrecognised difficulties which may not become obvious until entry to post-primary education.

The report therefore recommends that an early recognition system should be in place in all post-primary schools – this should include close liaison with feeder primary schools before transfer as well as information from parents on incoming students. Obviously, the production of such a comprehensive document with clear recommendations for all to see and follow is commendable.

It is also known that there are social implications to literacy difficulties and a number of prison studies in many countries – UK, Sweden and USA, for example – have shown that anything from 35–50 per cent of the prison population will likely show signs of dyslexia (Reid and Kirk, 2001; Elbeheri, Everatt and Al-Malki, 2009).

Wagner (2000) reports that low achievement in literacy correlates with high rates of poverty and unemployment. The impact of these realities is significant to society and the consequential socio-emotional risks for these individuals are profound.

Importance of literacy assessment for teachers

Assessment has long been an area of concern in all phases and areas of education. The literature is full of debates around the purposes and practices of assessment. Formative assessment, however, is pivotal to any approach to teaching and learning that gives value to children's ideas, since finding out their ideas initially and then frequently checking to find out how they have changed is a prerequisite to teaching for understanding. There is a body of evidence that suggests that formative assessment is an essential feature of classroom work and that development of it can raise standards. Formative assessment can also be preventative and pave the way for early identification, particularly for children who are at risk of dyslexia.

Comprehensive assessment and evaluation seeks to accurately identify a student's patterns of strengths and needs. A comprehensive assessment and evaluation should use a valid and most current version of any standardised assessment and use multiple measures, including both standardised and non-standardised assessments and other data sources, such as case history and interviews with parents, educators, related professionals and the student (if appropriate), as well as evaluations and information provided by parents. The term 'assessment' is used in many different contexts for a variety of purposes in educational settings, including individual and group, standardised and informal, formative and summative. Some professionals use assessment broadly to include both assessment and evaluation. Assessment refers to the collection of data through the use of multiple measures, including standardised and informal instruments and procedures. These measures yield comprehensive quantitative and qualitative data about an individual student. The results of continuous progress monitoring also may be used as part of individual and classroom assessments. Information from many of these sources of assessment data can and should be used to help ensure that the comprehensive assessment and evaluation accurately reflects how an individual student is performing.

Evaluation follows assessment and incorporates information from all data sources. Evaluation refers to the process of integrating, interpreting and summarising the comprehensive assessment data, including indirect and pre-existing sources.

The major goal of assessment and evaluation is to enable team members to use data to create a profile of a student's strengths and needs. The student profile informs decisions about identification, eligibility, services and intervention. The reason that comprehensive assessment and evaluation procedures are needed is because any type of learning issue can be manifested differently among individuals over time, in severity and across settings. That is why ongoing monitoring is important, as well as the review of intervention.

Literacy assessment process

Assessment of student needs is one of the most difficult and yet most important tasks that teachers have. Appropriate assessment leads to effective instruction and more efficient and successful learning. Assessment is ongoing and goal-directed to increase student learning. Without such a goal it ceases to have meaning in an educational context. As indicated in the previous chapters, assessment is more than test-giving and interpreting. It should incorporate various sources, which may include standardised tests, informal measures, observations, student self-reports, parent reports and progress monitoring.

When you look at some of the factors involved in literacy you can obtain some idea of the different aspects that need to be looked at in some way – either through standardised assessment or through observation.

These include:

- auditory factors
    - recognition of letter sounds
    - recognition of sounds and letter groups or patterns
    - sequencing of sounds
    - discriminating sounds from other sounds
    - discriminating sounds within words

- linguistic factors

  o   the flow of oral language does not always make the break between words clear
  o   retaining the sounds in memory
  o   articulating sounds
  o   recognising the sounds in written form

- visual factors

  o   recognising the visual cues of letters and words
  o   familiarity with left–right orientation
  o   recognising word patterns
  o   recognising letter and word shapes

- contextual factors

  o   acquiring vocabulary knowledge
  o   acquiring general knowledge
  o   using context as an aid to word recognition, comprehension and analogy skills.

Developing an observation schedule can be a useful way of incorporating these points. It is important, however, to consider the point made by Bell and McLean (2015), who suggest that, in the mainstream classroom, it can be easy to miss signs of SpLDs, particularly when students disguise these with bad behaviour, or by keeping a low profile, enabling them to remain undetected in a busy environment. They suggest that this can also be important in the case of adults with dyslexia, who can be well-practised at concealing weaknesses at work. As a result, they not receive the appropriate support and simple adjustments to their working practice which would help them carry out their roles more efficiently and possibly reduce stress and anxiety.

Planning

The assessment process must be well planned in order to ensure that it is comprehensive, orderly and efficient. At the start of the planning for assessment, the teacher or assessor involved must determine what is known, what is unknown and what needs to be known about the individual being assessed. Information will include learning potential, individual achievement levels, peer and adult interactions, social interactions, social/emotional adjustment, home and school environments and past school performance. Once information needs are identified, decisions can be made regarding the appropriate types of assessment procedures to be used, who will assess and their roles and the timeline for completion. The selection and use of tests in the assessment process is a critical decision. Used properly, tests can provide important diagnostic information, but poor selection and/or improper application of the tests can lead to confusion or, worse, inappropriate diagnosis. A major consideration in selecting a test must be its technical adequacy. Has the test been properly normed and is it reliable and valid? All such important questions and considerations must be addressed during the planning for assessment process. It can be useful to commence with a general screening test as well as some form of observation and data gathering (see later in this chapter).

Collection of information

The goal at this stage is to efficiently collect information through a variety of means that includes:

1   a review of historical information found in the student's records
2   a review of teaching strategies and current student performance diagnostic teaching
3   interviews with the parents, teachers, significant others and the individual concerned
4   observation of the student
5   any other formal and/or informal testing.

No single data source is sufficient for identifying students with SpLDs; this includes the data from any one quantitative formula such as a discrepancy between standardised ability and achievement scores. Comprehensive assessment measures, procedures and practices are necessary to enable multidisciplinary teams to differentiate learning disabilities from underachievement and other types of learning and behaviour problems.

Five critical assumptions have been widely identified concerning the assessment process:

1   the person giving the test is skilled
2   a certain amount of error will be present
3   the acculturation for the child being tested is comparable to the group on which the test was standardised
4   the behaviour sampling is adequate in amount and representative in area
5   present behaviour is observed, future behaviour is inferred.

The test examiner must be skilled in establishing rapport, correctly administering the test, scoring the test and interpreting test results. Two kinds of error are generally recognised: systematic error and random error. Systematic error is consistent in that it is built into the test instrument by the examiner. Random error is produced by the inconsistency of the examiner or the test instrument.

Analysis and interpretation

The collected information must be analysed and interpreted to determine its meaning. The analysis begins with a summary of the findings. Good summaries group the information in such a way that each piece can be given appropriate consideration in light of all the other information. Comparison of the information collected leads to the determination of the individual's academic and behavioural strengths and weaknesses. Once the strengths and weaknesses are identified efforts must be made to account for significant discrepancies found in the individual's performance. These include discrepancies between the individual's performance and the point of reference, as well as discrepancies within the individual's performance. Discrepancies in information collected by different individuals on the team must also be addressed and explained.

Synthesis

Synthesis is the process of putting the parts together to form a whole. The goal is to develop a comprehensive description of the individual as a learner in relation to his/her environment. The effects of the learner on their environment and the effects of the environment on the learner need to be included. The environment should include the classroom and the school environment so it is a good idea to start with some form of observation and this can take the environment into account.

Decision-making

The goal of the decision-making process is to increase student learning by initiating changes within the student's environment and/or educational programme. The decisions are to be logical extensions of the analysis and synthesis of the collected information. An educational plan and programme must be developed and implemented to meet the educational needs and to facilitate the necessary environmental changes (home, school, community and self) identified in the decision-making stage.

Forms of literacy assessment

There is evidence that for children with learning difficulties the form and format of the assessment being used will significantly influence the outcome. Both general screeners and curriculum-based assessment are well-known forms of assessment that are open and accessible for teachers. Below, we further investigate their importance and role in the assessment process, as well as how best to utilise them to enhance the utilisation of such tools to enable teachers to assess their students' literacy.

Curriculum-based assessment

Curriculum-based assessment involves the collection of repeated short samples of a student's behaviour within one or more curriculum areas. The data collected can be used to make eligibility and/or instructional planning decisions. The use of curriculum materials for measuring student performance repeatedly over time is analogous to physicians' measurement of individuals' vital signs, such as temperature and blood pressure (Rosenberg and Sindelar, 1982). In both cases the measures need to be direct, continuous and sensitive. An alternative starting point for curriculum-based assessment is at the conclusion of a few selected standardised, individually administered achievement tests. The administrations of either group or individual standardised tests serve the purpose of providing directions for the particular curriculum area(s) on which curriculum-based assessment should be focused.

Within the curriculum-based assessment system, the teachers are primarily responsible not only for collecting assessment data, but also for developing or selecting the assessment materials. As opposed to traditional models of educational assessment, curriculum-based assessment has the following distinct advantages:

1   Assessment data are related directly to instruction and teachers can utilise the data to better structure curriculum and teaching methods.
2   Frequent testing, which is required for curriculum-based assessment, can enhance student learning and motivation. It definitely provides more specific feedback to students and helps them become aware of their status in goal attainment.
3   Curriculum-based assessment is very time efficient as most of the assessment devices can be administered in one to three minutes.

In order to use the curriculum-based assessment to make eligibility decisions, local norms of peer performance on each of the academic measures need to be established. The referred student's performance is compared to the local norm and discrepancy ratios in the curriculum areas can be computed to help determine the appropriateness of special education placement. Curriculum-based assessment can be used to verify standardised individual achievement test results by collecting three rate and accuracy measures of randomly selected word lists, passages, maths facts or story starters from the student's current curriculum materials and analysing the types of errors.

Screening

The Dyslexia Screening Test (Fawcett and Nicolson, 1995) can be useful in providing a range of information that can be developed with further extended testing. The same applies to the screening procedures known as the Special

Needs Assessment Profile (SNAP) (Weedon, Long and Reid, 2012). SNAP is a computer-aided diagnostic assessment and profiling package that makes it possible to 'map' each student's own mix of problems on to an overall matrix of learning, behavioural and other difficulties. From this, clusters and patterns of weaknesses and strengths help to identify the core features of a student's difficulties – visual, dyslexic, dyspraxic, phonological, attention or any other of the key deficits targeted – and suggests a diagnosis that points the way forward for that individual student (see also Chapter 11, Developing an Assessment Framework).

Screening tools, however, can result in a false positive (i.e. a person is identified as possibly having a learning difficulty when, in fact, this is not the case) or a false negative (i.e. a person is not identified as possibly having a learning difficulty when, in fact, they may have one). These instruments can vary from a five-minute checklist to more in-depth assessments that can take one to two hours to complete. Screening tool results should be used in conjunction with other assessment tools to develop a clear understanding of the learner's academic needs and strengths. The more comprehensive screening instruments can (and should) be used to inform classroom intervention.

A positive result using any of the available screening tools may result in a referral to a professional diagnostician, such as an educational psychologist, for a full evaluation. Typically, the evaluation will include an intelligence test, such as the Wechsler Intelligence Scale (4th edition, WISC IV (WISC-V in US)) (Wechsler, 2008), and an achievement test such as the Woodcock Johnson® Psycho-Educational Battery (revised, WJIII) (Woodcock, McGrew and Mather, 2001) or the Wechsler Individual Achievement Test (2nd edition (3rd edition in USA and Canada), WIAT II) (Wechsler, 2005). Assessors can look for a discrepancy between intelligence and achievement, typically referred to as *unexpected underperformance*, but it is important to remember that this is only one factor in the diagnosis and may not be the most important aspect. The *DSM-V* allows for a discrepancy of between 1 and 2 standard deviations (American Psychiatric Association, 2013). Because individuals with learning difficulties do not necessarily suffer from cognitive impairment but usually perform poorly in certain academic subjects, discrepancy models are intuitively logical (Kavale, 2002, cited in Reynolds, Johnson and Salzman, 2012).

Role of literacy assessment in planning for learning

Children with dyslexia and the other SpLDs represent a unique group of students who present distinctive challenges to educators. No two children have the same set of needs and the needs of those with SpLDs are often complicated by difficulty in processing information, communicating and literacy and numeracy issues. Consequently, it is important that the assessment should lead to appropriate intervention. Early intervention, with successful modes of teaching and learning, can target areas of deficiency and help learners with dyslexia become proficient readers. Early intervention should focus on a teacher-directed approach in which specific skills are taught at the functional reading level of the child and progress is evaluated frequently to check for any further difficulties. This explicit instruction allows teachers to work on skills in a sequential manner and provide modelling, guidance and support during the learning process (Martin, Martin and Carvalho, 2008).

In the field of educational assessment, one of the crucial aspects, as indicated in previous chapters, is the linking of assessment with instructional planning (Zigmond, Vallecorsa and Silverman, 1983; Crombie, Knight and Reid, 2004; Reid, 2009). The type of assessment that involves collection of information that can inform teaching has traditionally been classified as informal assessment. Despite their crucial role in the teaching decisions, informal teacher-made tests have often been considered too simplistic to warrant much credit. Curriculum-based measures and traditional data, including quizzes, homework and test grades, are used to monitor student progress.

Diagnostic teaching allows the teacher to observe the student's performance and to compare this against the expected outcome and the level of the class. The purposes of diagnostic teaching as a source of information in assessment are: 1. differential diagnosis or 2. planning for learning.

In the case of differential diagnosis, the ultimate aim is to use strategies that will rule out distracting stimuli, slow learner characteristics, anxiety as an inhibiting factor in learning, motivation as a problem, inappropriate teaching and lack of learning opportunities.[3] In the case of planning for learning, the purpose is to:

a   find out what the student knows about how, what and why s/he learns
b   find out how the student formulated the answer and the 'why' of that particular answer
c   to test the hypotheses developed as a result of the synthesis of all the information gathered and analysed
d   to develop the instructional objectives and strategies that are necessary to meet the student's individual educational needs
e   to find answers to discrepancy questions
f   to determine the student's level of thinking and understanding of academic learning and life learning and allow a comparison of the student's success with a variety of instructional strategies.

Assessment of literacy: guidelines for teachers

Understand dyslexia/literacy difficulties

Assessment and evaluation are guided by a consistent understanding of what we actually mean by literacy difficulties or dyslexia. There can be misconceptions due to individual differences (Reid, 2009), the wide variation in severity (ibid.), popular myths (Fawcett and Reid, 2009) and academic controversy (Eliot and Grigorenko, 2014). Professionals with expertise in dyslexia are essential to conduct a comprehensive assessment. Usually educational psychologists will carry this out, but, as indicated in earlier chapters, in the UK there is now a robust series of training courses to enable appropriately qualified and experienced teachers to conduct assessments; there are number of courses in SpLD which include approved teacher assessor status and participants are awarded an Assessment Practising Certificate. The Professional Association for Teachers of Students with Specific Learning Difficulties (PATOSS) have a guide that can advise teachers on how to progress with assessing and reporting to ensure that their assessment is approved by examination boards (Jones and Kindersley, 2013).

Enable students to be part of their own learning process

Ideally, we should all be striving to help students with dyslexia become self-regulated learners, and be able to assess their work, identify its merits, locate its weaknesses and determine ways to improve it (Nicol, 2009; Sadler, 2009). Part of that judgment includes evaluating the appropriateness of their responses to assessment tasks and whether they have done what they were asked to do (Sadler, 2010). It also requires them to assess how good their response is in relation to the relevant academic achievement standards (Sadler, 2009).

Learners' understanding of the purposes of assessment and the processes surrounding assessment is part of the context within which they learn to make those judgements and become effectively self-regulating (Smith *et al.*, 2013). The literature here tends to suggest that learners' capacity to become successful self-regulated learners can be affected by various aspects of the assessment process.

We argue that, first, students need to understand the purpose of assessment and how it connects with their learning profile and preferences. Second, they need to be aware of the processes of assessment so they can anticipate the next steps. Third, opportunities for them to practice assessing their own responses to assessment tasks need to be provided so that students can learn to identify what is good about their work and what could be improved.

This approach is essentially metacognitive and Reid (2009) has suggested the following steps can be used:

- self-questioning
- self-clarifying
- self-understanding
- self-connecting
- self-directing
- self-monitoring
- self-assessment.

Students' capacity to develop the above requires a great deal of structured teaching and small steps, but helping learners with dyslexia develop their ability to assess their own work will enhance their learning outcomes (cited in Smith *et al.*, 2013).

Cultural and linguistic background when assessing literacy

Sensitivity to cultural and linguistic diversity in assessments and assessment procedures is a key factor and is receiving a great deal of attention in the reading and literacy research (Figueroa and Newsome, 2006; Wilkinson *et al.*, 2006). Although assessment instruments are now translated into Spanish, Chinese and other languages, particular care must be taken when assessing English-language learner (ELL) students whose native language is not English.

Literacy acquisition is even more challenging for students with dyslexia whose native language or culture differs from the language of literacy intervention. ELLs may have complex backgrounds and experiences that influence learning (e.g. interrupted or limited schooling, living through long separations from family, political turmoil or poverty). In addition, ELL children are twice as likely as their peers to score below basic levels in reading and writing skills and these achievement gaps (Grigg, Donahue and Dion, 2007; Perie, Grigg and Donahue, 2005).[4]

Because some ELL children have the additional challenge of a reading difficulty such as dyslexia, it is essential to distinguish those whose limited linguistic proficiency is due to a language difference from those who have a concomitant learning difficulty (Peer and Reid, 2000). Given the increasing diversity of the population in many countries, including the UK, educators and related service providers are becoming familiar with non-biased assessment techniques; assessment tools are available in different languages and there are protocols for selecting assessment tools that include norms that are sensitive to cultural and linguistic differences (Mahfoudhi, Elebeheri and Everett, 2009; Haynes *et al.*, 2009).

Professionals also are becoming more aware of the need to be able to interpret assessment results for parents and families, as well as other professionals on the team. Professional development opportunities are available that include more training in multicultural issues and non-biased assessments for school personnel. Increasing recruitment of professionals from culturally and linguistically diverse backgrounds is another means of improving services for an increasingly diverse student population.

Obtaining information from multiple sources

The goals of assessment for learners with dyslexia should be tied directly to teaching. This would be more appropriately and effectively carried out using a team-based, comprehensive approach. This would necessitate the collection of multiple forms of information, including standardised tests, qualitative analysis of learners' work samples, observation and self-report measures. Assessment should lead to appropriate programme planning, *whether or not* an individual student meets eligibility criteria for a diagnosis or a label.

Summary and concluding comments

It is important to have an understanding of the processes involved in literacy acquisition and some knowledge of what might go wrong and why. Coupled with this is an understanding of the process of educational assessment and particularly its significance in determining the diagnosis, the learning profile and the pathway to intervention for children who are at risk of failure. Educational assessment therefore provides a description of the student as a learner, resulting in decision-making that should lead, in turn, to increased and enhanced student learning.

Assessment is an ongoing team process. It is a well-planned sequence of events, which is cyclical in nature. It is universally recognised that solid assessment practices can result in providing a sound foundation for addressing the issues of literacy difficulties, diagnosis, appropriate teaching, enhanced learner awareness, parental confidence and appropriate planning for learning.

Notes

1 http://www.bdadyslexia.org.uk/about, accessed 1 January 15.
2 http://www.bdadyslexia.org.uk/dyslexic/dyslexia-and-specific-difficulties-overview, accessed 1 January 2015.
3 In the British Psychological Society (BPS) working party report, referred to earlier in this book, one of the hypotheses for dyslexia was the 'Learning Opportunities Hypothesis'.
4 Census data suggest that, by the year 2020, 25 per cent of all children in the USA will be considered ELL.

Chapter 4

Numeracy

Mathematics learning difficulties

Background

Dyscalculia and mathematics learning disability: features and definitions

Difficulties with learning mathematics can stem from several different sources. These include problems with less than optimal teaching experience (a child who has missed a large amount of school, for example), or they may be due to an underlying difficulty/disability specific to mathematics learning; though, equally, the underlying difficulty may be not be specific to mathematics learning but rather related to another type of specific learning difficulty/disability (SpLD), such as a general language disability. The terms 'dyscalculia' and 'mathematics learning disability' (MLD) have both been used to refer to individuals who have severe and persistent problems with mathematics that seem to stem from an underlying neurological difference compared to typical learners. A learning difficulty/disability such as dyscalculia or MLD has, typically, been seen as a specific problem with learning that is not necessarily due to low IQ. Hence, such individuals may seem bright, and perform well in other areas of the curriculum, but struggle with mathematics-related tasks. Although, as with any area of human behaviour, there are large individual differences in the specific problems presented by such children, individuals with an underlying difficulty/disability that leads to poor mathematics learning typically have been found to show difficulties understanding simple number concepts, and to have a poor intuitive grasp of numbers; they may also have problems learning number facts and procedures, including basic tasks such as counting; and they may show a lack of confidence in performing mathematical procedures or operations (see discussions in: Butterworth and Yeo, 2004; Chinn, 2014; Chinn and Ashcroft, 2007; Geary, 2004; Ramaa, 2000; Everatt, Elbeheri and Brooks, 2013). Hence, problems stemming from an underlying difficulty/disability may be evident even in the early stages of mathematics learning.

Although both MLD and dyscalculia have been used widely in the literature to describe similar developmental/neurological-based learning problems, they have also been used to contrast different conditions: experiential versus con-genital problems, or acquired versus developmental disorders (see discussions in Campbell, 2005; Geary, 2004). Hence, an understanding of the use of these terms by a practitioner/assessor is needed to be clear about where the problems experienced by a child may stem – a teacher reading a report will need to be clear about the use of these terms in the report – and, equally, definitions of the use of these terms may be needed to explain statements in reports that will be read by others. Additionally, although there is a growing body of work looking at MLDs, in comparison to work on literacy learning disability or dyslexia, research related to dyscalculia and MLD has been less common. Hence, there may be developments in the field that will lead to our necessary reconsideration of features and causes. However, current work focusing on this area of LD indicates a severe difficulty in mathematics that cannot be explained by general cognitive difficulties or educational opportunities, which seems to run in families (Shalev et al., 2001). Estimates vary as to the likely prevalence of the condition, but around 3–6 per cent of an educated popula-tion seems to be the likely level of incidence (Berch and Mazzocco, 2007; Geary, 2004; Lewis, Hitch and Walker, 1994; Wilson and Dehaene, 2007), suggesting about one child in every class of 30.

Persistence is another defining feature of a specific learning difficulty/disa-bility, with difficulties associated with dyscalculia/MLD continuing across grades (Shalev, Manor and Gross-Tsur, 2005). Indeed, facts learnt in earlier classes may be mis-remembered or mis-applied in later grades (Chinn and Ashcroft, 2007). Since an understanding of numbers (or values/amounts) and their relationships (Wilson and Dehaene, 2007) dominates the child's early experiences of mathematics, it seems likely that problems in this basic area are a potential source/feature of the underlying dysfunction associated with the LD. Consistent with this, relatively early features of problems related to dys-calculia/MLD are difficulties in understanding how numbers work together in patterns, such as recognising that one number has a larger value than another (Rubinsten and Henik, 2006). Additionally, there is likely to be a continued use of basic strategies in calculations (for example, using fingers to support counting – see Geary, Bow-Thomas and Yao, 1992) and evidence of anxiety and poor attitudes towards mathematics that are likely to inhibit performance (Beasley, Long and Natali, 2001; Maloney et al., 2010).

Finally, there is also evidence that the impact of dyscalculia/MLD can extend to areas outside of education, such as when telling the time or count-ing money (see Chinn and Ashcroft, 2007; Miles and Miles, 1992). These may be evident in negative emotional problems that stem from experiences of failure in mathematics and including anxiety when dealing with mathematics (when it comes to pay for something) or avoidance of situations that require mathematics (including areas of the curriculum that are perceived as requiring mathematics). Negative emotion can also emanate from feelings of embarrass-ment, frustration and anxiety when dealing with mathematical problems.

Children may feel stupid and may be teased or stigmatised by classmates, which can lead to low self-esteem, anxiety, avoidance and negative attitude. Adults may be blocked from certain professions, have difficulty managing money and a poor understanding of numbers/values that can influence decision-making. Anxiety related to mathematics also may interact with mathematic skills or underlying deficits associated with dyscalculia (Ashcraft and Krause, 2007; Maloney *et al.*, 2010). Therefore, even if some early problems are overcome, the lack of confidence that failure has produced may remain well into later schooling and adulthood. Any assessment process (whether conducted by a teacher or another professional) may well need to take into account the potential emotional responses that such experiences can prompt. Assessments, therefore, may need to be stopped to avoid emotional responses making interpretation of results inaccurate – and may have to be recommenced after some time to allow a clear profile of an individual's abilities and weaknesses to be determined.

Aspect of mathematics learning

Mathematics learning problems may not simply stem from a specific learning difficulty/disability. They can also derive from poor learning experiences and/ or problems more associated with other SpLDs (such as dyslexia). In order to appreciate these potentially diverse causes, and their links to mathematics, we need to consider some basic models of mathematic skills development. Models describing the way in which children develop mathematic skills to adult levels (see Nunes and Bryant, 1997) argue for a series of interacting but distinct components – as such, some components may be functioning well whereas others may not. Also, development of some skills may require prior skills to have been learnt. For example, an appreciation of amount (that there is more of one thing than another) may be one of the first mathematics-related skills to develop: most children seem to be able to tell the difference between a group of three toys versus two toys, even if the latter are larger toys and may take up as much space as the three toys. Dealing with this concept of amount in non-symbolic forms may support associations with numerical symbols – hence, concepts of amount are associated with names of digits and possibly counting. Learning the names of written digit symbols, as well as their order in counting, also are early indicators of acquisition of mathematic skills. In addition, learning of the procedural aspects of performing arithmetical calculations, as well as applying basic reasoning skills (Bryant, 1985; Geary and Widaman, 1992), will support skilled learning.

Each of the basic components of mathematical ability mentioned above will be influenced by underlying (cognitive) skills, as well as learning, and some may be influenced by achievement in other academic fields. For example, although an understanding of number concepts seems to be something that children (and even animals) seem to develop very early, such a skill may still be influenced by learning (see the sub-section on intervention below). Similarly, the learning of mathematics procedures will depend on those procedures been taught in a clear and systematic way. A child who has missed school when a basic procedure is taught, or misunderstood the procedure, may struggle in areas of mathematics related to that procedure, but show few problems in other areas. Similarly, the conceptual nature of mathematics may mean that a child can work well with basic procedures but struggles to follow some of the logic behind the problem-solving nature of mathematics. This may stem from a lack of ability in the area, possibly related to generally low intellectual functioning, but it could also be due a more specific problem with language understanding, since many mathematics concepts are taught verbally. Furthermore, if concepts are taught via reading a book or solving written mathematics problems, weaknesses in learning may stem more from reading skills (dyslexia). These latter problems may also influence later mathematics learning. Hence, progress in developing basic mathematic skills may suggest no problems, but a lack of learning experience, or a learning problem that is not specific to mathematics (e.g. a language weakness or attention deficit), may cause problems within any area of a mathematics curriculum. Reasonably comprehensive assessments may be required to determine if the problems stem from poor learning of a specific area of a curriculum or an underlying difficulty. Teachers with experience of the child's history of learning can be a valuable source of information here, both in terms of their own assessment of potential problems and in support of assessments by others, such as those specifically trained in assessment procedures.

Specific disability and sub-types

Neurological data also argue for subcomponents of mathematic skills that may relate to different types of learning problems (Dehaene, Spelke and Pinet, 1999). For example, an understanding of number seems to be related to activity in the intraparietal sulcus (sometimes shortened to IPS). This region of the brain seems to be involved the comparison of numbers, approximation and estimation, as well as in non-symbolic tasks related to mathematics (Dehaene *et al.*, 2003). In contrast, the angular gyrus seems to be related to mathematical tasks that focus on procedural or drill-type learning; as in learning the times-tables. However, the angular gyrus also seems to be involved in the more verbal aspects of mathematics, such as in the retrieval of arithmetic facts. The reason why these may be important for understanding potential areas of mathematics learning problems is that they seem to relate to data from individuals with acquired mathematics problems (i.e. problems with mathematics that follow some sort of brain damage, such as after a stroke). For example, Lemer *et al.* (2003) discuss one patient who was found to have difficulty with counting and fact recall (such as times-tables), but was able to approximate well, in contrast to another individual who struggled when required to make approximations but was able to recall addition and multiplication facts.

The characteristics associated with mathematics learning problems discussed in the previous subsections, and the brain areas that seem to be involved in mathematical procedures and understanding mathematical concepts, both argue for several potential causes of mathematics learning problems, which may suggest a number of sub-types of dyscalculia/MLD. Although several such sub-typing theories have been proposed, none has been uniformly accepted; and there may be alternatives to the sub-type explanations for the range of characteristics and potential causes covered above (see next paragraph). For example, Wilson and Dehaene (2007) discuss the possibility that there may be sub-types focused around problems in:

i   number sense, which is closest to the specific area of difficulty associated with dyscalculia/MLD discussed above – in this case, the child would be expected to show difficulties in conceptual understanding of number, which will potentially lead to problems in most elements of mathematics, except perhaps simple fact retrieval, as in counting – for many children, these problems should occur in non-symbolic tasks, as well as tasks involving digits;

ii   verbal aspects of mathematics, which would lead to difficulties in counting, fact retrieval and word-based problems – this form may be associated with language-related learning problems, including dyslexia;

iii executive functioning (or working memory), which may be associated with difficulties in fact retrieval and strategy/procedure use – and may also be associated with attention deficits;

iv   spatial processing, which may lead to specific difficulties in processing patterns, such as in geometry work, and non-symbolic quantities – this form of mathematics learning problem may be most clearly linked with non-verbal learning disabilities (see Rourke, 1989).

Although different terminology may eventually be agreed upon to describe these potential sub-types, each one may influence an assessment in different ways – and may be linked with different intervention procedures. Therefore, a consideration of each will most likely need to form part of an assessment process that aims to inform education plans. For the first sub-type, mathematics-specific measures may need to be developed. For the latter three, each may be assessed by evidence of poor mathematic skills in a related area, plus measures of language, non-verbal and attention that would be expected to form the basis of assessment procedures undertaken by trained assessors (such as an educational psychologist) – for example, most IQ-related tests will have sub-tasks that target verbal and non-verbal ability, as well as allowing an assessment of attentional functioning. A team approach by teachers and trained assessors may be the only way to fully understand the underlying reason for learning problems in such cases.

An alternative to the sub-type perspective (and mentioned in the previous paragraph) is that dyscalculia/MLD may co-occur (or be comorbid) with other learning problems. For example, as many as half of those with dyslexia may have weaknesses in mathematics (see Chinn and Ashcroft, 2007; Miles and Miles, 1992); and there are overlaps between the two conditions (Willburger *et al.*, 2008). Similarly, problems related to dyscalculia/MLD can be found in children with specific language impairments and ADHD (see discussions in: Adams *et al.*, 1999; Donlan, 1998). Therefore, sub-types may be more a feature of the range of skills in mathematics leading to children with other underlying difficulties, which are not specific to dyscalculia/MLD, struggling with certain aspects of mathematics. However, there are studies that have shown that a group of children with specific mathematics learning problems can be identified. For example, despite the large potential overlap between dyscalculia/MLD and dyslexia, research suggests that most dyslexics show more specific deficits in phonological skills, whereas dyscalculia/MLD may be more associated with inefficient number comparisons (Landerl *et al.*, 2009; see also Durand *et al.*, 2005; Rubinsten and Henik, 2006).

Assessment

The identification of dyscalculia/MLD has followed the same general principles that guide the assessment of any SpLD. Initially an assessment of the individual's ability in mathematics would be considered. In formal diagnostic procedures, this might be determined using a standardised test (see examples below), but teacher-based assessments or measures that compare performance against a point in a curriculum have also been used in many parts of the world, particularly where formally standardised tools do not exist. Typically, some agreed criteria would be used to determine learning problems: figures such as two years behind that expected of children at a certain level in school education, or below some centile score determined by standardisation norms, might be used. However, the exact figures will vary depending on the organisation accrediting the assessment and legislative requirements of the education system or government. Also, a teacher's personal experience of the learning shown by a child may provide an indication of a problem later identified more specifically by a full assessment by an educational psychologist.

In addition to mathematics level assessments, a measure of intelligence (typically based on IQ) would often be used to rule out general learning difficulties, or to determine a discrepancy between IQ-determined expected performance and actual performance on a mathematics test, or to identify general areas of weakness such as in language, attention or non-verbal skills (see discussions of the inclusion of IQ in assessments in Elbeheri and Everatt, 2009). The use of an IQ-based assessment would require the involvement of a trained assessor, such as an educational psychologist. Measures of mathematics ability and IQ will also be accompanied by measuring underlying skills related to poor performance in mathematics, or considered to be a cause of the learning problems. The previous subsection should give an indication of the sort of skills that would be tested, but again these may vary across assessors depending on their theoretical position. Finally, some process of eliminating alternative potential causes of mathematics weaknesses may be undertaken by a trained assessor: interviews may be used to determine the educational history of the individual (this might include teacher reports, school records and discussions with parents); information may also be sought on birth problems, serious illnesses, or psychosocial disorders in the past (again school records or parents will be surveyed); and dyslexia, ADHD, dyspraxia, or other such developmental learning/behaviour problems may be considered.

A comprehensive assessment of mathematics learning should involve a range of measures/tests; though given that difficulties related to dyscalculia/MLD are developmental and influenced by educational experiences, assessments should be related to developmental levels as well as the point on a curriculum that a child is expected to have reached. For example, the ability to count has been seen as an important building block for development and, therefore, often forms a part of the assessment of basic skills. As suggested by the discussions above, number sense is another area that has been seen as a basic underlying skill for mathematic development and, therefore, may be tested via symbolic number comparisons, non-symbolic comparisons and/or simple estimations. Finally, mathematical knowledge might be tested via basic arithmetic or specific procedures taught at various curriculum levels. Although there are quite a few tests designed to measure mathematic skills, a few have been more extensively used in the identification of mathematics learning problems (including by researchers investigating dyscalculia/MLD) and these are mentioned below to provide a basis against which to consider appropriate measures/tests.

The Test of Early Mathematics Ability (Ginsburg and Baroody, 2003) was developed with children aged three to eight years in mind. This test focuses on basic numbers, number-comparison facilities, numerical literacy, mastery of number facts, basic calculation and concept understanding. In contrast, the Comprehensive Mathematical Abilities Test (Hresko et al., 2003) targets skills that seven- to 19-year-olds would be expected to have developed. This test focuses on addition, subtraction, multiplication, division, problem-solving and the use of charts, tables and graphs, though it also includes supplemental tests of algebra, geometry, rational numbers, time, money and measurement. Another example of a highly comprehensive test of mathematic skills is KeyMath (Connolly, 2007). This tests numeration, algebra, geometry, measurement, data analysis and probability, as well as operations such as mental computation and estimation, addition and subtraction, multiplication and division, and applications including the foundations of problem-solving and applied problem-solving. An additional useful feature of the KeyMath set is that problems identified in specific components of mathematics are linked to remediation materials which can be used in schools. Other tools widely used by assessors, as they are reasonably well researched and include tests of mathematic skills, are the Wide Range Achievement Test (Wilkinson and Robertson, 2006), which, as well as reading measures, includes measures of basic mathematics computations through counting, identifying numbers, solving simple oral problems and written mathematics problems, and the Woodcock-Johnson (Woodcock, McGrew and Mather, 2001) battery of measures, which includes a range of cognitive and achievement measures. The availability of such standardised tests varies across contexts, and some require certificated training to access from publishers, but each can be used to attempt to identify the specific area of difficulty experienced by the child in order to support learning. Most of the tests are standardised on English-speaking populations – and most have USA norms – hence, the identification of an appropriate test for a specific context may require a search for alternatives, but a consideration of these tests will provide clues as to what to look for in an appropriate standardised test. The test chosen should also be easily linked to a curriculum by an educator, meaning that even if the difficulty experience by the child is more experiential (and not due to an underlying LD), then a process of supporting learning should be possible: for example, the child may be struggling with a specific area of the curriculum because they did not follow a previously taught concept or procedure – many standardised tests, such as those above, should provide an indication of where this lack of understanding/learning lies, allowing the educator to re-teach, or reinforce, that skill.

However, although tests (such as those in the previous paragraph) have been developed to assess mathematics learning skills quite comprehensively, no formal diagnostic tools specifically targeting dyscalculia/MLD have been agreed. Despite this, a number of (mainly English-language) screening tools have been proposed (see, for example: Butterworth, 2003; Chard et al., 2005; Mazzocco and Thompson, 2005). The Butterworth computerised screener[1] has the feature that it assesses basic mathematical concepts and, hence, does not depend greatly on skills such as reading, language or short-term memory, or on the child's educational experience. The tasks used in the screener are consistent also with most views about the characteristics of dyscalculia, as well as the data in the literature discussed above. As such, it may be more likely to identify the underlying deficits associated with an SpLD than those related to poor learning experience or difficulties not specific to dyscalculia/MLD. The screener measures the time taken to answer questions in comparison with the average for the child's age group. Those with dyscalculia/MLD have been found to perform the tasks in the screener less efficiently (or less fluently) than their peers.

Similar tools/screeners have also been developed for non-English-speaking populations: see work in French by Dehaene and colleagues (Wilson and Dehaene, 2007), and in German by Landerl and others (e.g. Landerl et al., 2009). And this has extended to work in non-Western cultures and education contexts: see Ramaa and Gowramma (2002), for work in Indian languages, and Everatt et al. (2014) in the Arabic language. These latter contexts suggest that specific deficits may not be related to particular languages, learning contexts or curricula, but rather that there may be a universal, and fundamental, cause of dyscalculia/MLD. For example, as well as language and cultural differences, in the education context targeted by Everatt *et al.* (ibid.), mathematics is taught in a much more rote/drill-based way than in many Western schools, and the number symbols taught in school are based on a written form that differs from that used in Western schools. Despite these differences, Arab children with severe and persistent problems with learning mathematics have shown deficits in conceptual tasks similar to those used in the Butterworth screener and consistent with the hypothesised number sense/concept cause of dyscalculia/MLD (ibid.). These Arabic children with specific problems in number concepts could also be distinguished from those with problems with reading and writing (i.e. those with features of dyslexia), despite both groups of children showing problems leading to weaknesses with certain aspects of mathematics.

Hence, problems with the concepts underlying mathematics have the potential to support the identification of dyscalculia/MLD across learning contexts. Furthermore, screeners based on non-symbolic and basic symbolic comparisons also hold the potential to predict future performance in mathematics prior to formal learning beginning: see Mazzocco and Thompson (2005) for evidence of prediction from behavioural measures in kindergarten. This may allow educators to implement appropriate interventions before experiences of failure (and the negative consequences of low self-esteem, frustration and anxiety that accompany failure) become the primary facet of the individual's mathematics learning.

Intervention

Following an assessment of a problem through an appropriate assessment process, some process of support or intervention should be planned and implemented. A good assessor will give indications of the type of teaching and support procedures that may be advantageous, but the educator too will be aware of procedures that may help: many of the techniques used for children with difficulties are based on those for use with children without developmental LDs since good pedagogy is good for all (see Gersten *et al.*, 2009). Intervention in schools, provided by mainstream teachers can be particularly useful: see examples in Fuchs and Fuchs (2001), and discussions of response to intervention procedures for children with dyscalculia/MLD in Bryant and Bryant (2008) – and see further general strategies below and elsewhere in this book. Special programmes are also available for those with more severe MLDs, two of which can be found in Butterworth and Laurillard (2010) and Wilson *et al.* (2006).[2] These specific support methods need to take account of the educational context and the learner (see discussion in Miller and Mercer, 1997), but training in number sense or conceptual understanding of number is often the target. This underlying skill/function shows evidence of change/development (see Ansari and Dhital, 2006; Lipton and Spelke, 2003) and, therefore, should be amenable to intervention. Programmes that focus on teaching this skill, or that provide strategies for learning basic concepts, should be highly useful and might be easily transferred across educational contexts.

However, many of the guidelines for those with dyscalculia/MLD also apply to children with LDs in other areas (see discussions in Bird, 2009; Butterworth and Yeo, 2004; Chinn and Ashcroft, 2007; Yeo, 2003). For example, teaching targeted at children with LDs has been considered more effective when taking account of the child's strengths and weaknesses, as well as their interests. Repetition of information or concepts that have been learnt poorly will be required with many such children, and such repetition can reduce the need for memorisation that can often cause problems for those with LDs. Multisensory learning methods can be useful in that they can be used to reinforce ideas by presenting information in different ways, thereby avoiding boredom produced by simple repetition learning. It is also vital to ensure that learning is structured, using logical steps to build on learning and help reinforcement. Chinn (see Chinn and Ashcroft, 2007) gives the example that most children with mathematics learning problems can, with the right support, learn simple multiplication facts for 1, 2, 5 and 10. The ability to perform such multiplication procedures can then be used to access other facts: for example, teaching that 9 times calculations are simply 1 times calculations less than the 10 times calculations, which have already been learnt. Hence, a basic level of skill can be used to teach strategies to deal with additional mathematical problems.

Experience of teaching children with LD also suggests that greater benefits will be found when strategies and concepts are taught explicitly. This should also be the case with generalisations – for example, from concrete examples to abstract problems – and when forming links between examples and the actual procedures that need to be learnt. Furthermore, the learning of concepts and procedures needs to be tested appropriately. Non-threatening questions about concepts can get the individual engaged and thinking, and ensure that appropriate generalisations have taken place. Assessments of learning need careful implementation to avoid associations with failure that can lead to negative affect, avoidance and poor motivation, particularly for children who may experience difficulties in an area. In contrast, concrete examples, or familiar objects/situations, that illustrate ideas will allow the child to relate to the information, thereby supporting understanding and interest. Clearly, making learning active and fun, and using things with which the child is familiar and enjoys, should maintain interest, increase motivation to learn and provide the basis on which learning is made easier both for the child and the teacher.

Conclusions

Research evidence suggests that there is an SpLD in mathematics that can lead to problems with education and activities outside of school. This SpLD can be both severe and persistent (particularly without appropriate intervention), and there is evidence for a neurological basis and genetic predisposition. Problems with the concept of number, and relationships between numbers, are the most likely underlying difficulty specific to dyscalculia/MLD[3]. However, such problems can be identifiable early and seem to be susceptible to change, which suggests that, with the right intervention tools, many of the problems faced by children with dyscalculia/MLD may be overcome. In addition to this potential specific characteristic of dyscalculia, though, there is evidence for wider deficits in mathematics that may be associated with poor learning opportunities or related to other developmental problems (such as language-related LDs). Again, such difficulties are amenable to intervention: basic principles common to supporting children with learning problems are as relevant to the area of mathematics learning as any other areas of education. Therefore, despite the need for more research to better understand dyscalculia/MLD, there is still a great deal that educators can do to support individuals with problems related to poor mathematics learning.

Notes

1 Available via *GL assessment* at http://www.gl-assessment.co.uk/products/dyscalculia-screener; but see also discussions in Butterworth, 2003, and Butterworth and Yeo, 2004.
2 Wilson *et al.*, 2006, is available at http://www.thenumberrace.com/nr/home.php
3 See Chinn http://www.mathsexplained.co.uk and the work on OG and Maths by Marilyn Waldropp.

Chapter 5

Teacher assessment
Movement

Introduction

Although the concept of a specific disorder of motor function has been recognised for almost 100 years now, awareness of the condition has been gradually increasing among health professionals, researchers and practitioners over the last 30 years. First recognised in the *Diagnostic and Statistical Manual, 3rd Revised Edition* (*DSM-III*) (produced by the American Psychiatric Association in 1987) as clumsy child syndrome, the disorder has also been known by a number of labels including dyspraxia (Denckla, 1984) and 'specific developmental disorder of motor function' (World Health Organization, 1992). Currently, it is generally referred to as 'developmental co-ordination disorder', or DCD for short (Henderson and Henderson, 2002; Sugden and Chambers, 2005).

Four diagnostic criteria are currently used to distinguish the condition:

a   the child has substantially lower motor performance expected, given his chronological age and measured intelligence
b   the disturbance in the first criterion significantly interferes with academic achievement or activities of daily living
c   the disturbance is not due to a general medical condition
d   if mental retardation is present, motor difficulties are considered not the associated secondary conditions (as cited in Tsang, Stagnitti and Lo, 2010).

DCD is diagnosed in children who, for no known medical reason, fail to acquire adequate motor skills. Typically, motor milestones are generally achieved rather late, while core aspects of this disorder can include difficulties in manual dexterity, ball skills and/or balance. Such marked impairment has a significant, negative impact on activities of daily living, such as dressing, eating, riding a bicycle and/or on academic achievements, primarily as a result of poor handwriting skills (Barnett and Henderson, 2005).

DCD affects around 5 per cent of school-aged children, with a prevalence of boys over girls (3:1). Although apparent in the early years, it is usually not diagnosed formally before the age of five. It has a varying, but significant, impact throughout the lifespan, and its symptoms are consistent across culture, race, socio-economic status and gender (Zoia *et al.*, 2006). Children with DCD usually have difficulties undertaking self-care tasks such as feeding and dressing, and in school have difficulty with tasks such as handwriting, and playing team sports such as football or netball. Presentation of signs and symptoms may vary depending on the age of the child and on demands presented to him/her. Recent evidence has shown that difficulties persist into adulthood. In addition, it is now well known that motor difficulties are apparent in a number of developmental disorders, such as autism spectrum disorder (Mari *et al.*, 2003), ADHD (Martin, Piek and Hay, 2006), dyslexia (Ramus *et al.*, 2003) and specific language impairment (Hill, 2001; Zoia *et al.*, 2006). It has also been suggested (Gibbs, Appleton and Appleton, 2007) that motor skills difficulties occur on a continuum with many more children having milder degrees of difficulty than those with a high level of difficulty, as might be indicated by a diagnosis of DCD.

A study by Sullivan and McGrath (2003) demonstrated that children with significant motor difficulties at four years of age were more likely to have academic or behavioural difficulties and need additional support when they reached eight years of age. A longitudinal study by Cantell, Smyth and Ahonen (2003) also explored long-term outcomes for 65 children who were assessed as having motor difficulties at five years of age. They found that by 17–18 years of age those who continued to have DCD had the lowest WAIS scores, shortest school careers and lowest self-perception of athletic and scholastic competence (as cited in Bond, 2011).

Importance of fine motor skills in the learning process

Every movement that we make that is repeated over and over again to reproduce the same end result, for example the formation of a letter, is dependent on a correctly learnt motor plan or sequence. Writing, in terms of letters written on a page, is dependent on deeply embedded, subconscious motor memory; we write with a level of automaticity that does not require conscious thought. According to Cohen, Kiss and Le Voi (1993), automatic processes occur without awareness, are highly efficient, difficult to modify and involuntary and have no capacity limitations. Children can adhere to changes when their primary focus is forming a letter in a particular way, but when another task is the primary focus – for example, thinking of ideas and writing independently – then the over-learnt motor sequence swings into action and handwriting reverts to what has been erroneously learnt and firmly established. It is clear, then, that because over-learnt complex tasks can be performed without engaging conscious processing, once they are established they become extremely difficult to modify (as cited in McMurray, Drysdale and Jordan, 2009).

An appropriate understanding of fine motor skills is necessary to determine their impact on learning generally and reading and writing in particular.

Fine motor skills are the co-ordination of groups of small muscles to complete a task or to participate in an activity (Case-Smith, 2001). These muscle groups are concentrated in three main areas:

1 the face (which includes the mouth, the eyes and the ears)
2 the hands
3 the feet (Dove Ministries for Children, 2012).

Many researchers have acknowledged the importance of fine motor development and have included fine motor skills as a component in studies and assessments focused on school readiness and scholastic adjustment (Bart, Hajami and Bar-Haim, 2007; Decker *et al.*, 2011; Pagani *et al.*, 2010; Seung-Hee and Meisels, 2006). Fine motor skills are an important foundational skill and can positively impact a student's progress in school. Researchers have found a relation between well-developed motor skills and better school achievement, as well as a relation to positive social behaviours (Bart, Hajami and Bar-Haim, 2007). A student is said to have proficient fine motor skills if s/he is able to efficiently and successfully complete age-appropriate fine motor tasks and activities. Proficient motor skills help a child transition to the academic demands encountered when beginning school.

Proficiency in fine motor skills, such as cutting, gluing, colouring, writing and folding, provides a strong foundation upon which a student may build further academic abilities. Contrary to this, deficits in fine motor skills negatively impact areas of a child's school progress. Poor fine motor skills can contribute to the early identification of students at risk for school failure (Grissmer *et al.*, 2010; Seung-Hee and Meisels, 2006); fine motor deficits have been connected to learning disorders, behavioural disorders, language disorders and attention deficits. In addition, the extent of the motor deficits can be a factor in determining academic achievement during the first three years of school (Ericsson, 2008). Second, fine motor deficits impact self-care skills needed at school. Children will have difficulty dressing, buttoning, zipping, tying shoes, feeding themselves and practising good hygiene (Case-Smith, 2001). Finally, deficits in fine motor skills impact a child's self-concept. Children with poor motor skills are more likely to be socially inept, to be lonely, to have low self-esteem, to be anxious and to be withdrawn (Bart, Hajami and Bar-Haim, 2007). These children may be less likely to join in physical and social activities.

Relationship between fine movement and literacy

In educational settings, good muscle tone in the neck, back and stomach is necessary for students to maintain posture, to stabilise the shoulders and to hold the head upright for long periods while reading or writing (ibid.). In 1992, McHale and Cermak took a closer look at how much classroom work required fine motor skills during a typical day. The study found 'that 30% to 60% of the school day was allocated to fine motor activities'. For students moving into the intermediate grades and middle school, fine motor skill execution and learning must often take place simultaneously. This integration of fine motor skills, learning, reading and writing may prove too demanding when fine motor deficits are a factor (as cited in St John, 2013).

Motor skills and literacy

In looking at fine motor skills and their functions, a direct correlation to literacy skills can be seen. Grissmer *et al.*, in their 2010 study on school readiness, also acknowledge this connection. One possibility that might partially account for a motor–cognitive causal link is that most activities that build or display cognitive skills also involve the use of fine motor skills. Writing requires fine motor skills with the hands as well as hand–eye co-ordination. Speaking requires fine motor skills that control the production of sound.

Reading requires the use of fine motor skills controlling eye movement for word tracking. Reading and fine motor skills are connected through vision (St John, 2013); reading requires scanning, visual vigilance and visual sequencing (Case-Smith, 2001). Scanning is a student's ability to rapidly change fields of vision. The eyes must quickly team together to meet the demands of both near and far vision. A student can view a book up close, switch to focusing on what the teacher is writing on the board and then switch back to the book. His/her fields of vision may change several times within a short period. When a student has the ability to handle many simultaneous visual elements, the student is said to have visual vigilance. The eyes must maintain attention while looking for details or patterns. A student does this when s/he looks at the letter order within words or details in pictures. Visual sequencing is the acknowledgement and remembrance of visual orders. When a student automatically remembers the sequence 'a-p-p-l-e' and recognises it in print as the word 'apple', s/he is practising visual sequencing (as cited in St John, 2013).

A student must be able to maintain visual attention on the text while looking at the forms of the letters, the sequence of the letters and the order of the words, all while processing the message of the words as a whole. Reading also involves directional skills. A student must be able to move his/her eyes and hands and to bring both together in the middle. Information from one side of the body must be relayed and co-ordinated with the other; both sides must then work together to accomplish a task. This process is known as bilateral integration (Case-Smith, 2001). Bilateral integration requires the student to cross the midlines of the body both horizontally and vertically. To read, a student must be able to cross the midline of a page, a picture and of the book itself; be able to track the print from the top of the page to the bottom and from the left side of the book to the right; and be able to grasp and turn the pages of a book from right to left. In 1989, Dennison and Dennison stated that once mastery of bilateral integration is achieved, one has 'an ability fundamental to academic success'.

Young children mostly learn motor skills implicitly, simply by doing them, with very little explicit teaching of how to perform the task (Orban, Lungu and Doyon, 2008). This is called procedural learning, which seems to apply to motor sequence learning, when a child needs to learn the correct sequence of movements that together comprise the motor action (e.g. brushing teeth, getting dressed, or buttering bread). However, later in life, when learning to tie shoelaces or to write, explicit teaching is frequently the method of choice to explain the correct order of movements. Until now, it has not been established which of these two methods is the most effective to teach children motor skills in the initial stage of learning (Savion-Lemieux, Bailey and Penhune, 2009).

Assessment of fine motor skills

The assessment of motor behaviour is an important and integral part of the intervention process and the nature of the initial assessment can influence the form that an intervention takes, as well as its final goals (Wilson, 2005). The most recent internationally agreed recommendations are that intervention should 'contain activities that are functional and are based on those that are relevant to daily living' (Sugden, 2006). This supports the use of motor assessments that focus on functionally relevant tasks (Barnett, 2008).

Diagnosing children with DCD in the UK is usually undertaken by a clinician, such as a pediatrician, and an occupational therapist or physiotherapist observing the child and using a standardised test in order to measure the level of motor impairment. In the UK, the most commonly used test to measure these impairments is the Movement Assessment Battery for Children-2 (Movement ABC-2) (Henderson and Sugden, 2007), which has norms up to 16 years of age. The Bruininks–Oseretsky Test of Motor Proficiency-2 (2005) is used in the USA and has norms up to the age of 21 years (Bruininks and Bruininks, 2005). However, assessment for DCD for those over 16 years of age is fraught with difficulties. Few pediatricians and adult physicians have experience or training in the assessment and diagnosis of DCD in adolescents and adults. This problem stems partly from a lack of standardised tools and protocols to do so, and also little awareness of the continuing nature of the disorder and the heterogeneity of the condition (as cited in Kirby et al., 2008).

Although the motor co-ordination difficulties of children with DCD are readily observable, both in classroom and physical education settings, children with DCD are commonly under-recognised until academic failure begins to occur (Fox and Lent, 1996; Miller et al., 2001). Classroom and special education teachers are often the initial source of referral in cases when they notice poor skill development interfering with classroom work and overall academic performance (Sugden and Wright, 1998). While teachers do identify some children with DCD, the literature suggests that teachers miss many children who may be experiencing motor limitations in their classrooms and that this may be related to a number of factors (Dunford *et al.*, 2004; Green *et al.*, 2005; Junaid *et al.*, 2000; Piek and Edwards, 1997). One solution to the problem, teacher checklists, has not worked well as they are often lengthy (Henderson and Sugden, 2007) and may have poor sensitivity (Junaid *et al.*, 2000). It is important to learn more about teachers' perceptions of what constitutes a motor problem (as cited in Rivard *et al.*, 2007).

Inter- and intra-individual variability within DCD is well documented and might interfere with the development of appropriate screening tools. In early infancy, proper identification of signs and symptoms is hampered by the lack of reliable tests and baseline data to the point that when motor difficulties are persistent, parents seem to be the ones who readily pick up the problems (Wilson and McKenzie, 1998; Jongmans, 2005). Standardised measures of movement skills are more readily available for children of school age. In recent years, a number of researchers have developed measures to aid with the identification of young children with DCD (Zoia *et al.*, 2006). The changing nature of DCD is affected by the changing environmental demands on the child. As the child grows up, new challenges, such as learning to ride a bike, present new problems, as well as increasing academic and social demands in secondary school. The change from junior school to secondary school may act as a 'tipping point' for the young person. Poor skills will also be recognised by peers and may result in the young person becoming isolated and leading, especially in boys, to an increased risk of having secondary psychological consequences of DCD such as anxiety (Sigurdsson, Van Os and Fombonne, 2002).

If motor assessments are to be useful, they must provide valid and reliable measures of motor behaviour. To be valid, an assessment instrument must measure what it purports to measure. To examine the validity of an assessment it is first necessary to define the construct under examination. As already mentioned, there are problems with conceptualisation of the term 'co-ordination'. However, when used in the context of DCD, the term is usually taken 'to mean a general level of proficiency or motor ability' (Wilson, 2005; Barnett, 2008). Children with DCD are often identified by classroom teachers and the identification process relies heavily on teachers' perceptions. Teachers' perceptions may be influenced by a child's gender, behaviour and the type of motor problem they demonstrate. To date, the influence of these factors on teachers' perceptions of children with DCD has not been empirically tested (Rivard *et al.*, 2007). Classroom teachers are therefore encouraged to develop and utilise their own observational frameworks for children with DCD, which may include answers to the following questions:

1   What types of tasks does the child find difficult?
2   What types of tasks does the child avoid?
3   Is there a physical or sensory component to those tasks?
4   Are behavioural or attention problems linked to specific activities?

5   Does the child appear to understand the instructions?
6   At what point does the breakdown occur?

If a child is listening and reading appropriately for their age, but is having difficulty with copying, written expression, handwriting and other motor-based activities, DCD should be suspected. Referral to other service providers, as well as the provision of adaptations by special educators and classroom teachers, can help children to be more successful in the school environment (as cited in Missiuna, Rivard and Pollock, 2004).

Many of the programmes and activities available are suitable for kindergarten through middle school, perhaps even high school. The programmes require just a little tweaking to fit the ages of the students. One programme that is easily adapted for multiple age groups is Bal-A-Vis-X: Rhythmic Balance/Auditory/Vision Exercises for Brain and Brain-Body Integration by Bill Hubert (2001). The programme uses bean bags, racquet balls and balance boards. The Bal-A-Vis-X exercises target the following:

1   visual tracking and focused attention on the bag or ball
2   hand–eye co-ordination
3   listening skills that focus on auditory rhythm as the bags exchange hands or the balls bounce
4   use of movements that engage both fine motor and gross motor muscles to manipulate the bags and balls. The activities are both fun and engaging for students.

Another programme that is easily adapted for multiple age groups is Brain Gym: 'Brain Gym is a series of simple body movements used to integrate all areas of the brain to enhance learning and to build self-esteem' (Cohen and Goldsmith, 2000). There are several exercises in *Brain Gym: Teacher's Edition*, revised by Dennison and Dennison (1989), that specifically address reading skills (St John, 2013). The Manchester Motor Skills Programme (MMSP) has been developed in response to a lack of assessment tools and intervention programmes for use in schools. Following on from the work of Wright and Sugden (1998) and Sugden and Chambers (2005) the MMSP adopts a broadly cognitive motor approach to intervention, which focuses on direct skills teaching, adaptation and task analysis. The programme is designed to take place daily for eight weeks, or three or four times per week for 12 weeks, with children being assessed pre- and post-using the MMSA.

The structure of MMSP sessions is based upon Cartlidge's work (as cited in Ripley, 2001). Sessions last for 20 minutes and are quite fast paced and active. Activities are repeated, ideally for five sessions, in order to build confidence and provide opportunities for high levels of distributed practice. The emphasis of the sessions is very much upon self-esteem building and collaboration. The session begins with a group warm-up. This is followed by skill development practice, which might involve working on two to three fine or gross motor activities for two minutes each. These activities are evaluated in terms of individual progress in relation to personal targets the children set. The session ends with a collaborative activity, praise and personal target-setting (as cited in Bond, 2011).

Importance of early intervention

It is essential that early years teachers are aware of the importance of appropriate early intervention, ensuring correct letter formation once a child is 'ready' to write, and that if 'readiness' is elusive then there may be underlying difficulties requiring closer examination (Macintyre, 2009).

The importance of effective early intervention is critical. Montgomery (2007) describes how the voluntary cortex of the brain is responsible for learning motor skills, putting together all the parts. With reference to handwriting and letter formation, she contends that because the cognitive system is involved in the learning process the child must have guided practice from the outset. Large movements should be encouraged – for example, in the air, in sand, on a board and, eventually, on paper. All these movements should be supported by painting and drawing to strengthen the muscles. Montgomery asserts that children should not be shown the model and then left to copy or trace over letters as habits can develop that are later difficult to change. While the child is endeavouring to learn this new motor skill the cerebellum is memorising all the complex muscle actions involved in any skilled movement and eventually takes control of the movement: 'this leaves the main brain free to think about new things' (ibid.).

There is extensive evidence of DCD overlapping with dyslexia and ADHD in between 35 and 50 per cent of cases (Kadesjo and Gillberg, 1999; Kaplan et al., 1998; Pitcher, Piek and Hay, 2003). Among school-aged children 5–6 per cent have movement difficulties that are not due to specific neurological problems or cognitive impairment, and which limit their classroom potential and affect their long-term academic achievement (American Psychiatric Association (APA), 2000). Everyday functional tasks such as dressing, printing, cutting with scissors, copying from the board and ball skills are problematic for these children and cause daily frustration (Cermak, Gubbay and Larkin, 2002; May-Benson, Ingolia and Koomar, 2002; Missiuna, 2003). It has been clearly demonstrated that children with DCD are known to develop serious secondary sequences that are not limited to the presenting motor difficulties. Several studies have shown that, over time, children with DCD are more likely to demonstrate behavioural and social/emotional difficulties, including poor perceived social and physical competence, social isolation, academic and behaviour problems, poor self-esteem, low self-worth and higher rates of psychiatric problems (Cantell, Smyth and Ahonen, 1994; Geuze and Borger, 1993; Losse et al., 1991; Rasmussen and Gillberg, 2000; Rose, Larkin and Berger, 1997; Rose and Larkin, 2002; Schoemaker and Kalverboer, 1994; Skinner and Piek,

2001; Smyth and Anderson, 2000). In addition, they are less likely to be physically fit or to participate voluntarily in motor activity (Cairney *et al.*, 2005; Watkinson *et al.*, 2001). Children with movement problems identified at an early age may benefit from intervention that includes the education of teachers and parents about how to make tasks easier for them (as cited in Missiuna, Rivard, and Pollock, 2004).

Macintyre (2009) provides some very clear guidance on the areas that should be targeted in an observation schedule in the early years in relation to movement and co-ordination issues. She suggests the following need to be focused on and can point the way for further assessment:

- appears un-co-ordinated
- poor at naming/locating body parts
- difficulty judging force in ball throwing
- poor balance/posture
- lack of dominance
- running, hopping, jumping difficulties
- difficulty with buttons, laces
- poor kinaesthetic memory
- cannot use two hands together for skills
- poor spatial awareness
- poor directional awareness.

Without early intervention or later remediation, many children with motor skill deficits will have these deficits for several years (Ericsson, 2008). Difficulties in motor skills do not remediate themselves, nor do they disappear. Avoiding or ignoring fine motor deficits year after year may negatively impact the reading and writing abilities of many students and may be labour intensive to remedy later if incorrect motor plans are allowed permanence (McMurray, Drysdale and Jordan, 2009). Professional development in the identification of fine motor deficits and their remediation is necessary to educate teachers so that students experiencing delays can receive the necessary help (ibid.). A school's occupational therapist is a great resource who can share a wealth of information and knowledge with staff.

Handwriting

'Handwriting is an integration of letter forms (orthographic codes), letter names (phonological codes), and written shapes (grapho-motor codes)' (Medwell and Wray, 2008). This co-ordination of letter knowledge and fine motor skills is known as orthographic integration (Christensen, 2004). A significant relationship between orthographic integration and a student's ability to produce a well-composed text has been shown to exist (St John, 2013). Writing is a co-ordination of many components related to fine motor skills and requires multi-tasking from multiple modalities, which not all students are able to do. To write, students must have: 1. the awareness of where the arms and hands are in space (kinaesthesia), 2. stable joints above the hand, 3. hand manipulation skills to hold the pencil and control the hand, 4. the ability to track the letters and words being written, 5. the ability to cross the midline of the body and 6. co-ordination of both sides of the body (ibid.). Before beginning to write letters or words, a child must be able to hold and manipulate a writing tool. This process is facilitated by a proper pencil grasp. A tripod grip is the ideal grasp where the thumb and pointer finger grasp the pencil with an open web space, while the pencil rests on the middle finger (Case-Smith, 2001). With a proper pencil grasp in place, stamina and hand muscle strength will continue to develop. But why does a teacher need to worry about pencil grasp? Improper pencil grasp can contribute to hand fatigue, can make handwriting more difficult to execute, and can drastically affect the speed in handwriting (as cited in St John, 2013).

Reading skills and writing skills go hand in hand: 'Literal reading is a prerequisite for writing. Letters have to be recognised visually before they are written' (Ardila, 2004). Learning to write is a complicated process (Ritchey, 2006). A student needs to write letters and spell words, with spaces in between, all while thinking and organising the content and message of what s/he will write (St John, 2013). Handwriting is a multisensory process that involves the integration of the visual, motor, sensory and perceptual systems (Case-Smith, 2001).

In writing, automaticity is the quick and easy formation of letters and words that lessens the amount of cognitive resources necessary, allowing for another writing process to happen simultaneously. In a review of research in 2004, Colette Gray concluded that 'an association between deficits in automaticity and difficulties in reading, reading comprehension, reading fluency, writing, numeracy, spelling, memory, speed, hearing, vision and balance' exists. In writing, automaticity will impact both handwriting fluency and content quality (Medwell and Wray, 2008). Promoting automaticity in handwriting should not be confused with rote learning or endless practice drills of letter formation (Gray, 2004). Instead, it should be thought of as creating a motor plan for each and every letter using multiple sensory systems, and then storing each plan as a motor memory. The more a student utilises a successful motor plan, the more refined the execution becomes (Case-Smith, 2001). The brain can then easily, and automatically, retrieve the needed plans when writing occurs (as cited in St John, 2013).

Teachers should be aware that lack of automaticity is not age-specific, nor is it a conscious choice. Some students in elementary, middle and high schools are still thinking about how to form a letter or letter sequence while they write; as a result, they struggle to keep up with the pace of their peers. This difficulty may also affect students' attitudes towards writing (Graham and Harris, 2006). Students may avoid writing in general, believing that they cannot write, and become static in their writing development stage. Difficulties with handwriting may even inadvertently change the writer's intended message or the reader's perception of the writer. This may be due to incoherent content, poor legibility, or incorrect spellings (Graham, 1990; Graham and Harris, 2006). In addition, students may use simpler sentence structures to limit how much they must write; they may choose simpler vocabulary choices to avoid difficult spellings. Medwell and Wray (2008) found that letter automaticity is the 'single best predictor of length and quality of written composition in the primary years … in secondary school and even in the post-compulsory education years'. For writing, Ritchey (2006) suggests modifying the writing tools, the writing surface, or the paper. Placing a pencil grip on a pencil enables the student with weaker hand muscles to better grip the pencil. The use of golf pencils, small pieces of chalk and broken crayons will improve pencil grasp and increase hand strength (as cited in Zoia *et al.*, 2006).

Visual perceptual difficulties can also be a key area in both reading and writing. Macintyre (2009) suggests the following should be considered:

- poor planning and layout of work
- poor spacing of words
- variation in size of letters
- difficulty in remembering an image when it is removed, e.g. copying from the board
- poor visual sequential memory
- remembering a series of visual images in order.

Dyspraxia: challenges

The limitations of a child with dyspraxia can be seen in the initiation and planning of movements and sequences and also in perception, causing problems in the legibility of handwriting, organisation skills and visual processing within reading, numeracy and physical education (Addy, 2003). Within the primary school a child with dyspraxia will display problems including delayed acquisition of motor skills, perceptual problems and language difficulties. Handwriting is particularly difficult for children with dyspraxia due to the highly complex inter-relation of motor, cognitive and language demands involved in letter formation (Malloy-Miller, Polatajko and Anstett, 1995).

A child with dyspraxia has specific difficulties in learning new movement patterns, yet learning handwriting involves the development of many new movement patterns (Lockhart and Law, 1994). He or she will therefore be slower and require more practice to develop automaticity. He or she will also likely experience difficulties when reading, organising, fastening clothes, manipulating toys, sequencing and concentrating (Portwood, 1999).

Tips for classroom teachers

a   Teachers can vary the writing surface. A slant board may help support a student's hand as s/he gains strength and stamina for writing. It can also change the visual field, making it easier to see while writing. Paper modifications may assist a student.

b   Testing out a variety of writing papers may help a student identify which type works best for him/her. The addition of a darkened line or a highlighted line can aid a student visually. For students who have both visual and motor difficulty staying within the lines, bump paper, where the bottom line is raised to provide the student with a tactile cue for positioning, is available.

c   Teachers can also modify assignments. Teachers should provide large work spaces and avoid visual overload. The length of an assignment may also be adapted to fit a student's abilities. If a student can demonstrate understanding in fewer problems or in a shorter paragraph, this should be allowed (as cited in St John, 2013).

d   A multi-sensory approach to teaching handwriting (Lockhart and Law, 1994). Students should practice the sequence of the letters using large motor movements in the air to facilitate recognition of the motor sequence. The motor sequence should then be practised in other media such as sand, salt, or shaving cream before taking it to the paper.

The visual, vestibular, kinaesthetic and tactile experiences send messages to the brain and promote the development of motor plans and automaticity (McMurray, Drysdale and Jordan, 2009). Some students may benefit from the use of reading trackers. These cards have a transparent, coloured window in the centre to highlight one line of text at a time and reduce visual overload. For younger students, pointers help develop one-to-one matching while reading. For all students, visual displays in the classroom can reinforce letter learning and remind students about letter formation (Gray, 2004).

e   Children with dyspraxia will also benefit from repetition and additional practice when learning handwriting. These children require 'over-learning' (Lockhart and Law, 1994). Through repetition, the new motor plans are developed, stored and gradually become more automatic. Bundy, Lane and Murray (2002) state: 'A learned motor skill must be practised to be stored and retrieved in a way that supports expertise. Practising movements is essential to skill development.' A child with dyspraxia has great difficulty in generalising skills, so specific skills need to be taught and rehearsed before moving on to the next set of skills (as cited in McMurray, Drysdale and Jordan, 2009).

f   Classroom teachers can adapt and modify activities to allow children to achieve curriculum expectations with less emphasis on the motor components of those activities. One of the most effective types of classroom modifications for children with DCD involves reducing the amount of writing required and allowing extra time to complete written assignments. It is important to decrease the motor (output) part of the task, though, without changing the cognitive expectations. For example, having the child draw the story instead of writing it may decrease the cognitive requirements of the task without altering the outcome.

g It is more difficult to decrease the motor requirements in physical education where motor performance is the focus. Strategies can be used, though, to encourage children with DCD to make progress within their own abilities, to foster self-esteem and promote the value of physical activity for long-term fitness and health.

When teaching physical activities to children with DCD, an emphasis should always be placed on encouraging fun, effort and participation rather than proficiency. Non-competitive games, in which goals are measured against one's own performance and not that of other children, may be helpful. Another strategy is to divide the class into smaller groups when practising skills as there will be fewer obstacles to avoid.

h Children with DCD are often the last to get ready to go out for recess, especially in the winter months, and missing recess time only adds to their already diminished opportunities for physical development. They are also hesitant to play in the playground and are often socially isolated and excluded by others (Smyth and Anderson, 2000); as a result, they may be deliberately slow at dressing to avoid going outside. Allowing extra time to get ready for recess, ensuring a bench or safe location for the child to sit while dressing, or pairing with an older student may be helpful. The complexity of self-care tasks can also be reduced by the use of Velcro, jogging trousers, sweatshirts, t-shirts and easy fasteners (as cited in Missiuna, 2003; Missiuna, Rivard and Pollock, 2004).

Concluding comments

This chapter has clearly shown that teacher awareness of dyspraxia, DCD and dysgraphia is crucial. This can help develop more effective observational assessment and pave the way for early identification. As indicated in other chapters in this book, early identification and appropriate classroom adaptations are of paramount importance in order to prevent the child from failing and experiencing learnt helplessness and low self-esteem. It is also important to consider the overlap (often referred to as co-morbidity) between DCD and other specific difficulties such as dyslexia and attention difficulties. The research does indicate that co-morbidity is the rule rather than the exception (Snowling, 2012). It is therefore important that a broad approach is taken in relation to assessment and that the focus is on more than motor development, but also incorporates areas such as working memory, naming speed and attention issues.

Chapter 6

Behavioural problems

Attention deficit hyperactivity disorder and emotional and behavioural disorders

Background

Problems most clearly associated with SpLDs in the classroom are those educational issues related to the acquisition of literacy (reading, spelling, writing) and/or mathematic skills (as discussed in the previous chapters), with movement difficulties also been evident (see Chapter 5). However, despite the important emphasis on educational outcomes, many children with LDs also show a higher than expected prevalence of behavioural, emotional and/or social problems (Lauth, Heubeck and Mackowiak, 2006; McConaughy, Mattison and Peterson, 1994; McKinney, 1989; Michaels and Lewandowski, 1990; Swanson and Malone, 1992). This relationship is most likely reciprocal in nature – that is, increases in one probably lead to increases in the other and vice versa. However, either area of problem could be the starting point: a behavioural, emotional and/or social problem could lead to problems in school that lead to poor learning; equally, the LD could be the starting point and lead to negative behaviours, emotions and/or interactions with others. The potential for one to lead to the other is, therefore, the reason why a reciprocal relationship is likely.

Relationship between learning and behavioural problems

Although the negative psycho-social consequences of learning problems in school have been less of a focus than those of low qualifications and poor employment opportunities, they have been discussed for as long as the educational and employment consequences (see Critchley and Critchley, 1978). For example, Gates in the 1940s was arguing that 'personality maladjustment is frequently found to co-exist with reading disability' (Gates, 1941, cited in Athey, 1982). Subsequent research has supported this hypothesised link: Maughan (1995) cites evidence that students with learning problems are more likely to suffer psychiatric disorders after middle childhood than their peers; and, similarly, Huntington and Bender (1993) cite evidence that adolescents with a history of learning difficulties/disabilities demonstrate more frequent and more serious bouts of depression (see also Livingstone, 1990) and higher rates of suicide than adolescents without such disabilities. Those with learning difficulties/disabilities also present increased evidence of attentional and behavioural problems (Hinshaw, 1994). In the early years of school, low achievers have been identified as vulnerable to conduct problems, and links have been reported between learning problems in school and disruptive behaviour problems, aggression and delinquency (Hinshaw, 1992; Jorm et al., 1986; Ritchman, Stevenson and Graham, 1982). Relationships have also been reported between learning problems and hyperactivity (Stevenson et al., 1993) and increasing correlations between negative behaviours and learning problems have been found from nursery school to first grade (Pianta and Caldwell, 1990). Negative emotion/behaviour-related responses to failure to acquire literacy skills can also lead to greater problems for intervention procedures (see Miles, 2004; Murray, 1978).

Such associations between negative behaviours and educational problems can be found across cultural/educational contexts. For example, in an Arabic-speaking context, with a relatively different educational system compared to those where much of the research has been undertaken, relationships between negative (off-task) behaviours and education achievement have been found in mainstream populations (Everatt et al., 2011), and there is evidence for a higher than expected incidence of dyslexia-related problems among adolescents in offender institutions (Elbeheri, Everatt and Al-Malki, 2009). These psycho-social problems may interfere with the child's ability to fully attend to and engage in instructional activities. For example, Miles (2004) has argued that a child who does not overcome his/her difficulties with learning early in school will experience higher stress levels, causing an undermining of motivation and negative consequences in educational development. Similarly, Lindquist and Vicky (1989) have argued that children with learning problems may disrupt a class (maybe becoming the class clown) in order to protect their self-esteem because they believe the classwork is too difficult for them. Furthermore, Edwards (1994) suggests that the feelings of frustration and isolation caused by the individual's educational problems lead to negative consequences, with individuals potentially being bullied or isolated by peers, parents and teachers.

The potential reciprocal relationship becomes clearer when one considers the effects of learning problems on how an individual views themselves – that is, the individual's self-awareness or self-esteem. McLoughlin, Fitzgibbon and Young (1994) found that individuals with dyslexia have poor perceptions about their spelling abilities even though they may not be as bad as they consider, and Butrowsky and Willows (1980) found that poor readers had low expectations of success not only in reading, but also in drawing, suggesting that poor self-worth feelings can extend beyond the initial area of difficulty. Hence, experiences of failure in education may lead to individuals with LDs developing a perceived self that may be further from their ideal self than their abilities should suggest. Such findings suggest a potential downwards spiral of poor achievement leading to poor self-esteem, which further affects performance (see also Terras, Thompson and Minnis, 2009).

Equally, good self-awareness may be a factor in a successful adult life for the individual with a learning problem (Goldberg et al., 2003; Leather et al., 2011), and positive experiences of overcoming challenges (with the right support) should lead to more resilience against future difficulties (see Ofiesh and Mather, 2012; Sorenson et al., 2003). Interestingly, the development of self-esteem seems to involve two integral components: the individual and their interactions and experiences within their social world, plus the evaluation of these interactions or experiences against their existing self (see discussions in Burden and Burdett, 2005; Riddick, 2010). Hence, while self-esteem initially emerges as a global entity, it most likely differentiates into separate areas, potentially becoming hierarchical in nature (Coopersmith, 1967). This suggests that some aspects of self-esteem may be evaluated as more negative than others, which has the positive feature that well-planned/targeted learning experiences can lead to positive self-image and resilience (see discussions in Everatt and Reid, 2010), but also means that continual negative experiences may impact on global self-esteem (see Ofiesh and Mather, 2012). If left to the individual, protection of their own view of themselves may lead to some areas of behaviour (the more positive, successful areas) being promoted as more important than others. If these 'more important' areas involve negative behaviours, the protection of self-esteem may be maintained by actions that lead to further loss of learning. Good educational practice would endeavour to avoid this negative spiral.

As the above suggests, SpLDs can lead to (and have been found to be associated with) negative emotion and behavioural responses. Equally, however, emotions and behaviours that are negative may lead to poor learning. The following two sub-sections consider two general conditions that are often associated with poor educational consequences and which may be evident in typical classrooms. The emphasis here is to provide the most useful examples – it is not possible to cover every condition in one book of this size. However, the features and possible practices discussed below should also be useful with other areas of difficulties.

Emotional and behavioural disorders (EBD)

When considering the relationship between LDs and emotional, behavioural and social problems, the most obvious group of individuals on which to focus are those students who might be considered under the broad assessment of emotional and behavioural disorder (EBD). Note that this term is not universally used, but provides a basis on which to discuss the broad range of relatively serious behavioural, emotional and social problems that a child might show – we will cover a more specific (though no less controversial) term in the next sub-section of this chapter. Problems associated with EBD can be found in fairly sizeable groups of children within a school-age population (typically around 5 per cent, though some estimates suggest that this can rise above 10 per cent) and have a high co-occurrence rate (probably over 25 per cent) with LDs (Adams *et al.*, 1999; Reid *et al.*, 2004). As the name suggests, individuals can show evidence of problem behaviour and/or negative emotion (see discussions in Rutherford, Quinn and Mathur, 2004). Problem behaviours can include verbal and physical aggression or other types of inappropriate behaviours such as persistent lack of obeying school or societal rules. There can also be difficulties with interactions with peers and adults. Emotional problems often manifest as persistent unhappiness or withdrawal, as well as a tendency to develop potentially irrational fears associated with personal or school problems. More internalised forms of EBD can lead to a child suffering from severe depression, and showing evidence of anxiety and loneliness, as well as other problems such as eating disorders. Such children often experience a loss of interest in social, school or general life activities, and may be hard to spot in busy classrooms even though problems can be severe. Children showing externalised aspects of the disorder often exhibit more extrovert problems, including a lack of control and more evidence of acting out: these problems can be associated with ADHD (see below) and conduct disorders (a term used to refer to students who show prolonged periods of antisocial behaviour, including defiance of social norms and classroom rules).

Clearly, the student showing more externalised problems is often more noticeable than those who do not. They are likely to act out their emotions instead of holding them in, and can show negative behaviours such as fighting, bullying, cursing and other forms of violence. These behaviours can negatively influence their interactions with peers and adults, as well as impacting on their educational experience (Cullinan and Sabornie, 2004; Lane *et al.*, 2008; Walker, Ramsey and Gresham, 2004). Without appropriate intervention, such behaviours can become firmly established and lead to long-lasting negative outcomes (Lane *et al.*, 2006; Walker, Ramsey and Gresham, 2004). Overall, students with EBD perform less well than their peers in school assessments and examinations, they show higher rates of school drop-out than found among most other groups of students and often go on to have negative employment outcomes, increased likelihood of antisocial behaviours and a high need for mental health services (Bullis and Yovanoff, 2006; Walker, Ramsey and Gresham, 2004).

Consistent with the relationship between learning and emotional, behavioural and/or social problems, students with EBD exhibit a broad range of deficits in school areas, including in language, reading, writing and mathematics (Anderson, Kutash and Duchnowski, 2001; Greenbaum *et al.*, 1996; Lane *et al.*, 2006; Trout *et al.*, 2003), and there is evidence of a lack of improvement in these academic deficits over time (Anderson, Kutash and Duchnowski, 2001; Reid *et al.*, 2004). However, there is some indication that such negative consequences may be related to the type of behavioural problems presented by different groups of children with EBD. For example, Abikoff *et al.* (2002) found that a co-occurrence of disruptive behaviours and attention deficit was more indicative of academic underachievement relative to other disorders. Similarly, Nelson *et al.* (2004) found that poor performance in reading, mathematics and writing was more likely in children showing externalising behaviours (i.e. more verbal and physical aggressive) rather than the more internalising behaviours associated with negative emotional responses, such as depression and anxiety. Such findings argue for a closer relationship between academic underachievement and problems of conduct and attention. Indeed, the potential relationship with attentional problems mean that these too need to be considered, with the most widely cited disorder in this area being ADHD.

Learning difficulties and attention deficits (ADHD)

Similar to EBD, there is a relatively high co-occurrence (or comorbity) between SpLDs and ADHD. It has been estimated that between 20 and 50 per cent of those diagnosed with ADHD also have learning/academic problems (Barkley, 2006; Hinshaw, 1994; Semrud-Clikeman *et al.*, 1992). Given that ADHD is typically diagnosed by professionals outside of the school context, we will cover this area in more detail as the teacher may need to follow the reports presented by another professional – or understand possible features of the condition prior to providing information to another professional (see also Barkley, 2006, for a similar discussion).

ADHD is a disorder characterised by three symptoms: inattention, hyperactivity and impulsivity. Inattention involves having problems with sustained attention, distractibility and alertness. Hyperactivity is characterised by high levels of motor and/or vocal activity. Impulsivity refers to behaviours such as having problems waiting in turn, and responding too quickly to situations and without considering the consequences, which may lead to dangers and risk-taking behaviours. There is also evidence that individuals with ADHD show deficits in (i) behavioural inhibition and self-regulation, (ii) sustained attention and resistance to distraction and (iii) executive function and planning (Barkley, 2006) – and such a range of difficulties can have negative effects on the person who experiences them in general life, as well as in schooling. Generally, for a diagnosis of ADHD, symptoms need to be long lasting and lead to difficulties that are apparent across contexts. The condition has been found across many countries and educational environments, and not just in Western contexts. Again using research in the Arab world as an example of a very different cultural and educational context from that in which much of the research has been conducted, several studies investigating the percentages of children with ADHD have identified numbers similar to those reported worldwide and found that those students who showed evidence of ADHD symptoms also performed poorly academically (see Farah *et al.*, 2009).

However, despite the evidence for the condition, there has for some time now been considerable debate regarding the use of the term 'attention deficit hyperactivity disorder' and the general notion of attention disorders as a separate and discrete syndrome. This debate has accrued further interest with the publication and implementation of the *Diagnostic and Statistical Manual of Mental Disorders* (*DSM-V*) (fifth edition, American Psychiatric Association (APA), 2013). As in previous editions, *DSM-V* acknowledges that there is no single test to diagnose ADHD and that it can overlap with other categories. The diagnostic standard set by *DSM-V* is recognised internationally and can provide guidance to education authorities in all countries. Some of the important changes made in *DSM-V* (*DSM-V* replaced *DSM-IV*, which was published in 1995) in relation to ADHD include:

1   symptoms can now occur by age 12 rather than by age six;
2   several symptoms now need to be present in more than one setting rather than just some impairment in more than one setting;
3   new descriptions were added to show what symptoms might look like at older ages;
4   for adults and adolescents, age 17 or older, only five symptoms are needed instead of the six needed for younger children.

It is also important to acknowledge that, although *DSM-V* presents criteria for diagnosis of attention difficulties, only trained professionals (usually psychologists or medical professionals) will be able to diagnose ADHD.

DSM-V states that children and adults with ADHD will show a persistent pattern of inattention and/or hyperactivity-impulsivity that interferes with functioning or development. The following provides details of these potential problem areas/symptoms.

Inattention – six or more symptoms of inattention for children up to age 16, or five or more for adolescents 17 and older and adults; symptoms of inattention have been present for at least six months, and they are inappropriate for developmental level:

- often fails to give close attention to details or makes careless mistakes in schoolwork, at work, or with other activities
- often has trouble holding attention on tasks or play activities
- often does not seem to listen when spoken to directly
- often does not follow through on instructions and fails to finish schoolwork, chores, or duties in the workplace (e.g, loses focus, sidetracked)
- often has trouble organising tasks and activities
- often avoids, dislikes, or is reluctant to do tasks that require mental effort over a long period of time (such as schoolwork or homework)

- often loses things necessary for tasks and activities (e.g. school materials, pencils, books, tools, wallets, keys, paperwork, eyeglasses, mobile telephones)
- is often easily distracted
- is often forgetful in daily activities.

Hyperactivity and impulsivity – six or more symptoms of hyperactivity-impulsivity for children up to age 16, or five or more for adolescents 17 and older and adults; symptoms of hyperactivity-impulsivity have been present for at least six months to an extent that is disruptive and inappropriate for the person's developmental level:

- often fidgets with or taps hands or feet, or squirms in seat
- often leaves seat in situations when remaining seated is expected
- often runs about or climbs in situations where it is not appropriate (adolescents or adults may be limited to feeling restless)
- often unable to play or take part in leisure activities quietly
- is often 'on the go' acting as if 'driven by a motor'
- often talks excessively
- often blurts out an answer before a question has been completed
- often has trouble waiting his/her turn
- often interrupts or intrudes on others (e.g. butts into conversations or games).

In addition, the following conditions must be met:

- several inattentive or hyperactive-impulsive symptoms were present before age 12 years
- several symptoms are present in two or more settings (e.g. at home, school or work; with friends or relatives; in other activities)
- there is clear evidence that the symptoms interfere with, or reduce the quality of social, school, or work functioning
- the symptoms do not happen only during the course of schizophrenia or another psychotic disorder; the symptoms are not better explained by another mental disorder such as a mood disorder, anxiety disorder, dissociative disorder, or personality disorder.

Based on the types of symptoms related to ADHD, there are three kinds (presentations) of ADHD that can occur:

a   *Combined presentation*: if enough symptoms of both criteria, inattention and hyperactivity-impulsivity, were present for the past six months.
b   *Predominantly inattentive presentation*: if enough symptoms of inattention, but not hyperactivity-impulsivity, were present for the past six months.

c   *Predominantly hyperactive-impulsive presentation*: if enough symptoms of hyperactivity-impulsivity but not inattention were present for the past six months.

Given that symptoms can change over time, the presentation may change over time as well.

There are some key issues to consider in relation to ADHD and these include:

1   *Situational variability* – ADHD is a condition whose symptoms may or may not be present, depending on the situation. It is important to obtain information from people who observe the child across different settings. This should certainly include input from parents and teachers.

2   *Secondary or co-occurring problems* – problems children with ADHD experience very often go beyond the disorder itself and overlap with other disorders. This means that an assessment for ADHD should address not only primary ADHD symptoms, but also other aspects of the child's behavioural, emotional and social functioning. In other words, a full comprehensive assessment is necessary.

It is important, therefore, to gather information from a range of sources and one of the best means of doing that is through the use of rating scales.

Assessment of behavioural, emotional and social difficulties

Most theories related to ADHD argue that it is a neurological condition which affects different psychological processes such as attention, control, behavioural inhibition and executive functioning (Barkley, 2006), and these have been associated with genetic factors and specific areas within the brain; potentially related to areas associated with frontal lobe activity, though differences between the brains of ADHD individuals and those without ADHD have been noted across a range of brain areas. However, a combination of factors can lead to an individual showing symptoms associated with negative behaviours. These include genetic factors, but can also be related to pregnancy complications, biohazards, inappropriate nutrition or malnutrition, problem home environments etc. (Bender, 1997; Barkley, 2006; Rutherford, Quinn and Mathur, 2004; Zentall, 2006). Hence, a simple focus on cause will not provide the basis on which to identify conditions such as ADHD.

However, the effects of having a student, or students, with such behavioural problems in a classroom can be highly disruptive (see discussions in Barkley, 2006). Such disruptive behaviours can affect concentration on task and entice other students to copy the disruptive behaviours; this may be particularly the case when the disruptive child is getting most of the attention. Furthermore, as the teacher's attention is often on the 'problem' student, there may be less time spent on the teaching and learning of other students. Moreover, having a student with behavioural difficulties in the classroom can increase student–teacher frustration and tension. For the student with attention and/or behavioural difficulties, much of a lesson may be missed as a result of fidgeting, moving about, talking excessively, or negative behaviours with other children, all of which decrease on-task activities. For children with emotional problems, withdrawal may also lead to missing sections of class time or poor interactions with fellow students during group work. For children with more specific ADHD problems, impulsivity can lead to answering teacher questions too quickly, or to writing down the first thought that comes to their head, which may not necessarily produce the 'right' answer (Zentall, 2006). Inattention and off-task behaviours can also affect concentration leading to less on-task time, or the child moving from one task to another without finishing the first. An inability to sustain attention for long periods of time may lead to the child being generally less productive academically compared to other students in the same classroom. Such children may have problems pacing the progress of work and, therefore, may tire easily or finish prematurely.

Hence, there is clear evidence for relationships between a potential lack of learning within a classroom and the behavioural, emotional and/or social problem discussed above; this will be the case whether the learning problems was the initial cause or the behavioural, emotional and/or social problems. Clearly, an assessment at any one point in time is unlikely to determine the starting point of the problems. However, documented information over time, including school and teacher records, may be able to give clues as to the source of the problem, which may enable better planning for support. A child with an underlying attention/behavioural difficulty, such as ADHD or EBD, would be likely to show problems in most, if not every subject and/or activity. Observation and data gathering from a range of people involved with the student in all aspects of the curriculum, therefore, should be very helpful. And information obtained from parents should also provide clues as to the underlying reason for the problem behaviours.

There are many tools, mainly checklist/questionnaire based, that can be used to indicate problems associated with ADHD/EBD or related difficulties. A good basis tool designed for use by researchers, clinicians and educationalists is the Strengths and Difficulties Questionnaire (SDQ), originally developed by Goodman (1997). It provides a reasonable coverage of student's behaviours, emotions and relationships in a relatively short questionnaire format which has been evaluated against other measures and translated into a range of different languages.[1]

Self-esteem can be measured through questionnaires such as the Coopersmith Self-Esteem Inventory (Coopersmith, 1967), which has been translated into several different languages, or the Rosenberg Self-Esteem Scale (Rosenberg, 1989), which is often used to assess level of global self-esteem. The Harter's Self-Perception Profile for Children (revised) (Harter, 2012) can be used to elicit specific information about the child's level of scholastic competence and their academic self-esteem.

Observations inventories can also be used to assess children's behaviour in classrooms – and these have been developed in a range of different educational contexts (see, for example, Lauth, Heubeck and Mackowiak, 2006). Assessments specifically targeted at attention deficits are usually based on questionnaires incorporating some or all of the characteristics of ADHD (see sub-section on ADHD above) – and, again, these can be found in a range of contexts (for example, see Attention Hyperactivity Questionnaire in Arabic by Al-Sharhan, 2012). The Conners Scales are perhaps the most popular and there are a number of different tests within the Conners suite of tests, such as the Conners Continuous Performance Tests (CPT-3™) and the Conners Continuous Auditory Test of Attention (Conners CATA™). The CPT-3 provides objective information about an individual's performance in attention tasks, complementing information obtained from rating scales. The age range is eight and over; it includes measures on (i) inattentiveness, (ii) impulsivity, (iii) sustained attention and (iv) vigilance.

Interventions

Despite the complexity of behavioural, emotional and social problems related to the conditions discussed in this chapter, there is a great deal of evidence that they can be overcome or reduced by appropriate intervention (Barkley, 2006; Rutherford, Quinn and Mathur, 2004). Approaches aimed at improving school and classroom environments, including reducing the negative effects of disruptive or distracting behaviours, can enhance the chances that effective teaching and learning will occur, both for the students exhibiting problem behaviours and for their classmates (Adams and Christenson, 2000; Kern et al., 2001; Lee, Sugai and Horner, 1999; Umbreit, Lane and Dejud, 2004). Many studies have shown the usefulness of medication-based interventions in decreasing disruptive behaviour, either on their own or in combination with other interventions (see discussions in the MTA Co-operative Group, 1999; though see also Conners et al., 2001). However, the long-term success with medication-based interventions alone is questionable, and there may be side effects to stimulant medications such as negative emotion, sleep disorder and weight problems (see discussions in Barkley, 2006); some studies have indicated disruption in growth (Faraone et al., 2008). In particular, although positive effects of medication-based interventions can be found on educational measures, several longitudinal studies have shown negligible long-term effects of medication-only based interventions on academic performance (MTA Co-operative Group, 1999; Swanson et al., 1995). Hence, long-term academic success may be best achieved through more combined approaches, particularly where medication is used only when necessary and over a short time period, and where interventions are implemented in, or supported by, targeted classroom practice.

One of the main alternatives to medication-based interventions aimed at decreasing unwanted behaviour in students has been more cognitive-behavioural strategies. Previous research on cognitive-behavioural intervention methods has indicated that they can help children and older students behave positively (Baer and Nietzel, 1999). Such methods include parent training, peer tutoring and teacher interventions, as well as self-monitoring and strategy training, and psycho-social interventions (see Cobb *et al.*, 2006; Pelham and Fabiano, 2008). For example, previous research has suggested that self-regulation methods, where the student is taught how to control certain behaviours and thoughts, has the potential to increase academic performance (Conderman and Hedin, 2011; Mooney *et al.*, 2005). In addition to positive effects reported in the literature, self-monitoring techniques, such as positive self-talk, have the advantage that they are relatively cost-effective and easily learnt and practised. They can also be taught (and supported) by teachers and/or parents, as there is no requirement for large numbers of rules and procedures that the student must follow. Additionally, some of these interventions can be generalised to other aspects of a student's life, potentially influencing social and emotional issues. Once learnt, students can practise on their own, independent of outside assistance, especially in the case of self-talk. Such independence has the potential to promote positive outcomes for the student, fostering a sense of self-worth and self-reinforcement. The student may not have to wait for external praise from a teacher or parent, but rather comes to internalise abilities and control. Similarly, relaxation methods have also been argued to be effective in reducing negative behaviours and feelings, as well as improving outcomes, across different learning contexts (Paul, Elam and Verhulst, 2007; Stuck and Gloeckner, 2005). The rationale for relaxation methods is that, particularly at certain points (such as at examination time), school life can be considered stressful – and, for the student with an LD, such stresses can be aggravated by difficulties related to their disability. Relaxation techniques are argued to reduce such stresses, and the negative behaviours associated with stress, potentially improving academic performance.

In relation to educational or classroom practice, the following may be considered:

- classroom adaptations
- task analysis
- investigation of the student's learning preferences
- working in groups
- ensuring opportunities for discussion
- allowing scope for creativity but providing some kind of structure
- ensuring active and interactive learning
- providing 'why' questions
- providing a lot of visuals, colour and music.

Hughes and Cooper (2007), in their book on teaching approaches for ADHD, suggest the following:

- avoid confrontational situations
- show the child respect
- listen to the child's concerns
- avoid distraction
- keep instructions to a minimum – one at a time
- provide reassurance on tasks
- split tasks up – short tasks with breaks
- enable them to complete tasks
- scaffold the child's work
- provide routine
- provide outlets for active behaviour
- provide a clear structure in the class.

Clearly, all of these points will benefit children with ADHD and help to mini-mise anxiety and disruption in the classroom. Yet one must consider a funda-mental point – each of these measures will also be beneficial for children with dyslexia, dyspraxia and, indeed, it might be argued all children! This emphasises, in many respects, the futility of teaching to syndromes and the efficiency and potential effectiveness of identifying the presenting characteristics, barriers to learning and attempting to re-structure the learning experience to help to meet those individual needs.

Tridas (2007) emphasises the importance of the environment for children with ADHD. Environmental adaptations should be seen as a part of the accommodation put in place, and these should be communicated to the home. This is essential to ensure success. Some strategies suggested by Tridas include:

- establishing of routines
- creating task lists
- organising the child's study area
- break routines and tasks down to small chunks to make it easier to accomplish
- sit child as close to the teacher as possible
- sit the child away from large windows or open doors
- use study carrels rather than desks
- avoid open-plan classrooms
- set realistic expectations.

Students with problems related to ADHD and associated behavioural disorders can also have difficulty with organisation and it may be necessary for the teacher to take an active role in helping the student organise their work pro-gramme. Such help could include ensuring that notebooks have dividers and that separate folders are used for different activities and that these folders are clearly labelled in addition to helping the student keep a daily record of tasks to be completed and those that have been completed. It should be acknowledged, however, that there are different degrees of organisation and some students can only tolerate a degree of imposed organisation. Nevertheless, it should be ensured that the student with attention difficulties is sufficiently aware of materials they will require and how to access the information they need for learning.

Presenting difficulties/the use of labels

Attention and behavioural difficulties, particularly those diagnosed as ADHD and EBD, have attracted considerable interest, but have also been the subject of confusion and controversy. It may, therefore, be an idea to focus on the presenting behaviour that may account for difficulties rather than the actual label. This is because children with all sorts of labels, and many without a label, can have attention/behavioural difficulties. Additionally, difficulties are often dependent on many other factors relating to the learning experience, including the nature of the task, how the task is presented, the learning environment and the students' learnt behaviours stemming from past learning experiences. Montague and Castro (2004) suggest that, because of the views held by some regarding the neurobiological nature of ADHD, interventions have tended to focus on pharmacological treatments. They argue, however, that the current trend is moving away from that perspective and professional organisations such as the 'American Academy of Pediatrics, as well as researchers, psychologists, and counselors advocate a multimethod, multi-informant, and multi-disciplinary approach to treatment … and rather than focus on the individual's deficits, emphasis is placed on identifying the strengths of an individual and building on those strengths' (ibid.). Montague and Castro also suggest that school accommodation plans are the key to intervention and these should be multi-faceted, involving all teachers, parents and children, and that it is important to provide optimal curricular and environmental conditions for learning. They suggest that 'collaboration and cooperation among school, home and community agencies … should be the cornerstone of an intervention programme (for ADHD)' (ibid.).

Similarly Lloyd and Norris (1999) suggest that sociological and environmental criteria can be influential factors in ADHD and that dealing with the presenting behaviours and the sociological causes can be more effective than, for example, prescribed medication. This view is also supported by the developmental, contextual perspective (Pellegrini and Horvatt 1995) that acknowledges the interaction between biology and environment as crucial in understanding and dealing with difficulties associated with ADHD. Giorcelli (1999), who has pioneered inclusive approaches to managing ADHD-type difficulties by considering both within-person factors and systems, suggests that a multifaceted approach is necessary to fully comprehend and advise on the difficulties associated with ADHD.

Reid (2011) indicates that there are a number of issues relating to the use of labels to describe SpLDs and these concerns also apply to children with attention and behavioural problems. These issues include: (i) the confusion relating to the overlap between the characteristics of individual specific difficulties; (ii) the criteria used for the identification of specific conditions and (iii) the most appropriate type of intervention and provision. Reid (ibid.) suggests that it might be more useful to focus on the actual characteristics rather than the conditions and, particularly, how these characteristics relate to the barriers to learning for the individual child. The overlap between many of the characteristics usually associated with different aspects of LDs can be confusing for both teachers and parents. A useful perspective to adopt, therefore, will acknowledge the role of the interaction between the learner and the environment and emphasise that individual learning preferences can have an influential affect on the learning outcome, as can environmental and classroom factors. This can be achieved through reversing any negative learning behaviours and helping to identify and acknowledge the 'optimal curricular and environmental conditions' for learning. It is important to appreciate the role of the environment in learning; the learning environment, as well as cognitive and curricular factors, need to be considered.

At the same time, however, a label can result in additional resources and more appropriate support being provided. A label or 'working definition' can bring a degree of understanding of the nature of the difficulty and this can be beneficial to all, including the child. Some terms or labels, however, used to describe SpLDs are not well defined and can be vague, controversial and misleading. This has, at various points, applied to ADHD, EBD, dyslexia, dyscalculia, dysgraphia, DCD and most other education-related conditions, each of which can be misleading and is not always easy to define and diagnose. Many of these are the subject of ongoing controversy, ambiguities and different theoretical positions. Although labels are commonly used for the above conditions the diagnosis can still be far from precise. Often a diagnosis emerges from clinical judgement that is based on evidence from checklists or screening tests. The diagnosis can be further compounded by the overlapping characteristics. The overlap between ADHD and dyslexia has already been noted and the same type of overlap can occur between literacy difficulties, attention difficulties, language difficulties and dysgraphia. In this situation it may be difficult to identify the principal difficulty(ies) experienced by the child.

It may, therefore, be more useful for the teacher to be aware of the specific characteristics of an individual child's profile. This also highlights the view that children can have different profiles for the same difficulty. For example, some children with characteristics of ADHD may also have significant difficulties in working memory, while other children may not. Characteristics, as opposed to labels, can take on a more descriptive role. Characteristics for a number of SpLDs can include, to a greater or lesser extent, aspects relating to:

- working memory deficits
- auditory processing
- fine motor difficulties
- phonological difficulties
- non-verbal difficulties
- literacy difficulties.

Reid (2011) suggests that the broad range of the difficulties associated with the term 'specific learning difficulties' can be subdivided into the following categories:

- language-related difficulties
- attention difficulties
- reading difficulties
- expressive written/oral difficulties
- social difficulties.

It has been noted, however, that some children may possess characteristics that fall into each of these above categories (Weedon and Reid, 2003). Weedon and Reid also point out that children who present with the same range of difficulties in the classroom situation, and may have the same label, can have underlying needs that are very different and, therefore, will need different responses from the school. This emphasises the view that SpLDs should be seen within a continuum. This continuum can range from mild to severe and there will be individual variations. This means that not all children within the same category will necessarily exhibit the same specific cluster of difficulties to the same degree. At the same time it also highlights the view that intervention should be contextualised to the individual and not to the category or label.

Concluding points

One of the key points that is reiterated in this chapter is that the presenting behaviours displayed by the child need to be identified within the learning context in order to establish reasons and strategies for overcoming the difficulties. It is also suggested that this should be accompanied by identification of learning preferences as this can lead to more effective intervention. This should include both cognitive (within child) and environmental perspectives. Much of this information can be obtained from observations of the child within the learning context. It is important to appreciate that identification of learning preferences will provide guidance on the nature of the classroom, curricular and environmental considerations that need to be made for the child and that these should not necessarily be seen in a fixed and prescriptive manner – flexibility is the key. It is crucial that the intervention for children with attention, behavioural, emotional and social difficulties is seen as an educational responsibility and not a medical one. Assessment and intervention can be controlled through analysing the learning habits and experiences for the child, as well as individual cognitive and performance assessments. It is important that the result should offer relevant and individually structured educational experiences for these children. The teaching approaches used and the accommodations implemented should be informed by the results of the assessment.

Note

1 See http://www.sdqinfo.com/a0.html for information.

Chapter 7

Assessment and the role of the educational psychologist

There is little doubt that in the UK the role of the educational psychologist in relation to assessment through testing is one that provides a confusing and, at times, a contradictory picture. Woods (2012) suggests that educational psychologists in the UK have two core roles: a formative role, in which they actively support the development of provisions for children and young people; and a summative role, in which they link specialised assessments of children and young people to available provisions.

For some years, however, in terms of practice the profession in the UK has wavered between 'testing' and 'consultancy' and to some extent has been at the mercy of both government policies and the views of their paymasters. There are unquestionable differences in how educational psychologists operate from area to area within the UK and this has been characterised by a general reluctance of LEA psychologists to conduct formal psychometric testing and, even more, by a reluctance to label children with, for example dyslexia, dyspraxia or ADHD.

The BPS working party report on dyslexia (BPS, 1999) has been helpful in providing some framework for dyslexia and in making suggestions on assessment and intervention, but the definition used for dyslexia in the working party report is vague and open to misinterpretation. It does, at least, provide a framework that can be used by educational psychologists as a platform for their practice.

One of the main dilemmas is the use of their time in testing individual pupils as opposed to consulting more broadly with schools. The current trend seems to favour the latter and this has arguably led to the emergence of independent private psychologists whose practice is almost exclusively based on testing and diagnosing the nature of the child's difficulties. In some countries such as USA and Canada, as well as the Middle East, conducting psychometric and standardised assessments is the expectation and conventional practice and this role of independent educational psychologists in private practice is both established and welcomed.

Individual testing versus system-based intervention

The dilemma referred to above between testing and consultancy is based on the premise that there can be a conflict, certainly in terms of time and consumer expectations, between individual testing and broad consultancy based on systems approaches. The latter approaches tend to pursue practices of analysing the processes and procedures of school systems, developing a research orientation and a more definitive involvement in teacher education.

Many of the examples of changes in practice have emerged from the changing theoretical and practical context in education in the UK, Europe, USA, Canada and in Australia and New Zealand. These changes are characterised by the rise of inclusion and the demise of special schools, as well as an increase in the accountability of educators. The statutory influences on psychologists have impacted on the current role they play in schools in influencing, formulating and monitoring educational policy and practice.

Farrell *et al.* (2006), however, report that the majority of educational psychologists' work within the field of SENs is focused at the individual level and that almost half of this relates to children/young people's social, emotional or behavioural needs. This is perhaps significant as children who fall into this category can often seem to have more urgent needs and needs that have a more disruptive impact on the school and the classroom. Woods (2011) touches on this dilemma encompassed in the educational psychologist's service model when he cites Baxter and Frederickson (2005), who suggest that the challenge to educational psychologists is that they need to be in a position to evaluate the effectiveness of their work in improving outcomes for children and young people. In other words, they need measurable outcomes.

Individual needs

The need to assess individual children often emerges from the demands of the school to engage educational psychologists in specific individual assessment and intervention work that they see as specialist in nature and outwith the scope of expertise of the school. This means that rather than see the psychologists as partners some schools would see them as a bolt-on to existing provision.

However, some educational psychologists may see conducting traditional assessments as almost a palliative attempt to deal with the challenges experienced by the school. They see working with individuals, although in some cases necessary, not to be a cost-effective model for working with schools in the long term.

An alternative model, which may be preferred by some educational psychologists, includes working with the schools through analysing school processes, administrative structure of the school day, professional development of teachers, school policies in literacy and classroom management, incentives schemes and home–school liaison. Clearly, there is scope for both models – individual testing and school consultancy operating with schools.

This fragmentation of the role of educational psychologists has, however, led to a rise in parental referrals to independent psychologists, which has become prevalent in the UK and is established standard practice in North America and the Middle East.

Testing times

Is testing the most effective model of assessing needs? If so what tests should be used and how should these results be applied? These are the questions that need to be considered by educational psychologists.

The re-conceptualisation of the purpose of testing is a big issue. At present psycho-educational assessments tend to be retrospective, focusing on the assignation of diagnostic label. According to Oakland and Cunningham (1999), there needs to be more emphasis on testing procedures that can promote self-understanding, self-regulation and self-motivation. This means administering test procedures in more authentic settings and broadening the assessment processes to incorporate qualitative information from classroom and curricular performances.

Performance oriented/evidence-based approaches can be complementary to the traditional psychometric-focused approaches. Essentially, school psychologists need to take a leading role in the developments in education in policy, research and practice. This includes embracing innovations stemming from new technology and being in touch with new trends in education and the needs of students and teachers.

There has, however, been considerable debate for some time now on the use, and indeed the misuse, of psychometric tests.

The most useful psychometric tests are those that can provide diagnostic information as well as psychometric measures. Some tests can be interpreted diagnostically while others have identifiable criteria for diagnosis. For example, the Gray Oral Reading Test (revised) (GORT-5) has standardised data available for reading fluency and reading comprehension, but in the administration of this test there is also guidance available to conduct a miscue analysis that can identify the nature of the students' reading errors. This means that both standardised and diagnostic data is available from the one test.

Ashton (2001) provides some interesting insights into the role and the origin of educational psychologists using standardised tests. He suggests that it originated in the use of IQ tests and, particularly, in the placement of low-ability children in special schools. He suggests that, even as recently as 20 or 30 years ago, it was widely accepted that children with IQs below about 70 were better off in special schools than in the mainstream. Ashton also provides an interesting view on why the IQ figure of 70 was thought to be about right. He maintains that Burt, and his employers at the Greater London Council (GLC), looked at the distribution of IQ scores in the school population and at the total number of places available in the GLC's special schools at the time. He then calculated the IQ score below which there would be just enough pupils to fill the places available – this, of course, is the administrative part of the work. It turned out that if those pupils with IQs below about 72 were selected, then there would be just about the right number of places available for them. Ashton argues that this fuels the debate regarding whether this is 'good science serving the best interests of children, or a cynical abuse of power in the interests of administrative convenience'. There is little doubt now, in today's climate of inclusion, equal opportunity and social equity, that such administrative measures would not be tolerated, but these do not represent the type of skills or applications that educational psychologists should be involved in.

Intelligence tests

Kaufman, Lichtenberger and Naglieri (1999) discuss the controversy over the use of intelligence tests. They suggest that critics have said intelligence tests are biased, unfair and discriminatory. They maintain, however, that today the current debate is on what IQ tests actually measure and how the results can be interpreted and applied to intervention. They suggest that three current controversial themes are associated with IQ testing. These are: opposition to the practice of sub-test interpretation, opposition to the actual use of IQ tests and that the practice of intelligence testing is sound but more 'contemporary instrumentation could improve the effectiveness of this approach' (ibid.). Many of the critics argue that the IQ test has few instructional implications but Kaufman, Lichtenberger and Naglieri argue that it is obvious that if a child has low verbal IQ but scores average to above in the performance area there will be clear instructional implications. Additionally, as Kaufman, Lichtenberger and Naglieri point out, all test data has to be interpreted by the examiner in order to provide instructional pointers. They argue that the examiner needs to use the data and scores to provide a profile of the student's strengths and weaknesses and to cross-validate this with observational information from background evidence as well as the information from standardised achievement tests.

Kaufman, Lichtenberger and Naglieri argue the Wechsler Intelligence Scale for Children (WISC) can also be seen as an achievement test in that it measures past achievements and is predictive of school success in the traditional subject areas. They also maintain the WISC should be interpreted within: an information-processing model – this means looking at the input and how information is received; integration – how it is understood and made meaningful; storage – how it is stored and organised; and output – how it is retrieved. They argue that the WISC can provide information to help understand the students' processing skills using this type of model.

An alternative or complementary test to the WISC can be seen in the Woodcock Johnson Psycho-Educational Battery (revised, WJ-R), particularly the tests of cognitive ability. In addition to providing a measure of '*g*' intelligence factor, the battery can also provide achievement measures such as maths, reading, written language and general knowledge and an aptitude–achievement comparison can be made.

The Differential Ability Scale (DAS) (Elliott, Smith and McCulloch, 1996) is also viewed as a good alternative to the WISC. The DAS can be useful in assessing the achievement and the intelligence in children and adolescents; Braden (1992) suggests it represents a psychometric improvement over existing techniques for measuring intelligence. Furthermore, the General Conceptual Ability index (GCA) of the DAS is seen to be useful in the identification of processing deficits in learning disabled children.

Another test that can be used is the Kaufman Assessment Battery for Children (K-ABC) (Kaufman and Kaufman, 2004). This battery is based on a theoretical framework of sequential and simultaneous information processing which, according to Kaufman, Lichtenberger and Naglieri (1999), relates to how children solve problems rather than what type of problems they must solve (is verbal/performance). The K-ABC distinguishes between problem-solving skills and knowledge of facts. Problem-solving is defined as intelligence, while knowledge of facts is seen as achievement. Although the K-ABC, like other intelligence tests, has been subject to controversy, it does have many unique and attractive features. It is well designed and the manual is clearly written, which aids ease of administration.

Elbeheri and Everatt (2009) suggest that the popular and political link with intelligence (normally referred to as IQ) has remained an important feature in dyslexia practice and that IQ and dyslexia have been associated in such a way that it is often impossible to disconnect the two in social/political discourse.

They suggest that even those who have argued against using IQ in definitions/diagnosis of dyslexia have often felt it important to make statements/arguments along the lines of 'dyslexics are not stupid'. For that reason alone the use of the IQ test can be valid.

It should be recognised, however, that this view is not without controversy; Siegel (1989, 1999; Siegel and Lipka, 2008), for example, questions the usefulness of IQ in the diagnosis of dyslexia. She suggests that the 'discrepancy diagnosis' uses an IQ test such as the WISC in order to work out a person's expected reading ability. The WISC, as argued by Siegel (1989), includes subtests that are either irrelevant to the types of abilities required to predict reading or tap abilities that would be impaired by having the learning disability.

In defence of the use of IQ, Thomson (2001) argues that 'it is quite clear that it is possible to examine the relationship between intelligence, however imprecisely measured, and reading'; he supports the use of the IQ test in, for example, an assessment for dyslexia. Turner (1999) also insists that the IQ component of any dyslexia assessment test though sometimes a distraction has a serious statistical utility.

An important consideration is that the individual scores and index scores that comprise the global IQ figure need to be considered. Reid (2008) indicates that the nature of the conventional IQ test means that some sub-tests are challenging for dyslexic individuals and that the aggregate score may not represent the individual's real intellectual ability.

Miles and Miles (1999) also makes this point, arguing that dyslexics are 'strong on some tasks and relatively weak on others'. Therefore, combining scores to produce a global IQ may mean that we underestimate the potential of the child. Miles worries that some researchers take the concept of global IQ for granted, uncritically citing IQ figures without paying any attention to the sub-skills that make up the IQ figure.

Role of psychologists and standardised tests

One of the issues about the use of standardised tests is the lack of a suitable alternative that can supply the type of information that schools need. Ashton (2002) maintains that educational psychologists have three roles. These are: ensuring the application of science, serving the needs of students and serving the employer, which in the UK is usually the LEA; in the USA and Canada this can be the school itself or the school district.

These roles, however, can be fraught with areas of tension and conflicting agendas. For example, Ashton suggests that some LEA officers may resent educational psychologists putting support of the child first, but there are probably many parents who fear that the educational psychologist who assesses their child is going to be too concerned about LEA policy at the expense of their child's best interests. Often educational psychologists are caught between these two sets of expectations and usually try to satisfy the legitimate pressures from both sides, while also adhering to scientific standards of procedure. At the same time, educational psychologists feel an obligation to persuade their schools to develop projects and initiatives through joint consultancy with educational psychologists and through staff development programmes. This can be seen as an alternative to conducting individual assessments and may be considered by the educational psychologist to be a more productive use of their time.

Working with schools

There are many examples of psychologists working collaboratively with schools. For example, in England and Wales the revised code of practice for schools and, in particular, the 'school action plus' component of the policy provides a role for psychologists to collaborate with schools. The policy states that there may be occasions where a child's needs are at a level that it is necessary to place them directly on school action plus to recognise the significant additional support they require in school. This means that, at an early age, some students will warrant further assessment which will also involve advice to schools on both assessment and intervention. The triggers for school action plus include that the student:

- continues to make little or no progress in specific areas over a long period

- continues working at National Curriculum levels substantially below that expected of children of a similar age
- continues to have difficulty in developing literacy and mathematic skills
- has emotional or behavioural difficulties which substantially and regularly interfere with the child's own learning or that of the class group, despite having an individualised behaviour programme
- has sensory or physical needs and requires additional specialist equipment, regular advice or visits by a specialist service
- has ongoing communication or interaction difficulties that impede the development of social relationships and cause substantial barriers to learning.[1]

In Scotland, Turner (Deputy Principal Educational Psychologist)[2] acknowledges that reports from independent psychologists can be useful, but suggests that they are more helpful if the report gives reference to the school assessment and 'context-based information'. She indicates that without this there can be an assumption that the independent report is the only piece of information that matters. From this situation various problems, including a lack of a willingness to focus upon interactional or contextual factors, can follow. The message from this is, therefore, that there is a need for collaboration between independent psychologists, the school management and school policy-makers.

Impact on classroom practices

Consultation

Internationally, for some years now, there has been a major thrust in the development of consultation services for psychologists in meeting the needs of schools and also children. Gutkin and Curtis (1999), in the USA, suggest that the inclusion of consultation into the working practices of school psychologists is seen by many groups as an essential aspect of the psychologist's work. They suggest that school districts and national professional organisations, such as the National Association of School Psychologists, agree with this view. Gutkin and Curtis suggest that consultation can be seen as the 'paradox of school psychology', as they argue that to serve children effectively they must, first, concentrate their expertise on adults. They argue that the period of time when school psychologists diagnosed and provided recommendations are long gone. They now need to provide a high-quality assessment, an accurate diagnosis, develop an effective intervention plan and become involved in the planning and the monitoring of the plan.

The development of consultancy as a working approach fits in well with the growing thrust towards inclusion in schools. This can involve periods of reintegration for children from special schools to mainstream and this process has relied heavily on consultations with school psychologists.

According to Gutkin and Curtis, the problem with consultancy is the actual term itself. The term 'consultant' is now almost meaningless as it is one that is widely used by many people from different walks of life and in wide-ranging professions. The other problem with the perceptions of being a consultant is that the professional does not provide services directly to the client; it is a more indirect service delivery model. Students tend to be seen as the client and the teacher with whom the psychologists consult as the consultee. Gutkin and Curtis also warn of the danger of school psychologist/consultants entering into the area of psychotherapeutic services with the consultee. It is important always to focus on the client's need and not the teacher's personal needs, even though these may be heightened by the work demands. This may be a legitimate form of work, but it is separate from school consultancy.

Ideally, consultation should help to make the consultees better problem-solvers – so often the aim of a consultation is not to provide the answers but the means and the processes to achieving the answers. This is important as, in order for consultation to be cost effective, it is important that the consultee acquires the skills, the confidence and the independence to begin to tackle the issues independently. This would make the school psychologist's role more that of training, by providing the means for teachers to acquire some of the skills that the psychologist has.

Research findings reported by Gutkin and Curtis support this view. They argue that effective consultation can lead to dramatic decreases in student referral rates, the generalisation of client gains to other children in the class or similar settings, transfer of consultee's skills to colleagues in the same setting and empirical evaluations of preventative programmes based largely on consultation methodologies. Zins and Ponti (1996) show how consultees' processing skills can be improved by exposure to consultation and to consultation training.

It seems that it is important for the participants to be actively engaged in the consultation process. Additionally, they must want to be involved in it and do so voluntarily. This has implications for school management in how they perceive consultancy and how they present it to staff as a desirable working practice with school psychologists. Much of the success of consultancy as a means of delivering services in schools rests on the teacher's perceptions of themselves and particularly the self-efficacy of the teacher (Bandura, 1993). Gutkin and Ajchenbaum (1984), in fact, found a positive correlation between teachers' perceptions of control over presenting problems and their preferences for consultative services rather than referral services. Gutkin and Curtis therefore suggest that increasing teachers' self-efficacy is a worthwhile goal that should accompany a consultancy form of service delivery. They also provide a number of criteria to help ensure the success in this. These include: designing strategies and interventions that the consultee (teacher) feels capable of carrying through; and ensuring the results of the consultation and the proposed intervention seem to be legitimate to the teacher and congruent to his/her perceptions of the problem. This means that the way in which interventions are presented to teachers is as important as the actual intervention itself.

Consultation models

Models involving school organisation are popular with school psychologists; these involve dealing with the school as an organisation rather than one individual student or client. This can involve school psychologists participating in learning environments, planning of facilities and buildings and organisational factors to develop a 'healthy' school – physically and mentally.

Reid (1998) and Reid and Hinton (1999) developed a programme aimed at reducing the levels of teacher stress in schools by taking an organisational approach and employing a consultation and training model. This approach was based on the perceived stress levels experienced by teachers and the perceived causes of these levels. It aimed to 'stress proof' the school rather than the actual teachers themselves; areas such as management concern, buildings and facilities, lines of communications within the school and perceived control over timetabling and other administrative aspects of the school were all dealt with. The results showed that this approach can be more enduring and more successful than therapy programmes focusing on individual teachers. This was because, although the individual programmes may well have worked up to a point, the teacher had still to function within the school system and it was often the system that was at the root of the difficulties experienced. Therefore, it was more successful to treat the system rather than the individual.

Comments

The above represents an example of how systems intervention can operate in practice and how an organisational approach can be taken. Borgelt and Conoley (1999) suggest a range of interventions can result from a systems approach. These include diagnosis; team building; intergroup activities; education and training; structural activities involving work design and communication procedures in the workplace; mediation; coaching; and technology management. Certainly, organisational psychology as well as behavioural and social psychology can lend much to systems consultation approaches, as can ecological psychology and family-focused system interventions. But as Borgelt and Conoley point out, there is no 'readymade' manual for dealing with systems. This was also found by Reid (1998) in relation to developing programmes for organisational stress in that the most effective approaches were those that were generated by the teachers who were, themselves, part of the system. This concurs with the view of Borgelt and Conoley, who suggest that the challenge of 'systems work is in the construction of various approaches to enlist the human resources necessary to solve organizational problems'.

Implications for psychological services and SpLDs

It can be suggested that trends in education, whatever form these might take, have persuaded psychological services to adapt the way that they serve schools. This is certainly the case in the UK, which has seen the concept of inclusion as one that has been continually evolving. Before the Warnock Report (1978, the categorisation of students was a major element of developing legislation and one that provided an important role for psychologists. It was often the case that students who were not achieving at the same level as peers were classified as 'special needs' and, in some cases, 'mildly mentally handicapped'. Some categories of students were actually seen as being 'uneducable'. The deaf and blind were educated in separate institutions and received specialised forms of education with specially qualified teachers. Wearmouth (2001) notes that, in seeking to develop a common national framework for the education of (nearly) all children, the creators of the 1944 Education Act were faced with decisions about how to construct an educational framework that would support the learning of a diverse pupil population. The legislators formalised a system of selection and segregation based on the results of assessment tests largely of literacy, numeracy and 'reasoning skills' that, they believed, could differentiate different 'types' of learners. Different curricula could then be designed for different learning 'types' to be educated in separate sectors of the system. Selection on the basis of the results of the '11 plus' examination operated between types of secondary school in mainstream: grammar, technical and secondary modern. Within individual schools, students were selected into ability 'streams' and academic or work-related programmes, according to measured 'ability'. Many students were segregated into special schools as a result of tests of 'intelligence'. Many commentators viewed the educational hierarchy that developed as equitable, both because pupils appeared to be able to rise to a level which reflected their ability and also because it was based on psychometric testing, considered largely reliable and valid at that time.

Clark *et al.* (1997), however, retrospectively commented on a number of factors that undermined the credibility of the system. For example, movement between different types of school was very difficult, regardless of the amount of progress made by individual pupils.

In addition, there were other factors that militated against the stability of the selective system – for example, a growing concern for equality of opportunity and social cohesion in society at large. The result was the establishment of comprehensive schools in mainstream education, the introduction of methods and curricula into the mainstream from special schools, through the addition of special classes and 'remedial' provision, and the integration of some children from special to mainstream schools.

The 1978 Warnock Report was a turning point in special education in the UK; it reviewed educational provision in Great Britain for children and young people whom, up to that time, were considered 'handicapped by disabilities of body or mind' and introduced the concept of 'special educational needs', recommending that it should replace the categorisation of 'handicap'. This brought about a change in role for educational psychologists and they soon saw themselves as working *with* schools rather than working *for* schools. Consultancy accompanied testing as a role for psychologists.

Consensus and pathways

It is interesting to note the consensus that emerged from the delegates of an invited seminar at the Institute of Education in London in October 2005 (reported by Hallam, 2006). The proposals at the seminar regarding the way forward for psychologists working in education included the following:

- the need to work with, and respect fellow professionals in other disciplines
- increasing the amount of inter-disciplinary work – emphasising the need to develop working partnerships in education
- improving communications with a wider audience, particularly communicating with teachers in a language they understand
- encouraging debate about research and educational issues
- focusing on topics of interest to teachers.

The seminar also recognised the barriers that may have prevented educational psychologists from achieving a revision in their practices and status in education. These include:

- competing pressures – such as publishing responsibilities, which clashed in terms of time with other responsibilities, including assessments and school consultancy
- obstacles preventing effective multi-disciplinary working – such as alternative understanding of needs and conceptual and practical agenda differences
- the credibility factor – this relates to misunderstandings of what psychology can and cannot do, as well as the recent trend for educational psychologists in training not to possess a teaching qualification. This can be an obstacle since the majority of their work will be with schools
- the need to become aware of current issues in education and to help to implement new initiatives within school authorities.

In one sense these factors represent the ideal, but, in practice, often educational psychologists are burdened – indeed, overburdened – with statutory work which is time consuming. This often involves SN assessments from pre-school to young adult.

It is interesting to compare these issues and concerns with those stemming from a meeting of a similar nature to the 2005 seminar, held in 1993 – 12 years earlier. At that meeting of the BPS, an accompanying document included in its title the phrase 'challenges and changes for the future of our profession', which almost notes a feeling of gloom over what was to come in the field. In the document Williams suggests that the profession's esteem has diminished and its role has been limited. He talks of statutory work (in relation to SENs) becoming a 'chain round the neck of educational psychologists'. He also claims the profession of educational psychology has had great difficulty in coming to terms with the world where more up-front accountability is being demanded from professionals. Controversially, he asserts that 'there is still, unfortunately, an element of "conspiracy" between schools and psychologists, where both can convince each other of a job well done'. Although Williams accepts that there are opportunities ahead for educational psychologists, he is not convinced that all educational psychology services are in a position to maximise these opportunities. He urges the profession not to be afraid of change and indicates, in general terms, some of the different attitudes that need to be considered in relation to the type of tasks performed by psychologists: the need to be accountable and to embrace the market forces that prevail and even to be prepared to give away expertise – rather than allowing resistance to this to inhibit the development of the profession.

Problem-based working practices

A considerably more positive perception is encapsulated in the 'problem-based learning' approach. The emphasis in this is to encourage and facilitate trainees to develop problem-based learning skills that could equip them to apply their knowledge and skills in real-life contexts; that is, not to equip the trainees with the knowledge – the content area – needed to become educational psychologists, but rather with the skills of understanding the learning processes they will embark on when dealing with problems in practice. They argue that students taught in this way will be able to apply their skills more effectively in new contexts.

It is interesting to note, therefore, the responses from a group of trainees who were taught in this manner. Using a four-point scale, almost 70 per cent of the sample indicated they were reasonably well prepared to undertake research at school/organisational level and 78 per cent at the school/classroom level. Not surprisingly, 78 per cent felt they were also reasonably well prepared to deal with problem-solving situations and 61 per cent felt they had 'very well-developed' skills in collaborative working.

This example serves to pinpoint the changed ethos and the more positive perception within the profession – certainly one that is clearly characterised by confidence to adapt and perceived competence to respond to the current and changing demands in education.

Conclusion

This chapter has touched on a number of issues that have a direct impact on the current working practices of school and educational psychologists in relation to the professional, professional working practices, special needs and specific difficulties, such as dyslexia.

The dilemma and the conflicts inherent in the individual and the systems approaches can often over-burden the school psychologist. It is important, however, that – whatever options are selected – the quality of collaboration between school/family and identifying the individual educational needs of children who are at high risk of failing is given a high priority. This, along with professional integrity, is the essence of effective service delivery and it is this that will best serve the profession in the long run and ensure that the needs of those children who are at risk of failing are recognised and dealt with.

Notes

1 Adapted from Criteria for school action/school action plus, available at: http://www. tgfl.org.uk/tgfl/custom/files_uploaded/uploaded_resources/1733/Criteria-for-School-Action.pdf, accessed 20 July 2009.
2 Personal communication, 26 February 2013.

Chapter 8

Recognising and dealing with self-esteem, motivation and emotional needs

Self-esteem, self-perceptions and locus of control

There is ample evidence that children with SpLDs are more likely to incur low self-esteem, learnt helplessness and lower levels of motivation (Burden, 2005; Burden and Burdett, 2007; Everatt and Reid, 2010). There are, however, different views on the notion of what exactly represents self-esteem. The typical view focuses on how closely an individual's 'perceived' self matches their 'ideal' self. Self-esteem has also been linked to general self-concept, which includes behavioural, affective and cognitive appraisal of the self and may be influenced by cultural factors that can determine characteristics of the ideal self (Coopersmith, 1967). There is also significant evidence to show that academic self-esteem is vulnerable to underachievement from middle childhood, when the child becomes more aware of his successes and failures (Chapman, Silva and Williams, 1984). Further it has been noted that children with SpLDs have been found to have lower self-esteem than their peers (Huntington and Bender, 1993; Rosenthal, 1973).

It can be argued that individuals with SpLDs may be poor appraisers of their own abilities, meaning that their 'perceived' self may be further from their 'ideal' self than their abilities should suggest. This is a very important point and can have significant implications for children with SpLDs as they may have exaggerated lower perceptions of their abilities. For example, McLoughlin, Fitzgibbon and Young (1994) found that individuals with dyslexia had poor perceptions about their spelling abilities even though they might not have been as bad as they considered and Butrowsky and Willows (1980) found that poor readers had low expectations of success not only in reading, but also in drawing, arguing for the poor self-worth feelings to extend beyond the area of poor ability. Lawrence (1996) has argued that an individual's levels of achievement can be influenced by how they feel about themselves, suggesting a potential downwards spiral of poor achievement leading to poor self-esteem, which further affects performance. Equally, good self-awareness has been considered a factor in a successful adult life for the individual with a learning problem (Goldberg et al., 2003).

Locus of control

Self-awareness may also be related to feelings of being in control. Chan (1994) compared students with and without a disability, and looked at the relationship between motivation and strategic learning, finding a pattern of learnt helplessness – feelings of having no control of their lives was observed among many poor learners. When children with an LD experience failure, they may not look for internal factors, such as ability and effort, but rather external controls, such as luck, which may affect achievement motivation (Oka and Paris, 1987). Indeed, Mruk (1990) proposes that positive levels of self-esteem are linked with having an internal sense of control, which increases an individual's motivation and achievement in the learning situation.

Consistent with this potential relationship, Margerison's (1996) work has identified an association between self-esteem and locus of control in children with emotional problems and Humphrey and Mullins (2002) argue from their data that dyslexic children are more likely to attribute success to external factors, such as the teacher, rather than their own ability, which, as discussed above, may lead to feelings of learnt helplessness. Typically, continued failure leads to de-motivation and feelings of helplessness.

Control and success

The relationship between control and success has been studied in a small number of studies focusing on children with learning disabilities/dyslexia and the higher the internal and external control, the more likely an individual was to take control of their life and the higher was their ability to adjust to their disability and succeed in life. The work of Burden (Burden, 2005; Burden and Burdett, 2007) identified a relationship between improved academic performance and confidence (in terms of predicating success on a task) and personal control. These data were derived from work in a specialist school that produced positive attitudes towards learning, suggesting that being educated in an environment with a strong internalising focus may result in positive learning outcomes. A study by Everatt, Al-Azmi, Al-Sharhan and Elbeheri (submitted) investigated academic poor achievement indicative of learning disabilities among Arabic children and found that low self-esteem was characteristic of those with a poor level of literacy, though this was moderated by locus of control.

Overall, such findings with children and adults suggest that feelings of control may be related to overcoming negative emotional consequences and improve success, both within and outside educational contexts. This clearly has implications for assessment as the picture obtained from standardised tests may be contaminated by self-esteem, locus of control, learnt helplessness and low motivation.

Motivation and achievement

Measuring motivation has usually focused on two methods: assessment of continued engagement in a task and questionnaires used to elicit views about a task. Both can be used to support conclusions about motivation, though neither will necessarily give a full picture of the student's perspective. One measure of engagement that could be used to assess continued interest in school work in general is the Student Engagement Instrument (see Betts *et al.*, 2010); though see also the Student School Engagement Measure (see Hazel *et al.*, 2014) for a similar measure of engagement in schooling. Motivation can also be assessed via questionnaires: see the Inventory of School Motivation, which has been used across a range of contexts around the world (McInerney and Ali, 2006; Nasser, 2014) – and a range of other tools can be used to assess motivation, engagement and helplessness (see DeCastella, Byrne and Covington, 2013, for a discussion of examples). Motivation, however, is strongly linked to achievement, and, for the teacher, well-organised tasks and assessment of learning may be the most profitable way to determine the child's willingness to engage in work.

Individual perceptions and motivation

Achievement and the de-motivating impact of lack of achievement are influenced by the perception of the individual: for example, perceptions of the importance of literacy/mathematics, and school in general, can impact on the relationship between academic performance and negative affect (see Hettinger, 1982). Indeed, it can be quite illuminating talking to a group of high achievers. Some very successful learners are not aware of their own success. They may measure or perceive success in a different way from others. A student who is accustomed to obtaining straight 'A's may feel a failure if she/he obtains a 'B'; yet this can be a highly commendable grade. The 'must be best' syndrome is quite widespread in today's competitive society and, although this has some positive elements, it can be seen as one that can place enormous pressure on the learner. The key point here is: what do we mean by achievement? Achievement is not necessarily reaching the goal set by the teacher. Achievement depends on the learner and their readiness for the task. If a person does not achieve, then the task will need to be revised until they can achieve it. Motivation is related to what the learner has already achieved and this needs to be linked to current and future learning.

Self-esteem and motivational issues

There is a range of self-esteem inventories currently available (e.g. the Piers–Harris self-esteem inventory is useful as it also looks at academic and social self-esteem – second edition: Piers and Harris, 2002), but there are few self-esteem instruments that are focused on SpLDs. One such instrument is the Special Needs Assessment Profile – Behaviour (SNAP-B) (Weedon and Long, 2010).[1] SNAP-B is a bank of targeted questions that profile 12 problem areas under three broad headings:

Relationship with self

- Anxiety
- Explosive anger
- Implosive anger
- Depression

Relationships with peers

- Friendship deficit
- Instrumental aggression
- Attention-seeking from peers
- Hurtful towards peers

Relationships with adults

- Attention-seeking from adults
- Defiance towards adults
- Over-dependence upon adults
- Hurtful towards adults

There is also an optional assessment to profile educational and social self-esteem. The questions are presented in the 'pupil assessment pack' in question-naire booklets – for completion by pupil, parent and teacher(s) – for collation, analysis and profiling using the CD-ROM. The user's handbook provides full information for administering the package and interpreting the computer-generated profile. The focus is upon identifying specific skills a learner needs to be successful, rather than speculating about possible causes of any behaviour. SNAP–B suggests what action the teacher can take and provides specific advice about how to help that particular pupil, depending upon the pupil's profile.

Burden (2002) refers to Kelly's Personal Construct theory (Denicolo and Pope, 2001) as a means of helping students develop an awareness of their own perception of themselves as learners. This relates to how the individual sees him/herself as a learner and, importantly, the attributions that they make for their successes and failures in learning. If learners constantly fail at learning they will attribute this failure to themselves and their lack of ability. In fact, they may be failing because the task or the learning environment is not conducive to the learner's current level of knowledge or his/her learning style. The attributions – that is, the reasons children give for failure – are important and can provide useful information on the learner's self-perception and self-esteem.

If learners have negative perceptions of their learning abilities this can give rise to feelings of low self-worth and any repeated failure can result in a situation that can be referred to as 'learnt helplessness' (Smiley and Dweck, 1994). This means that the student loses motivation to learn as a result of an accumulation of failures.

Barriers to learning

The barriers to learning experienced by the child or young person with SpLDs essentially need to be identified at an early stage and strategies put in place to prevent further failure and 'learnt helplessness' from occurring. One of the main means of preventing learnt helpless is through ensuring the student has some early success. The use of a base line assessment is crucial for that and Came and Reid (2008) have developed a set of materials that can help to identify both concern and need. They suggest that it is crucial for teachers in the classroom to be the first to identify concern. This can be done through observation and from checklists and other pro forma materials looking at skills and attainments and checking on progress in the sub-skills of literacy and in other areas of learning.

This point is further highlighted in the results of the 'say no to failure' project,[2] which published a report in March 2008 in the UK. This report indicated that, overall, 55 per cent of all pupils who failed to reach expected targets for national standard tests (SATs) in the UK were found to be at risk of dyslexia. The sample size was 1,341 taken from Years 3–7 in 20 schools across three different authorities in England. The participating authorities included a large London inner city borough with a wide ethnic mix, a rural community in the south west of England and an authority in the north of England that included towns and a widespread rural community. The research also highlighted that a relatively greater proportion of 'at risk' children in Year 7 had more severe difficulties compared to those at risk in Year 3. This highlights the need to identify children at risk at an early stage. It is important to, first, identify the nature of their difficulties and, second, to minimise the potential for failure by planning and implementing ongoing monitoring and intervention. At this stage an appropriate individual educational plan can be implemented. This can help the teacher recognise and monitor the concerns that have been identified and pinpoint precisely which aspect of learning should be prioritised in a short-, medium- and long-term learning plan.

Such planning will help to both identify and deal with the barriers to learning. This is crucial if all students with SpLDs are going to be equipped to deal with the challenges of effective and successful learning in an inclusive educational setting. With respect to this, Riddick (1996) indicates that:

> a clear definition of both 'dyslexia' and social and emotional difficulties is problematic, so that comparing like with like is very difficult. ... much

research compares groups of pupils with and without difficulties in literacy development. Such studies mask individual differences between children. Those who experience difficulties in literacy but are well supported at home may have higher self-esteem than those with very difficult home circumstances but no literacy difficulties, for example. … it is likely that social and emotional experiences fluctuate over time and that the child's home and school context may change, all of which can affect the outcome. In addition, it is not clear if difficulties in literacy lead to poor self-esteem, or whether poor self-esteem leads to poor literacy acquisition. … what constitutes 'self-esteem' and also how to measure 'self-esteem' are highly problematic.

This view is further emphasised by Jones and Kindersley (2013) in their *Dyslexia: Assessing and Reporting*. They suggest that it is difficult to unscramble the different aspects that contribute to a child's specific difficulties and to understand the overlap and interplay between the different SpLDs. This can have implications for diagnosis and labelling.

Labelling

Pumfrey (2002) suggests labelling can be a contentious issue. He suggests that 'the label specific developmental dyslexia (or other similar labels) leads to a "pathologizing of normality"'. He feels that there is a slippery path from the recognition of such differences to the identification of defects and portrays this as an example of 'the slippery path from differences to defects [which] can lead to the pathologizing of normality – differences – deviations – difficulties – disabilities – deficits – defects'. Riddick (1996) examines the relationship between labelling and stigmatization, and quotes from Gallagher (1976) in discussing the positive and negative aspects of labelling. These are:

Positive:

1 diagnosis and appropriate treatment and alteration to the environment
2 to enable further research which may lead to better understanding, prevention and treatment
3 to act as a positive way to call attention to a particular difficulty and obtaining better resources through funding and legislation.

Negative:

1 the professionals labelling for its own sake, without suggesting any form of treatment or support
2 as a way of maintaining the status quo by keeping minority groups at the bottom of the social hierarchy.

Other factors that can account for failure and low self-esteem

Reed (2000) focuses on the wider context and discusses more fully the issues that arise from using the dyslexia label to describe difficulties in literacy experienced by students for whom English is an additional language. She considers that dyslexia offers too restricted a view for bilingual learners and risks ignoring the range of factors significant to their learning, being dependent on many contexts – for example, the contexts of the family, institution and society – and the interactional effects of, for example, physical or psychological problems, socio-economic and/or refugee status and degree of acculturation.

Developing learning competencies

There are two factors that are of importance here – one is the word 'developing' and the other 'learning competencies'. Taking the phrase 'learning competencies', the question we need to ask ourselves is: 'Competent in relation to what?' For example, there are many young people who are competent in kicking a ball and have learnt this skill over time, but they are not competent compared to the professional soccer player. Competencies need, therefore, to be matched to the learner and their zone of proximal development. This means that all competencies should be achievable. The difference, however, between 'learning' and 'competencies' needs to be made clear. One can achieve the competencies without necessarily having gone through the learning process. In the phrase 'learning competencies', therefore, the key word is 'learning' as it is important that learning actually takes place and that the learner is aware of how that learning was acquired.

There is no question, however, that learning does not automatically appear but is a developmental process. The word 'developing' implies a type of nurturing processing that takes time. It needs to be understood that learning also takes time and, during that time, the learner undertakes a number of learning processes relating to his/her understanding of the material. The well-established and accepted Blooms taxonomy – knowledge, analysis, synthesis, hypothesis and evaluation – is an example of that development, but each of these stages in themselves have also developmental phases. The work of Piaget and Vygotsky on constructivism and social constructivism highlights the important role that 'developmental stages' play in the acquisition of learning competencies. Nevertheless, it is important that developmental stages should not impose an unnecessary restriction on the development of learning competencies. There is a strong indication from the literature on learning styles, multiple intelligences and thinking skills that children are very likely much more capable than what we give them credit for.

Strategies for maintaining motivation

For many students with SpLD the sight, or indeed the thought, of certain types of tasks can be sufficient to de-motivate them. There is, therefore, an onus on teachers to develop achievable tasks that can sustain motivation. This can be the first major barrier that has to be overcome in order to maintain motivation. Some learners, if they have experienced repeated failure, will become totally de-motivated and will not want to engage in learning new material in any way at all. It is important that children can experience success before they become de-motivated. It is for that reason that great care must be taken when developing tasks to ensure that they are motivating and, even more importantly, that the learner believes the task is achievable. Breaking a task down into small steps, with every step representing an achievable and rewarding outcome for the learner, can be both rewarding and motivating. (For further details about such strategies, see Reid, 2007.)

Although rewards are useful, they should be seen as a short-term strategy – a step towards self-motivation. Rewards are normally only successful in the short term and can help children who need a boost, particularly if they are finding the task challenging. Rewards also must be achievable and the learner must value the reward. Ideally, it is best if the reward is negotiated with the learner. This needs to be considered carefully in terms of the feedback given to the child, who may be struggling. Every learner needs feedback to ensure he/she is on the correct path. However, feedback is often used as a means of grading or correcting. In using feedback this way, the teacher runs the risk of de-motivating the learner. Particularly for the child with a difficulty, it is important that feedback is seen as different from correcting work. Feedback should be continuous and formative and not necessarily come at the end of a task. Moreover, feedback should be positive or framed in a positive manner. Clearly, rewards and feedback can be dealt with separately, but giving rewards at the same time as negative feedback may be, at best, confusing, but more likely self-defeating.

Learning experiences

It is important also to consider the complete learning experience and appreciate the importance of the environment (ibid.). Social interaction can be beneficial for learners with dyslexia as it can help develop important social skills, such as turn-taking and sharing and listening to other people's opinions. The process of helping and working with others can in itself be motivating. Group dynamics can be positive or negative and it is important to ensure that the composition of the group is beneficial to all. A constructive and positive group working harmoniously can be a significant motivator. A motivated group will be able to pull the resources of all the members of the group together and this can be a strong motivating force. In fact, one can take this a step further and focus not on the individual student but on the notion of the motivated school. School ethos, school culture and school climate are important factors that can promote a healthy school (Dunham, 1995; Killick, 2005; McLean, 2004). This can provide the supportive learning environment that is required by students who are vulnerable to de-motivation and failure.

Intervention, affect and motivation

Both motivation and achievement are influenced by many factors. In the child who is struggling to achieve expected levels of performance, this relationship can be just as complex, though the link from low achievement to poor affect, low self-concept, loss of control and feelings of helplessness can cumulate in de-motivation that negatively influences achievement. This spiral of negative consequences will need to be overcome in many children with SpLDs for interventions to be successful. Miles (2004) believes if a child overcomes his LDs early in school, then this will increase confidence, allowing the individual to better cope with pressures in later life. However, a child who does not overcome his/her disability will experience higher stress levels, causing them to undermine their motivation, which can lead to consequences in the child's educational development.

Lewis (1984) found that a structured group counselling programme improved reading achievement, as well as self-concept, among elementary school children, and similar effects may be apparent for children with LDs, particularly those in middle school (see review by Elbaum and Vaughn, 2001). This argues for a combined educational and psychological response, particularly for older children who may have developed negative feelings of self-worth following failure in educational achievement which may be coupled with de-motivation. However, strategies targeted at improving self-esteem and feelings of control may be implemented best once gains in achievement have started and are likely to continue.

If gains in achievement are short-lived or perceived as external to the individual, then there is likely to be little effect on self-concept or on motivation. For example, strategies that build on strengths have been found to have positive effects on educational achievement in older children with learning problems when trying to remediate areas of weakness have been less effective (see Weeks, Brooks and Everatt, 2002). Clearly, further work is necessary, but this strategic combined approach may prove useful, particularly for older children who have experienced a prolonged period of failure during their education. Building positive self-concept, through achievable goals (and potentially good counselling support) will improve motivation and enhance the positive effects of interventions targeted at improving learning. Ignoring these influences of negative affect and de-motivation will reduce the likelihood of intervention success.

Implications for practice

Two general implications can be noted. The first is to attempt to avoid/reduce the LDs and the consequent negative emotion/motivation through appropriate teaching methods and learning environments. Well-trained teachers (particularly those working in early learning contexts, such as the first year or two of formal learning) equipped to deal with a diversity of learners, including those with special teaching needs, and schooled in up-to-date teaching methods are the most effective response to reduce the negative relationships discussed in this chapter. For example, early phoneme awareness and letter-sound training can reduce the subsequent incidence of literacy-learning problems associated with dyslexia (Elbro and Petersen, 2004) and interventions based on similar themes show good outcomes when implemented early in literacy learning (Torgesen, 2005).

The second implication is that if learning problems are not recognised early enough, then interventions will need to focus much more on the whole person (i.e. the causes and consequences of the LD, as well as the developing differences between individuals that will influence the manifestation of difficulties and the success of interventions) rather than literacy alone. The evidence argues that, even with older children with dyslexia, interventions including the phonological awareness and phonological decoding training referred to above can be successful (Gillon, 2004). However, a range of tools will be needed to support learning and allow access to the curriculum (see previous section). Above all, motivation will need to be maintained by allowing the child with special needs to do things they are good at and that they enjoy – although literacy learning can be integrated into many areas, including play, sport, art, drama and music. Special needs teacher training, as well as teams of additionally qualified professionals working with the mainstream classroom teachers, will be needed to develop further, and implement, such a range of tools if education is to become a truly inclusive system for all.

Notes

1 Available at: http://www.snapassessment.com/about2.htm
2 Availableat:http://www.xtraordinarypeople.com/news/15/Groundbreaking-Report/

Chapter 9

Identifying and utilising learning preferences and styles

Approaches to assessment

There are well over 100 instruments especially designed to identify individual learning styles. Many of these focus on relatively narrow aspects of learning style such as a preference for visual, auditory, tactual or kinaesthetic input. Others are far more elaborate and focus on factors primarily associated with personality issues such as intuition, active experimentation and reflection (Gregorc, 1985; Kolb, 1984; Lawrence, 1993; McCarthy, 1987).

Some assessment approaches attempt to identify how individual students process information in terms of cognitive style; others emphasise the cognitive/physiological aspects of learning, including laterality preferences (Hannaford, 1995). It is a good idea for the assessor wishing to pinpoint the learning preferences of students with SpLDs not to get too embroiled in the learning styles debate but to view learning styles from a practical perspective. The question is 'How can knowledge of a child's learning preference or style inform your teaching?' Once this has been established it is essential that the learning plan using the identified learning preferences is closely monitored; the teacher needs to be able to adjust the teaching and the materials if necessary. The message here is that learning styles should be seen as being flexible rather than fixed!

Style inventories

Cognitive style

Riding and Raynor (1998) use the term 'cognitive style' rather than learning style. This includes basic aspects of an individual's psychology such as feeling (affect), doing (behaviour) and knowing (cognition) and the individual's cognitive style relates to how these factors are structured and organised.

Kolb's learning style inventory

Kolb's (1984) learning style inventory is a derivative of Jung's psychological types combined with Piaget's emphasis on assimilation and accommodation

(Piaget, 1970). Kolb's 12-item inventory yields four types of learners: divergers, assimilators, convergers and accommodators.

Dunn and Dunn's learning styles inventory

The Dunn and Dunn approach utilises the learning styles inventory (Dunn, Dunn and Price, 1975, 1979, 1985, 1987, 1989). The inventory contains 104 items that produce a profile of learning style preferences in five domains, with 21 elements across those domains. These domains and elements include: environmental (sound, light, temperature, design); emotional (motivation, persistence, responsibility, structure); sociological (learning by self, pairs, peers, team, with an adult), physiological (perceptual preference, food and drink intake, time of day, mobility) and psychological (global or analytic preferences, impulsive and reflective).

The learning style inventory (LSI) is comprehensive and assesses elements in combination with each other. It asks students to answer the questions as if they are describing how they concentrate when studying difficult academic material. The instrument can be completed in approximately 30–40 minutes by elementary/primary and secondary students. After answering all the questions on the LSI answer form (the test itself), each student's answer sheet is optically read and processed individually. Each student then receives his/her own LSI individual printout – a graphic representation of the conditions in which each learns most efficiently.

Given's learning systems

Given (1996) constructed a model of learning styles derived from some key elements of other models. This model consists of emotional learning (the need to be motivated by one's own interests), social learning (the need to belong to a compatible group), cognitive learning (the need to know what age-mates know), physical learning (the need to do and be actively involved in learning) and reflective learning (the need to experiment and explore to find what circumstances work best for new learning).

Interactive observational style identification (IOSI)

Given and Reid (1999) decided to use learning styles in terms of an assessment framework rather than an inventory. Observation and self-report, by themselves, may not be sufficient to fully identify learning styles and preferences, but Given and Reid found that the use of a framework for collecting observational data can yield considerable information and can also verify and extend formal results from a self-report instrument.

A number of arguments can be put forward to support the use of interactive observation or an observational framework. For example, observation can be diagnostic, flexible and adaptable. It can occur in a natural setting, it is interactive and feedback can be ongoing. This is highlighted below.

Diagnostic:	Observations provide intermittent and ongoing opportunities to analyse student responses in different learning situations.
Flexibility:	Interactive observations can be used across subjects, settings and interactions to surface how children learn best.
Adaptability:	The interactive observational framework can be adapted to different ages, classrooms and learning situations. This contextualisation allows for a holistic picture of the child's learning preferences.
Natural setting:	Consistency of social behaviours, academic performance and study habits across a range of tasks can serve as an initial indicator of learning needs and preferences.
Interactive:	Observations can be more illuminating if some form of interaction is introduced. This can be achieved by obtaining oral responses from questions, or from the student's responses to a task. Posing questions that ask children to reflect on how they tackled a particular learning task can provide the assessor with information about children's understanding of how they learn.
	Engaging students in experimentation and exploration of what environmental, social and physical conditions work best for them can make the observational process highly interactive.

Metacognitive-type questions will facilitate interaction with the student. These include questions such as:

- how did you do that?
- do you think you were successful?
- why do you think that?
- what steps did you take to complete this?

Throughout the interaction, this type of questioning can reveal information on students' learning processes and how they organise their learning. This can also provide information on students' self-perception and whether they believe the performance was due to their own skills and efforts, or due to an external factor such as the teacher, or others in the group or class. This latter point relates to attribution theory (Dweck and Licht, 1980), which is an important aspect of learning. It is crucial that learners are able to attribute the outcome of learning tasks to themselves when the outcome is successful and not to some external factor. This can reinforce self-belief.

Teachers can use observational data to encourage students to think analytically about their learning style preferences. Since there are no correct or incorrect style preferences, IOSI encourages students to experiment with various ways of learning and to take responsibility for determining which approaches work best for them. IOSI can serve a valuable purpose by teaching children to observe their own behaviours and performances and to take responsibility for their own learning.

Pupil's Assessment of Learning Styles (PALS)©

Reid and Strnadova (2004) translated the above Given and Reid observational framework into two instruments: one a self-report instrument aimed at students to help them identify their own learning preferences, the other focusing on the teacher's observation of the student's learning preferences.

These instruments were piloted in both primary and secondary schools and the responses from the teachers who implemented the piloting were promising, indicating that the instruments provided information that could be used to implement teaching and learning materials to cater for the range of styles in most classrooms. The instrument has been refined three times following the piloting process and is in the form of a rating scale. An example of a component of the instrument is shown below.

Social

1   After school would you prefer to go home in a group rather than alone?
2   Do you like playing computer games with others?
3   Do you enjoy working in groups in class?
4   Have you got a lot of friends?
5   Do you like team games?
6   Do you enjoy being with a lot of people?
7   Do you like discussing topics in groups?
8   Do you like doing your school work with friends/others?
9   Do you enjoy spending your weekend with other people?
10   Do you see yourself as a leader?
11   Are you happy to share your desk with others?

Environmental

1   Is your desk/workplace neat and tidy?
2   Do you like quiet surroundings?
3   Does sound annoy you when you are studying?
4   Do you like having lots of space around you when you work?
5   Do you prefer to read when sitting at a desk instead of sitting on the floor?
6   Do you prefer light colours (white, yellow) in the room to darker ones (red, dark blue)?
7   Do you prefer learning indoors to outdoors?

Emotional

1   Do you change your mind about things a lot?
2   Do you often feel sad?
3   Do you find it difficult to make decisions?
4   Do you feel confident?
5   Do you worry a lot?
6   Do you consider yourself to be reliable?
7   Do you have often headaches?
8   When you start completing your task, do you finish it?
9   Do you consider yourself as having good concentration?

Cognitive

1   Do you enjoy doing crosswords puzzles?
2   Do you remember lists?
3   Do you like to learn through reading?
4   Do you enjoy picture puzzles?
5   Does drawing help you to learn?
6   Do you like to use coloured pencils a lot?
7   Do you learn best by watching a video or television?
8   Do you enjoy experiments?
9   Do you learn best by building things?
10 Do you learn best through experiences?
11 Do you learn best by visiting places?

Metacognitive

1   Do you like to make a plan before doing anything?
2   Do you usually think how you might improve your performance in any activity or task you have done?
3   Do you usually avoid making very quick decisions?
4   Do you usually ask a lot of people before making a judgement on something?
5   Do you find it easy to organise your ideas?

The key point about the use of instruments such as those above is that they need to be contextualised for the actual learning context. The instrument, therefore, is only valid if the user is aware of the need to use the instrument with flexibility and insight, particularly insights into the child's specific classroom context and ideally his/her learning habits over time. It is, therefore, crucial that any learning style or learning preference instrument that is used should be linked to practice, otherwise the information obtained is fairly meaningless.

Linking assessment with practice

As indicated above, the responses from a learning styles instrument should have practical implications for the teacher as well as for the learner. If there are 30 learners in a class then the teacher will have difficulty in catering for 30 different styles. It is almost certain, however, that there will not be 30 different styles and there will be some types of styles that the teacher can combine. For example, learners who are visual are often kinaesthetic and may also be global – meaning that they prefer to see the whole before the individual pieces of information – and prefer working in groups. This would mean that learners in this category would be able to access similar materials and respond effectively to similar teaching and learning approaches.

Empowering the learner

It can be suggested that students can become more independent in their learning and therefore more empowered as a result of knowing their strengths and weaknesses. Students can develop more effective learning strategies which they themselves can use outside the classroom. This should be one of the aims of administering a learning styles assessment.

Using learning styles

Coffield *et al.* (2004) cite the views of Alexander (2000) who distinguishes between 'teaching' and 'pedagogy'; and they argue that the learning styles literature is principally concerned with teaching rather than pedagogy. They take this as evidence that teachers need to be cautious about using the learning styles literature as a guide to classroom practice and argue that there is a need to be highly selective as some approaches are more relevant than others.

One of the key questions that needs to be considered by the teacher when planning on using learning styles is 'What is it being used for?' In other words, learning styles should not be identified in isolation but in relation to the learning environment, the task and the curriculum. Using a learning context for learning styles can be more meaningful and ensure that the approaches used and the materials developed are not developed only for the student but in relation to the task the student is to embark on. This means it is important that every subject teacher has knowledge of learning styles as well as the student's individual profile.

Although all learners' styles should be accommodated in every subject, there may be some variability and restriction depending on the subject. The important point is that the identification of learning styles needs to be linked to teaching plans, teaching methods and teaching strategies. It is for this reason that the framework described earlier in this chapter (Given and Reid, 1999) was developed. This framework allows for flexibility and can be used to accommodate the learning and teaching needs of all students in all subjects of the curriculum.

The learning process is integral to, and affected by, the interaction between teaching and learning style. It is important that this should be seen as a high priority even though the research to support this may not be abundant. Coffield (2005) argues that one needs to be careful about attempting to match teaching and learning style because of the conflicting research evidence. It is important, as Coffield also claims, that students and staff in schools and colleges reflect on their own learning and that of others. This should lead to learners being taught to set explicit, challenging goals and to identify strategies to reach these goals. This is one of the reasons why the identification of learning styles is important as it can help students become more aware of their own learning and be able to reflect more effectively on the actual learning strategies and the learning environment.

Learning styles and SpLDs

Key points about learning

It is also important to consider some of the key points that can be taken into account when planning learning for students with SpLDs. These include the following:

1   *Learning is a process:* it is important to consider this as it implies that learning will take place in a series of steps and, importantly, these steps have to be explicitly presented for students with SpLDs.
2   *Learning takes place over time:* this implies that students with SpLDs will need sufficient time to complete tasks and in many cases may need more than others in the class.
3   *Learning requires a period of consolidation:* this is important for students with SpLDs as it implies that over-learning is necessary. Often students with SpLDs may appear to have learnt something new – but they may not have consolidated that new piece of learning. This means that they require a period of over-learning in order to ensure they have automaticity in the use of that new learning. This means that often learning will take longer for students with dyslexia because they need longer to acquire automaticity.
4   *Learning is more effective when the content is familiar:* this is very important for students with SpLDs. One of the most effective means of achieving this is through pre-task discussion. This will ensure they have a good grasp of the concepts and a background understanding. Students with SpLDs need to engage in pre-task discussion before they can embark on a task independently.
5   *Over-learning needs to be planned:* this is essential for students with SpLDs. This should not happen by accident, it needs to be planned and it is

important to present the materials that have to be learnt in different teaching contexts and also to present them over a period of time. This enhances the opportunities for retention and understanding.

6   *Learning is holistic:* it is important to consider the emotional and social needs of students with SpLDs. Environmental factors are important and these should be considered in a learning programme for students with SpLD.

The learning process

Burden (2002) suggests that learning difficulties may arise at the input phase of information-processing because the learner may have an impulsive learning style or may suffer from a blurred or sweeping perception of incoming stimuli. This means that at the initial, vital stage of learning there is a breakdown in the learning process, which can therefore affect attention and make effective learning at this important input stage less efficient. Burden also suggests that, during the elaboration or cognitive phase, the learner may be unable to discriminate between relevant and irrelevant cues in defining a problem. This has been noted both among students in school and in tertiary education (Reid and Kirk, 2001) and can result in inappropriate responses to a problem or excessive elaboration, much of which is unnecessary. This excessive elaboration is often a compensatory mechanism because the student has not been able to grasp or access the key points.

Burden further emphasises the potential difficulties at the output stage of the learning cycle. He suggests that people with dyslexia may have difficulty being aware of the needs of the audience or the purpose of the activity. This can also be seen in writing where they may well be redundant pages of information.

Vygotsky (1962, 1978) differentiated between the 'cognitive' (i.e. learning how to do things) and the 'metacognitive' (i.e. a gradual conscious control over knowledge and learning), and being able to use that knowledge to help with further learning. Both cognitive and metacognitive aspects are important in Vygotsky's model, and both have been applied to many areas of assessment and learning. In particular, the cognitive aspects of learning and how it relates to the theory of social constructivism has been given some prominence. This, essentially, means that one needs to look at not only cognitive, within-child factors, but also how the child's understanding of language and learning is mediated by the learning context and the classroom environment.

Feedback

In order for the young person with SpLDs to develop learning skills, feedback is crucially important. Feedback should be provided throughout the task as well as at the end of the task and should offer:

- *Guidance:* the key point of any feedback is to provide the learner with guidance to ensure that he/she is progressing towards achieving the task.

Guidance can and should be framed in a positive way for students with SpLDs.

- *Positive reinforcement:* it is important to start with positive comments and then some points for development can be mentioned – it is important that positive comments are made both initially and at the end of any feedback session.
- *Assessment of progress:* ideally this should be done by the learner and the key point of this is to attempt to empower the learner sufficiently so that he/she can take on the responsibility of self-monitoring their own work. This highlights the need for learners to gain some control over their own learning.
- *Suggestions for further work:* it is also important that the learner is left with a framework and suggestions for development. Parents can also be informed about any further reading and additional resources that can be accessed.
- *Opportunities to develop self-monitoring and self-assessment:* essentially, this is what feedback is all about – empowering the learner to take control over his/her own learning. Constructive teacher feedback framed in a positive tone can help the learner achieve this.

Creativity and the 'gifted' student with SpLDs

One of the pitfalls about teaching a structured programme to children with SpLDs is that the programme can often be so structured that it stifles creativity and, perhaps, comprehension. It is important that teachers are aware of this and establish teaching procedures that can accommodate to the 'gifted' student to ensure that a preoccupation with remediating difficulties does not result in a restriction of higher-order thinking skills and enhanced comprehension.[1]

A good example of this comes from the work of Yoshimoto (2005), which has developed programmes and strategies for the 'gifted dyslexic' following the Orton–Gillingham (OG) approach. This ensures that critical thinking and learning skills are developed alongside the basic decoding skills needed by all dyslexic students and essential for reading fluency. Yoshimoto suggests that gifted learners with SpLDs can have:

- superior listening skills
- expansive vocabulary
- excellent general knowledge
- good abstract reasoning skills
- unusual capacity for processing information
- good problem-solving skills
- can be creative, original thinkers
- may be artistically/musically talented.

At the same time Yoshimoto claims that they can also:

- have a low self-concept
- use humour to divert attention away from perceived failure
- have low frustration tolerance
- react poorly to criticism
- try to avoid failure, which can result in refusal to perform tasks.

It is important, therefore, to ensure that differentiation caters for all abilities, as students with any of the SpLDs can be well above average in terms of their intellectual functioning and potential.

Some considerations

Some points that you may want to consider are shown below.

- Consider how learning can be made more effective for students with SpLDs.
- Consider why the learning process can go wrong for so many students with SpLDs.
- Consider learning strategies and reflect on how you might use these in your teaching and why you would adopt a particular approach for a particular student.
- Consider the importance of providing feedback to the student. Reflect on the different ways of doing this.
- Consider the importance of self-esteem in learning.
- Reflect on the role of creativity in learning for students with SpLDs and how you might develop this with your students.

The idea underpinning this chapter is to help the reader understand the underlying learning skills and preferences of children and young people with SpLDs. By focusing on their specific learning preferences this should help them develop self-knowledge and lead to empowerment and eventual success in learning.

Note

1 See www.gifteddevelopment.com and www.visualspatial.org

Chapter 10

Higher education and the workplace

There has been a great deal of progress in the area of higher education and, indeed, the workplace in terms of recognition and support of SpLDs, certainly over the last ten years and particularly in the UK and North America.

In the UK the path was set quite early on with the seminal HE working party report (Singleton, 1999) *Dyslexia in Higher Education*. This report was focused on dyslexia as it was noted that this was the most common of the SpLDs at university and one that was often the most difficult to pinpoint at that stage.

The report provided clear guidelines on assessment and support for students with dyslexia as well as guidelines for support staff and course tutors. Subsequently, a number of informative texts have become available aimed directly at dyslexia in adults (Reid and Kirk, 2001; Bartlett and Moody, 2000; Moody, 2009; McLoughlin, Leather and Stringer, 2002; Jamieson and Morgan, 2008; Pollak, 2009). Additionally, the BDA produced an *Employment and Dyslexia Handbook* (Smythe, 2009) which centred on the range of topics associated with identifying and supporting not only people with dyslexia, but also other SpLDs, and particularly the overlap of SpLDs and dyslexia (Kirby, 2006).

There also have been a number of reports commissioned and published, such as the Moser report on 'adult literacy' (Moser, 2000), the Adult Dyslexia for Employment, Practice and Training (ADEPT) report on best practice in assessment and support for adults with dyslexia, particularly focusing on the unemployed (Reid and Kirk, 2001), the report on adult literacy by Rice and Brooks (2004) and the BDA *Employer's Guide* (2005).

In the USA, legislation such as the Americans with Disabilities Act (1994) also provides a framework and opportunities for employees with dyslexia to resolve work disputes, although Gerber (1997) suggests that the ongoing reference to case law is still a powerful influence. Young (2001) cites some of this and, essentially, 'gives hope that identification and support in the workplace will become more easily obtained in the future'.

One interesting point to emerge from the UK study is the high percentage of students with dyslexia identified for the first time after entering university. In a UK study of over 100 institutions, 43 per cent of the total dyslexic student population was diagnosed as 'dyslexic' after admission to university (Singleton, 1999). There are likely a number of reasons for this, but, in the course of time, this number should be reduced as more students are identified at school level. Young people with dyslexia can be quite adept at developing coping strategies to compensate for their difficulties. It is important, therefore, that the student support services have open access and become more accessible and welcoming for the student.

In the UK the Disabled Students' Allowance (DSA) has been a significant source of support for students with SpLDs and the criteria indicates that a formal diagnosis of a 'specific learning difficulty like dyslexia or dyspraxia' is sufficient.[1]

Most universities have a web page providing details of the DSA and the support offered to students with SpLDs in terms of assessment and accommodations. For example, the University of Southampton indicates that it provides:

- an informal chat about your problems
- screening and diagnosis if appropriate
- help with applying for DSA
- arranging a needs assessment to access DSA funding
- one-to-one study skills tutorials
- group study skills workshops
- recommendations for special exam arrangements
- access to assistive technology
- working with faculties to explain your difficulties and needs
- information to help academic, or other, staff understand the difficulties faced by students with SpLDs and guidance on inclusive strategies to ensure teaching and learning are accessible to all students.[2]

Similarly, the University of Sheffield indicates the nature of the support it offers thus:

- copies of lecture notes and handouts in advance and/or in alternative formats
- support workers (such as note-takers or sign language interpreters) to ensure that students have an accurate record of what is covered in lectures
- the loan of digital recorders to record sessions
- support worker assistance in practical sessions (e.g. in labs) to ensure that students can work effectively and safely.[3]

Exam support is also a key feature in the accommodations offered and the University of Sheffield indicates the following supports can be available if appropriate:

- extra time
- use of a computer and assistive software
- rest or nutrition breaks

- permission to use specialist ergonomic equipment
- permission for students to sit their exams in a venue with fewer other candidates, or on their own
- exam papers in alternative formats (e.g. Braille or large print)
- modification of the language used in exam questions (generally for students who are deaf or hard of hearing or for those with an autism spectrum condition).

Stages of support

There are a number of different stages that students need to go through in order to obtain the most appropriate type of support at university or college. Each university will have its own specific guidelines and process for students to follow. It is important, however, that these guidelines are well publicised and the student is left in no doubt about what type of action he/she needs to take.

Some of the important stages can include:

Preliminary talk with course tutor or studies advisor This would help the student articulate his/her concerns and the tutor can advise on the most appropriate course of action. This would likely be a meeting with the student advisory service at the college.

Preliminary meeting Each university, certainly in the UK, will have a student support service and they will be able to listen to the student's concerns and make some decisions on the best course of action. At the same time, the course tutor may also have contacted the student services with the students permission.

The student services may well undertake a preliminary screening test with the student – either a pencil and paper one or one of the computerised screening (e.g. Quickscan™).

Kirk and Reid (2003) identified some of the difficulties associated with dyslexia in students – these difficulties can be used as a guide in the development of a checklist or screening for students in further and higher education and can be in:

- reading accuracy
- speed-of-reading
- persistent spelling errors
- grammatical structure
- sequencing in words and in ideas
- the need to reread text
- planning and organising written work
- memorising facts
- memorising formulae
- taking notes in lectures

- planning essays
- study skills
- transferring learning from one situation to another
- noting inferences in texts
- written examinations, particularly if timed
- technical words
- identifying main points
- a short attention span
- proofreading
- inability to read aloud
- poor sequencing, history, events, ordering information.

The next course of action will usually depend on the results of the screening test. It is important to remember that a screening test is not the same as a diagnosis and it is unlikely that there will sufficient information from a screening test to formulate a definitive diagnosis or to make specific recommendations. It can, however, inform the next course of action.

If there are enough indicators in the screening test the student services may recommend that the student is referred for a full psycho-educational assessment by a qualified and registered psychologist.

Prior to a psychological assessment

It is important that the student is briefed on what to expect prior to the assessment. This can be done either by the psychologist or through a procedures document held by the student services that will indicate what is involved in the assessment. The student therefore should be aware of the reasons for referral, the content of the assessment itself and the follow-up process. It is important that the student does not have to wait too long for the assessment and, more importantly, that the report on the results of the assessment are provided as speedily as possible – a week would be ideal.

Psychological assessment

An assessment should not be carried out in isolation. The assessment needs to be contextualised for the course of study and for the needs of the student. The demands and the skills required for different courses can vary considerably.

The demands of training in, for example, nursing will be quite different from those experienced in some science, engineering or teacher-training courses. Additionally, the person conducting the assessment needs to know about some of the other factors that may influence the outcome of the assessment and the student's performance in the course. Factors such as English being a second language and factors relating to the student's school and life experiences may also influence course performances.

It is important to recognise that dyslexia is about how reading difficulties affect individuals and how this can contribute to low self-esteem and other difficulties. It is for this reason that constructive feedback following an assessment is beneficial for the student. Such feedback can make a considerable difference to the self-esteem of the student, if handled sensitively.

The assessment

The assessment will usually be as informal as possible although the testing itself will use formal standardised instruments. It usually includes the Wechsler Adult Intelligence Scale (WAIS IV) and a range of adult literacy measures such as the Wechsler Individual Achievement Test (WIAT II) and the Wechsler Fundamentals Adult Skills (Wechsler, 2008) and perhaps some specific detailed tests on memory such as the Wide Range Assessment of Memory and Learning 2 (WRAML™). Additionally, some of the standardised tests used for children, such as the Comprehensive Test of Phonological Processing (CTOPP-2™) (Wagner, Torgeson and Rashotte, 1999) (up to age 25) and the Gray Oral Reading Test (GORT-5™) (normed to age 24), can also be used.

Ideally, the tests selected should be contextualised for the presenting difficulties and the reason for referral, but there will be a core set of tests that need to be used with, perhaps, some supplementary ones. The Comprehensive Test of Non-Verbal Ability (CTONI-4™) can also be used as it focuses on non-language skills and can be useful for students who are bilingual.

Post-assessment feedback to the student

It is important to spend some time after the assessment ensuring that the student is clear on the results and the implications of the assessment. It can be quite daunting for students to be assessed for a 'disability', and the results may come as a surprise to some students. Often, however, many students who are diagnosed as having an SpLD usually have a suspicion that they have some difficulties. Nevertheless, it is still important to provide full and informative feedback, which may well take the form of a counselling session. It is important that feedback should be clear and jargon-free. It may be necessary at this point to provide the student with encouragement; they may wish to meet other students with SpLDs, perhaps in the form of a study skills group. It is important also to emphasise that dyslexia, for example, is simply a difference in how information is processed and in some situations it may be a disability, but the disability aspect does not need to take prominence.

The workplace

While there have been significant strides in the area of higher education there has not been the same progress in the workplace, although the emergence of supports in colleges and universities will eventually pave the way for more enlightened workplace practices. The BDA have produced an *Employer's Guide to Dyslexia* (BDA, 2005) which has helped to establish a firm basis for developing awareness and effective workplace support for adults with dyslexia. The lack of employer awareness of dyslexia can have a profound effect on the worker; different countries will be referred to and how this might influence practice in the UK.

There is, however, significant evidence (Fawcett and Nicolson, 2008) that dyslexia is more than a reading difficulty. There is, therefore, a need to ensure that employers are aware of the nature of dyslexia and other SpLDs and that they understand how these factors can affect the employee in carrying out their daily work. There is also a need to understand the strengths that can be shown with people with SpLDs. It is important to dispel the notion that dyslexia equals disability as this may discriminate against employees or potential employees with dyslexia. Hence, the work by Nicolson and colleagues (Nicolson *et al.*, 2012) has done a great deal to develop the notion of positive dyslexia and provided a great deal of encouragement to people with dyslexia and, indeed, other SpLDs.

Disclosure

It is important to emphasise to adults with dyslexia that they must disclose they have an SpLD in application forms and at interviews. Many, however, are reluctant to do this because of the risk of employers discriminating against them – despite the anti-discrimination legislation that is in force in many countries. This is the reality of the situation and it is difficult to persuade dyslexic people looking for employment to put their trust in the system. Yet they must if they are going to get the support they will need once employed. It can be difficult to cover up for their dyslexia but many attempt to do this, as the extract below shows:

> No one at work knows I am dyslexic and I try to spot my mistakes before they do. When I am learning a new skill or task at work I need a base framework that is usually quite difficult as it takes time, but once I get that basic framework it is easier to learn and remember.

There are several important points here. First, a basic framework provides security for individuals with dyslexia – this also means that routine can be important and they need to establish a basic format for the tasks they have to undertake. The second point is that this particular individual has been successful, but many are not and need support to establish a basic framework or routine. If the employer does not know the employee is dyslexic then it becomes difficult to provide the understanding and the support needed. Often a crisis point is reached when the employer seeks to discipline the employee due to incompetence because they have no knowledge of the person's dyslexia (personal anecdotal interviews with author – not recorded).

Technology

It is fortunate that technology is now abundant and becoming highly sophisticated in the type of support it can provide to the employee with dyslexia. The BDA *Employer's Guide* (2005) highlighted this. The guide lists spellchecks, thesauruses, personal organisers, reading pens, voice recorders, predictive text, voice recognition, read-back scanners and software, as well as the increased portability of computers, as all being of benefit to the dyslexic individual in the workplace. The important issue is that employers have to realise that with these types of supports the barriers caused by dyslexia can be significantly minimised. This point is also made by Smythe (2009) in is aptly named chapter what's 'hot in technology': as Smythe points out, technology should be seen as another strategy that can help to reduce difficulties, but it is not a solution!

Empowerment and the social model of disability

There is an ongoing need for an awareness of SpLDs in society and in the workplace. This can be achieved through educating university staff and employers, which was the purpose of the BDA *Employer's Guide*, but it can also be achieved through more widespread and more accurate identification. This is particularly the case in the adult workforce where there are a great number of undiagnosed people with SpLDs.

McLaughlin, Leather and Stringer (2002), from the Adult Dyslexia and Skills Development Centre in London, suggests that if dyslexic people are to be fully included in society the emphasis should be on empowerment or enablement rather than a model of disability that perceives the dyslexic as a 'victim'.

He suggests that empowerment comes from:

- Self-understanding – dyslexia is often referred to as a 'hidden disability'. Dyslexic people therefore have to advocate for themselves, and can only do so if they have a good understanding of the nature of their difficulty, how it affects them and what they need to do about to improve their performance.
- Understanding by others, particularly employers – if dyslexic people have to deal with managers and colleagues whose understanding of the nature of dyslexia is limited it is likely the dyslexic person will be excluded, rather than included.

If employers are enlightened and informed, discriminatory practices should be minimised. This paves the way for rethinking the concept of disability along the lines of the social model of disability. The social model of disability opposes the medical model commonly used in the health professions, making an important distinction between the terms 'impairment' and 'accommodation'.

The implication of this for people with SpLDs is that society needs to recognise the diversity and the differences in methods of information processing displayed by different individuals. This has implications for education and for training, in particular for assessment and recognition of achievement. This also has implications for ensuring the learning environment at college and in the workplace is suited to the needs of the individual with SpLDs.

This means there needs to be a focus on support. At college and in the workplace this can involve support with the following:

- organisation of work area and of workload
- reading strategies – particularly reading fluency
- note-taking – and being able to organise and make sense of notes
- listening to instructions – and not feeling embarrassed to ask for them to be repeated or to be able to write them down
- writing reports – and being offered support to proofread and additional time to write the reports
- making presentations – identifying the key points can be problematic
- preparing for exams and generally trying to memorise information.

Career advice

Reid and Kirk (2001) show how many people with dyslexia have succeeded in a variety of occupations. McLoughlin, Leather and Stringer (2002), who indicate that being dyslexic is not necessarily a barrier to occupational success, support this view. They say:

> there are too many dyslexic people in all occupations to refute this, but some occupations are more dyslexia-friendly than others, tapping the dyslexic person's strengths rather than their weaknesses. There are undoubtedly dyslexic people who are in the wrong job, that is, they are in a situation where the demands on tasks they find difficult outweigh those on their competencies and strengths. Career guidance/counselling geared towards the needs of dyslexic people is arguably one of the most important, but under-resourced professional activities.

Without doubt, ongoing career advice is important. This will allow the young person to have several choices; if one does not work out, s/he will be able to discuss this with the careers person. Key points for career advice would be before subject choice in secondary school, before applying to college or university, when applying for a job and after having been in employment for a period of time, to discuss how the dyslexic person may advance in that career or an alternative one.

Self-advocacy

Self-advocacy is a crucial area. It is important in order to establish 'rights' which may not be easy to achieve without some form of struggle or lobbying. A shift towards greater personal responsibility, self-direction and self-advocacy is crucial to the attainment of employment success (McLoughlin, Leather and Stringer, 2002). Employment success may be dependent upon whether a disabled individual knows the dimensions of their disability well – and how, and when, to compensate for them within their job contexts because there may not be available advice. This could be because the employer is unwilling to provide support or, indeed, because they do not have a clear view of what would be beneficial.

Self-esteem

Riddick (2010) suggested that adults with dyslexia have relatively low self-esteem and, significantly, that this is not confined to academic self-esteem. This would imply that support may be needed in relation to a number of life and family factors. This means that literacy is only one aspect of a much bigger picture, and low self-esteem can affect performance in a range of life skills. One student with dyslexia, quoted by Jamieson and Morgan (2008), said that 'being dyslexic is a fundamental part of who I am. There are many things beside reading and writing that I find difficult.'

Riddick (2010) asked practicing teachers with dyslexia about the kind of coping strategies they used in the classroom. They stressed the importance of extra preparation and advance preparation. She cites one trainee teacher remarking that 'preparation is power'. Many, however, always carried a spell-checker or dictionary with them. She comments that, although all the trainee teachers had developed effective coping strategies, they were fearful of negative reactions from schools and would have welcomed support, such as mentoring or advice from experienced teachers with dyslexia.

Moody (2009) explains that the weaknesses of people with dyslexia that can affect efficiency at work include:

- literacy skills – following a technical manual, reading reports quickly and writing memos in clear English
- memory – remembering telephone numbers and recalling what was said at meetings
- sequencing ability – difficulty in filing documents in correct place and looking up
- entries in dictionaries and directories
- visual orientation – may have difficulty dealing with maps
- hand–eye co-ordination – can result in poor presentation of written work and figures

- speech – may talk in a disorganised way, especially at meetings and on the telephone
- organisational skills – may miss appointments; their work area can look disorganised
- emotional factors – may display anger, embarrassment and anxieties.

Concluding points

There does seem to be, rightly, some optimism that the needs of students and adults with dyslexia at college and in the workplace are, in some way, being dealt with. This is particularly the case in the UK in relation to university. Yet it is important that the needs of adults with SpLDs are not ignored.

In order for this to become a reality, the social model of disability needs to be acknowledged as well as the skills and potential of people with SpLDs. Legislation can help but, ultimately, it is the responsibility of society, including employers and educational institutions, to ensure that all who deal with students or employees with SpLDs have a realistic and positive awareness of their challenges and their needs. When the notion of disability is reframed in a positive and constructive fashion then people with an SpLD will feel more secure to assert their rights in study and in the workplace.

Notes

1 See https://www.gov.uk/disabled-students-allowances-dsas/eligibility, accessed 2 January 2015. There is further information on the DSA on the BDA website, http://www.bdadyslexia.org.uk/educator/hints-and-tips-fe-he#Disabled%20Students%20Allowances, including useful addresses (accessed 2 January 2015).
2 Adapted from University of Southampton web page, http://www.southampton.ac.uk/edusupport/study_support/index.page?, updated 22 September 2014, accessed 2 January 2015.
3 Available at: https://www.sheffield.ac.uk/ssid/disability/what-support-is-available, accessed 2 January 2015.

Chapter 11

Developing an assessment framework

This book has, in many ways, indicated that there has been considerable progress in the field of SpLDs and dyslexia. This has been reflected in the accessibility of appropriate tests, a more enlightened awareness of the assessment process, the incorporation of curriculum assessment, more appropriate adaptations to teaching and learning procedures and examination accommodations and support. Assessment is now more comprehensive and more robust. Many authorities and countries have guidelines for SpLD and dyslexia (quite apart from *DSM-V*), and these have been accompanied with definitions and intervention guidance, as well as criteria for teacher training (Rose, 2009).[1] These points augur well for the future and can help to ensure that children at risk of SpLDs and dyslexia are identified as early as possible and that parents, school management and teachers, as well as specialist teachers and other professionals, can all have a role to play in the process.

This chapter will, therefore, reiterate the key points in the process of assessment and discuss the importance of this framework in providing some form of structure for the assessment process.

Some key points

Historically, diagnosis was based on a 'medical' model, which focused on the child's difficulties and looked at ways of remediating those difficulties. This has been replaced, to a great extent, by a more interactive model (Wedell, 2000) which focuses on the barriers to students learning, meaning that curriculum approaches to assessment become a prime focus of the process.

It has been acknowledged that most countries now are very multicultural and often multi-linguistic. It is therefore necessary to take linguistic and cultural factors into account and this has implications for the development of tests and the planning of the assessment process.

Overall, there is no golden formula for addressing the special learning needs of students who experience SpLDs. For example, every such student should be treated as an individual; the context and the learning situation can vary and this needs to be taken into account.

Addressing the difficulties experienced by the child/student becomes a problem-solving situation and all aspects need to be considered – as well as the learner's cognitive profile. The need to obtain the learner's perspective is also seen to be important as there is now a major thrust in self-advocacy. It is also acknowledged, certainly in this book, that parents are a significant source of information and it is crucial that the assessment takes family factors into account.

The barriers to the student's learning in the classroom environment, including the curriculum, needs to be assessed and a holistic perspective taken – cognitive, social, emotional and environmental. It is important to reflect on what will best address those barriers to help the learner achieve success in the classroom situation (these points adapted from Reid and Green, 2009).

The use of tests – points to ponder

Assessment is a powerful educational tool for promoting learning. However, assessment activities should be appropriate to the aims of the assessment, to the objectives of the curriculum and to the individual student.

In the case of dyslexia, for example, it is important to identify the processing skills of the child. Often reasoning and understanding are unaffected, but the actual processing of information can be challenging. Areas such as accessing print, decoding and encoding print, processing speed and memory, as well as written output, are all processing activities necessary for literacy acquisition. These factors can also be relevant in other SpLDs such as dyspraxia and dyscalculia.

Cognitive measures

One of the most well-used practices in the assessment procedures for SpLDs is to obtain a measure of intellectual functioning as part of the investigation into discrepancies. Often the Wechsler Intelligence Scale for Children (WISC IV) is used as an ability measure as it is well standardised and translated into a number of languages (Wechsler, 2004). The use of ability measures, however, such as the WISC, according to Siegel (1989), rests on all or some of the following assumptions:

- that tests of ability or IQ are valid and reliable measures, so that there is some virtue in examining discrepancies between ability and achievement;
- particular sub-tests are valid instruments in the assessment of specific cognitive sub-skills;
- distinctive patterns may emerge that can be reliably correlated with learning difficulties;
- that IQ and reading share a causal dependency, with IQ factors influencing reading ability.

Some authors (e.g. Siegel, 1989; Siegel and Lipka, 2008), however, argue that the evidence in relation to these points is inconsistent. IQ tests do not necessarily measure intelligence, but in fact measure factual knowledge, expressive language ability, short-term memory and other skills related to learning.

There is evidence that children with dyslexia and other SpLDs can have difficulties in relation to cognition. Cognition essentially involves how children think and process information in order to understand it, to relate it to previous knowledge and to store it in long-term memory and these factors need to be considered in an assessment.

The other factor associated with SpLDs is output of information. It is interesting to note that, often, children with SpLDs do not perform to their full ability in tests because responding to test items involves immediate responses, many of which are in written form, and all of which have to be delivered without any help from the examiner. Yet, they may respond well to cues and 'assisted assessment', which can often reveal skills and aptitudes that are concealed in traditionally administered psychometric tests.

Assessment of processing skills

A significant breakthrough in terms of process assessment has emerged from the revision of the Process Assessment of the Learner (PAL-II™) diagnostic assessment for reading and writing (Berninger, 2007). Berninger suggests that intelligence tests such as the WISC IV may offer correlation data with measures of academic achievement, but do not explain why a child is experiencing poor learning outcomes or how to intervene to improve learning outcomes. It may indicate that a child needs intervention but it does not tell us precisely what kind of intervention would be the most effective. The process assessment (PAL-11) materials developed by Berninger offers clues to why a child may be underachieving in reading or writing and provides guidance on how such difficulties can be tackled.

The sub-tests of the PAL target those neuro-developmental processes most relevant to reading and writing. These include: orthographic skills, phonological skills, morphological and syntactic skills, rapid automatic naming, silent reading fluency, word-specific spellings and narrative compositional fluency. The test is very specific and extremely well conceptualised. The reading-related sub-tests are in the form of domains such as orthographic coding, phonological coding, morphological/syntactic coding, verbal working memory and rapid automatic naming. For each of these domains there are at least two to four specific sub-tests. For example, orthographic coding contains sub-tests on receptive coding and expressive coding. The receptive coding sub-test is used to measure the processes involved in coding written words into memory and analysing units of the written word without having the child writing or pronouncing them. This suite of tests can provide an alternative, or at least reduce the dependency on the use of measures of intellectual functioning.

Similarly the Wechsler Individual Achievement Test (WIAT II) (WIAT III in the USA and Canada) provides comprehensive insights into literacy acquisition and the scores can be correlated with the measures on the WISC. While there is a range of skills taken into account in the WIAT II, it is still up to the examiner to attempt to use the data diagnostically. Essentially, the results inform us on the extent of the child's difficulties but do not provide guidance on the areas within the reading process that can precisely account for these difficulties. The WIAT II does provide composite measures on key aspects such as reading, mathematics, written language and oral language and, although the reading composite includes a test on pseudo-word decoding, it does not inform us of the reasons for the child's difficulties. For example, difficulties in pseudo-word reading can suggest difficulties in applying phonetic decoding skills but do not tell us what kind of phonological difficulty the child experiences.

This emphasises the need to use tests selectively and purposefully. It is important to obtain measures of the extent of the difficulty, but, equally, it is important to obtain evidence of the nature of the difficulties experienced and reasons for these difficulties. This information is necessary if appropriate and effective intervention is to be put in place.

There are more specific tests that can accompany some of those mentioned above and can provide diagnostic criteria as well as age/grade-related measures. One such example of this is the Comprehensive Test of Phonological Processing (CTOPP-2) (Wagner, Torgeson and Rashotte, 1999). The authors have placed the test within a theoretical framework that pinpoints three types of phonological processing relevant for mastery of written language – phonological awareness, phonological memory and rapid naming.

Phonological awareness refers to an individual's awareness of and access to the sound structure of oral language. It is important to assess phonological awareness as this is often seen as one of the principal difficulties in dyslexia and some other SpLDs; studies show that children who are weak in phonological awareness display improved reading performance after being given intervention designed to improve their phonological awareness (Torgeson, Morgan and Davis, 1992; Torgeson, Wagner and Rashotte, 1997).

The other areas in the CTOPP theoretical model are phonological memory and rapid naming. Phonological memory refers to coding information phonologically for temporary storage in working or short-term memory. This is often referred to as the 'phonological loop' (Baddeley, 1986; Torgeson, 1996). Difficulties in this area can restrict a child's abilities to learn new material. Phonological coding in working memory thus, according to Wagner, Torgeson and Rashotte (1999), plays an important role in decoding new words – particularly multi-syllabic words.

The third aspect of the model underpinning the CTOPP is rapid naming. This relates to the efficiency with which young readers are able to retrieve phonological codes associated with individual phonemes, word segments and entire words. This is important as it has been shown that individuals who have difficulty in rapid naming usually have difficulty in reading fluency; those who have difficulty in both rapid naming and phonological awareness (double deficit) will have greater difficulty in learning to read than individuals with deficits only in one or the other (Bowers and Wolf, 1993). This type of test not only provides precise diagnostic information, but also can be used as a means of monitoring and evaluating a child's progress with the intervention that is being used.

A similar process is used in the Woodcock Reading Mastery Tests (revised) (Woodcock, 1998). There are three main areas to the model used in this test battery: reading readiness, basic skills and reading comprehension. For readiness, visual/auditory learning and letter identification are included; for basic skills, word identification and word attack; and, for reading comprehension, word comprehension and passage comprehension. This provides a comprehensive model using dimensions of reading that can lead to a diagnostic understanding of the child's difficulties. Additionally, there is a word attack error inventory that records the child's errors on target sounds and target syllables. This type of reading inventory is formal and structured. There is also some benefit in using more informal measures to record precise reading errors such as the system of recording miscues. The Gray Oral Reading Tests (GORT-5) does precisely that. This particular test looks at both bottom-up and top-down processes. It includes the recording of errors in graded passages to obtain accuracy scores and timed reading for fluency, as well as questions on the passage for the reading comprehension component. Additionally, however, it includes a miscue analysis system to record miscues. The miscues are divided into five types: meaning similarity – word error in relation to the meaning of the story; function similarity – word error in regard to the grammatical correctness of the word substituted in the sentence; graphic/phonemic similarity – the appropriateness of the word error as to its similarity to the look and sound of the printed word; multiple sources – this refers to the word error that has a combined meaning, function and graphic-phonemic similarity to the word; and self-correction – the occasions when a word error is immediately corrected by the student (Wiederholt and Bryant, 2001). This system will provide useful diagnostic information that, in itself, can inform planning.

Contextualising assessment with a view to intervention

It is important to ensure that the assessment process and results from any tests used are contextualised in relation to the curriculum and the nature of the child's learning situation. Sometimes factors within the classroom and the materials that are being used may account for the difficulties the child is displaying as much as the child's own attributes. Came and Reid (2008) tackle the issue of assessing literacy from the perspective of identifying concern and empowering the teacher to be in a position to do this. In their publication *Concern, Assess and Provide (CAP) It All!* (ibid.) Came and Reid provide a range of materials that can be used in the classroom context and focus directly on the student's current work.

They ask the key question 'What is literacy?' and suggest that the answer to that question will determine selection of information to undertake an assessment. This can mean addressing the functional aspects of literacy (technical) or the purpose of literacy (meaning). One of the important features of this is to have efficient and effective monitoring mechanisms in place to ensure that all aspects of the reading process are addressed. Unlike some other tests, they include assessment of children's inferential understanding of text as well as the literal meaning of the passage. Identifying the inferences in texts is an important element for developing higher-order thinking and processing skills – and particularly important for children with dyslexia as, often, their main focus is on mastering the bottom-up sub-skills of reading; the inferential meanings of the text are sometimes lost.

This emphasises the view that assessment should not be carried out in isolation. It needs a context, a purpose and appropriate linkage with intervention. Similarly, teaching reading should not be carried out in isolation. Assessment is the starting point, but it is important that the time allocated to assessment is used appropriately and productively. That is why a range of materials should be used and the teacher and specialist teacher need to be empowered to take some responsibility for the assessment process – to observe, to diagnose, to monitor and to plan appropriate intervention based on a solid and sound framework.

The problem to solution approach (ibid.) provides a useful focus. This includes the following five areas:

1   clarifying the concern
2   getting the evidence
3   planning for learning
4   action/implementation
5   monitor/review.

Clarifying the concern

Some questions the assessor should ask include:

- Can I define the problem?
- Who has a problem?
- Why are there concerns?
- What do I want to achieve?
- What strategies have been attempted that work/don't work?

Getting the evidence

- Look at the full range of evidence already available.
- Further assess the extent of the difficulty.

- Consider further assessment.
- Establish a starting point for intervention.
- Is this a balanced view, has everyone been consulted?

Planning for learning

- What strategies/programmes will be used?
- Who will implement them?
- What are the specific short-term targets?
- How can I involve parents?
- Who will monitor the progress?
- How will progress be measured?

Action/implementation

- Obtain agreement from all.
- Gather the materials.
- Conduct the programme.
- Keep parents involved.

Monitor/review

- What is going well?
- When is it working?
- Has progress been measured?
- Is progress evident?
- Has monitoring informed future targets?
- Should the plan continue?
- What are the future targets?

Self-assessment

Self-assessment is an important aspect in assessing the learner's progress. Every effort should be made to help the learner become more aware of how to tackle a question and to monitor his/her progress. This gives the learner some ownership and responsibility over his/her learning and this can also help learners develop an awareness of their own learning strengths and strategies. It is important that they are guided through the following stages shown below.

- Questioning – *why, what, where, how?*
- Clarifying – *I see, but what about this?*
- Understanding – *right, I get it now*
- Connecting – *I did something like this last week*
- Directing – *okay, I know what to do know*

- Monitoring – *maybe I should do this now; that does not seem to be correct*
- Assessing – *so far, so good; I think I am on the right track*

Ideally, you should try to get students to carry out these stages themselves, but, to begin with, they will need some support; eventually they should be able to do this unassisted.

Problem-solving and assessment

There is no golden formula for identifying and addressing the specific learning needs of every student who experiences SpLD. Addressing difficulties is a question of problem-solving and looking at the inter-relationship and interaction between the characteristics of the individual learner, the requirements of the curriculum and factors related to the learning environment and teachers' pedagogies.

We understand, however, that dyslexia should not only be identified through the use of a test. The identification of dyslexia is a process and that 'process' involves much more than the administration of a test or a group of tests. The assessment needs to consider classroom, cultural and curriculum factors and the learning preferences of the child, as well as specific difficulties and strengths. In summary, it needs to consider the task and the curriculum as well as the learning environment and the learning experience. It is worth considering the following four points as a general framework for understanding SpLDs as this also has implications for assessment.

Four general points

The four points in this framework in relation to SpLDs are:

1 the differences are personal
2 the assessment is dynamic
3 the intervention is educational
4 the understanding is scientific.

These points indicate that we need to focus on the individual characteristics of the learner. It also implies that assessment is more than administering a test; it includes looking at other aspects of learning and appreciating that we need to look at the learner in different contexts over different time periods.

It is also important to appreciate, from the points above, that the intervention is educational. This may at first seem quite obvious, but many interventions claiming to have powerful results are what might be described as 'non-educational' and, in some cases, can be medical and neurobiological. While these are not discussed here, some of the alternative interventions (see Everatt and Reid, 2009) can be useful as complementary to the main focus of intervention – educational programmes and access to the curriculum.

The fourth point mentioned above, that understanding is scientific, is an important one. In the UK there has been a great deal of debate and controversy, particularly regarding Eliot's work on the vulnerability of the concept of dyslexia. While this view has been hotly and successfully disputed, it is important that we have an awareness of the scientific foundation of dyslexia and other SpLDs (Galaburda, 2014; Knight and Hynd, 2002; Kirby, 1999; Kirby et al., 2010).

A specific framework for assessment

The list below includes a number of areas that need to be considered in some way throughout the assessment process. The idea is that this is a comprehensive list and it needs to be adapted and contextualised for the individual requirements of the assessment, depending, of course, on the type of challenges the child displays. It is important, however, to keep an open mind when conducting an assessment and ensure that a wide range of tests and other procedures are used. The following points can be used as a guide:

*   *Sensory assessment:* hearing, vision in particular and especially for young children.
*   *Information from parents:* this is essential as parents have much to offer and they can have a very detailed understanding of their child's needs, as well as strengths and weaknesses. Parents need to be consulted at the outset, but also throughout the assessment and, particularly, at the end in the feedback session.
*   *Word recognition test:* this is important as it can be a good test of decoding skills. The child is not able to use context, as only individual words are presented. He/she either has to decode the word, read it visually or access the word from their established lexicon. This type of basic reading test can also be a useful diagnostic instrument and you should always attempt to analyse the type of reading errors made.
*   *Non-word recognition test:* this is a pure test of decoding. Because non-words are used learners will not be able to read them visually and will not have seen them before, so they have to decode them. This will provide an indication of their phonological skills and their understanding of word rules.
*   *Spelling test:* it is always important to use a spelling test – perhaps several – as spelling errors can be diagnostic and can reveal a great deal about the learner's literacy development. You should try to identify a pattern of errors – for example, the use of silent letters, word endings, plurals, vowel digraphs and spelling rules. The WIAT II has a good word spelling test and the Test of Orthographic Competence (TOC™) focuses on visual spelling ability by providing part of the word; the child has to complete the word – this is, essentially, a visual spelling test. It is also important to use a spelling

in context test so you can compare the child's spelling using single words with his/her spelling in a piece of free writing.

- *Phonological assessment:* this is particularly important for younger children and very important if dyslexia is suspected. There are many appropriate phonological tests but they should show if the child recognises beginning, end and mid sounds in words and if s/he can recognise the onset and rime parts of words. Rhyming is important in a phonological test and you should be able to obtain information that can reveal whether the child can recognise and generate rhymes.

- *Miscue analysis:* assessment should be diagnostic as well as standardised; miscue analysis, irrespective of the particular system or code used, is a very useful tool with which to analyse reading errors and obtain a pattern of difficulties.

- *Reading/listening comprehension test:* both reading comprehension and listening comprehension are important. In some cases, as might be found in children who have severe dyslexia, listening comprehension can be the most useful as it does not include being able to read accurately. It is interesting, however, that many children who may not score highly in terms of reading accuracy can perform quite well in reading comprehension – their score is often higher than their accuracy score. It is important that both are used.

- *Free writing:* this can be very revealing and very informative. There are many different things to look for here – for example writing speed, spelling errors, grammar and punctuation, quality of writing in terms of content, the use of vocabulary and the structure of the written work. The WIAT II has a number of writing tasks for all ages of children and young adults. Those for younger children are highly structured and may involve joining sentences together, as well as sentence generation. For older children, titles are provided and they have to write a story based on these titles. The Test of Written Language (TOWL-4™) utilises picture cues; the stimulating picture is provided and the child's response is measured using the scoring criteria provided in the test manual. This includes spelling, structure, content and quality and quality of the response.

- *Curriculum information:* it is important to contextualise the assessment and to include information obtained from the child's performance in class. For that reason communication with the class teacher is crucial.

- *Observational assessment:* this has been detailed in earlier chapters of this book; it has been acknowledged that this is important for all SpLDs – literacy, numeracy, movement and attention factors can all be incorporated into an observational schedule that can be implemented in the assessment.

- *Movement assessment:* this is particularly important if dyspraxia is suspected and it is important to obtain information on both fine motor and gross motor skills. Fine motor skills would involve handwriting and delicate-type tasks such as the bead-threading task in the dyslexia screening test (DST); this type of task can have relevance for dyslexia and dyspraxia.

Gross motor skills would involve body awareness and spatial awareness and often be noted in extreme clumsiness and co-ordination difficulties. It is useful to obtain this type of information for all SpLDs.

- *Maths assessment:* it is important to carry out several different types of maths assessments, irrespective of the type of SpLD that is suspected. This should include mental maths, which can have relevance for dyscalculia, dyslexia and attention difficulties. It should also involve maths problem-solving skills using both concrete practical examples and more sophisticated problems using text. It is important to observe how the learner tackles the problem; you may be able to get more information by looking at his/her working and the steps he/she took in order to get a response.

- *Attention issues:* this is clearly essential if ADHD is suspected; there are a number of standardised rating scales for this. But information on 'attention' can also be noted through test observation, which can be useful for all SpLDs. The digit span sub-test can be a test of attention, as can any of the speed tests used.

- *Additional relevant information:* it is important to go into an assessment with a fairly open mind and see it as a problem-solving exercise. While it is useful to have an established test battery, it is useful if you can see that battery as flexible and not fixed. You may not need to use the full battery for every assessment and there are some assessments when you may have to, for whatever reason, use a test you may not normally use. It is important to seek information from as many sources as possible and as many relevant tests as possible. You, obviously, need to keep in mind the length of time taken for an assessment. It is too easy to over-test a student, so you need to use the test materials and the time available prudently.

It is useful to have a framework and to be able to justify the inclusion of different tests and approaches within that framework. In many ways, this has been the purpose of this book – to not only provide you with information on an assessment, but also to help you justify why you may want to use a certain test or approach for that particular assessment.

It is important to consider a point that has been made throughout this book – that is, to acknowledge the individual needs of each learner. Ideally, therefore, the assessment should be tailored towards meeting the assessment and learning needs of the individual child. Tom West – in *In the Mind's Eye* (1997), a seminal text in this area and one that was well before its time, paving the way for ground-breaking initiatives in positive dyslexia and taking the needs and learning preferences of the individual student into account – suggests:

> We ought to begin to pay less attention to getting everyone over the same hill using the same path. We may wish to encourage some to take different routes to the same end. Then we might see good reasons for paying careful

attention to their descriptions of what they have found. We may wish to follow them some day.

This is, perhaps, a fitting manner in which to close this chapter and this book. Many points have been made relating to preserving the individual needs and the dignity of the learner and every effort should be made to make assessment a rewarding and learning experience and not only a 'testing' one.

Note

1 Also see BDA web site, http://www.bdadyslexia.org.uk/, on quality assurance criteria on teacher training.

Chapter 12

Sources and resources for assessment

This chapter will provide an overview of a range of sources of information and key resources that can be used to assess children with SpLDs. Perhaps the most important resource is the human resource! That is, the role different professionals can play in the assessment process. A brief resumé of this is shown below; then a range of the tests and websites that can be accessed will be discussed.

The role of professionals in assessment

Psychologists

Educational psychologists are highly qualified professionals in psychology and education who have an understanding of the cognitive processes involved in learning. For that reason they are permitted to use cognitive tests, such those that measure intelligence.

The benefit of this, in the case of dyslexia or any of the other SpLDs, is that other reasons for lack of progress in learning or in attainments, such as low IQ, can be eliminated. If the IQ does come out low, then the educational priorities can be different from a child who has a higher IQ, but is not performing to their ability. For example, the child with a low IQ may need to focus on language comprehension, while in the case of a child with dyslexia with a higher IQ, reading accuracy may need to be prioritised. It should, however, be noted at this point that the IQ test, because of its focus on language, can discriminate against children with, for example, dyslexia and the IQ score may not reveal their actual potential.

The IQ test usually used by the educational psychologist is the Wechsler Intelligence Scale for Children (WISC IV) (for adults the equivalent test is called the Wechsler Adult Intelligence Scale (WAIS IV)). These tests, however, can be supplemented by other tests some such as the Wechsler Individual Achievement Test (WIAT II and III) and these can correlate with the WISC IV. The educational psychologist can therefore access a battery of tests.

In most countries it is the educational psychologist who provides a diagnosis of SpLDs, although this is always best acquired through collaboration with the school.

An assessment by an educational psychologist is usually carried out after the school, or the parents, suspect that the child is not making the progress that would be expected given his/her abilities in other areas. It can also be carried out privately. The British Psychological Society (BPS) publish a list of chartered psychologists which is updated annually and contains details of the qualifications and the specialisms of every registered chartered psychologist. This directory can usually be referred to in the public library. Most psychologists now have to be registered with the Health and Care Professions Council (HCPC) in the UK, which is responsible for maintaining standards and dealing with quality assurance issues among its members.

Specialist teacher

Some schools have access to trained and experienced specialist teachers who can carry out a school-based assessment. These teachers will have completed a recognised course of training in dyslexia that should include a sizeable component on assessment. For example, the British Dyslexia Association (BDA) awards accreditation status (Associated Member of the British Dyslexia Association (AMBDA)) to those teachers who have completed an approved course (a list of approved courses can be found in the BDA Handbook, published annually). Registration is now necessary through the Professional Association for Teachers and Assessors of Students with Specific Learning Difficulties (PATOSS), who also run approved courses. Teachers who hold PATOSS registration are eligible to assess for examination accommodations.

An assessment conducted by a specialist teacher will provide diagnostic information on the child's level of reading, spelling, writing and number work. Reasons for any lack of progress should be offered and recommendations on teaching programmes and strategies should be made, including what parents can do at home.

The class/learning support teacher

The class teacher is well placed to obtain first hand and detailed knowledge of the child's difficulties and strengths, as well as the learning preferences and learning style of the child. Many class teachers also have some knowledge of dyslexia, although the extent of this can vary considerably. Information from parents can also be accessed by the class teacher who can liaise with the school learning support teacher or SENCO, who will usually have specialist knowledge in the use of tests.

Standardised tests

It is important that, if standardised tests are used, the assessor checks the nature of the standardisation of the test. What is the age range of the standardisation;

did it incorporate different cultures and socio-economic factors; was the standardisation recent?

Standardised/psychometric criteria

Standardised or norm-referenced tests provide some form of score or measure, which is compared with the average scores of a standardised sample. From this type of test one can obtain, for example, a reading age or IQ score. As well as providing an indication of the pupil's progress in relation to his peers, these tests can also provide information that can be used diagnostically. Important factors in standardised tests relate to test construction and, particularly, aspects relating to validity and reliability. Standardised tests must have high validity and reliability, and this is usually indicated in the test manual. This means that the tests are well constructed, so the assessor can use the data from the test with some confidence. It is, however, important to check that the test has been constructed soundly and has high content validity and high reliability.

Standardisation

If one is attempting to standardise a test that can be used nationally across different populations of children or, indeed, selecting a standardised test for use, it is important to note a number of important points:

The sample: It is important that the sample is a representative one. Factors that should be considered include urban/rural locations, cultural background, age and sex, first language and size and selection of sample. It is important, therefore, for users of tests of any type to check the standardisation procedures that were used in the construction of the test. It is also important to check the nature of the piloting that was carried out before the standardisation data were gathered.

Reliability: This refers to the reliability in obtaining the same responses from the test if repeated under similar conditions. Reliability can be called 'replicability' or 'stability'. It, essentially, refers to the extent to which a child would obtain the same score in a test if he or she had done the test on a different day. It can be measured by determining how far the score on one question can be predicted from the same pupil's score on other questions in the test. The reliability can be calculated using the Kuder Richardson Formula 20 (KR20).

Validity: This refers to the design of the test and whether the test actually measures what it was designed to measure, such as IQ, decoding, verbal comprehension or spelling. This is not the same as reliability. A test may well be reliable and give consistent results over time, and this would mean the test is a good measure of something, but not necessarily the item it is intended to measure. Sometimes, the term 'content' or 'face validity' is used to describe validity. This refers to the extent to which the questions in the test conform to expert opinion of what good questions for that test should be. This may refer to the language used and the age appropriateness of the test material and whether cultural and social factors have been considered in the development of the test items.

Confidence interval: This refers to whether the pupil, if he or she took the test repeatedly, would obtain around the same score.

Homogeneity: This means that if the different items in the test actually measure the same skill or attainment then it should be expected that, over a group of pupils, test items should show high levels of inter-correlation. At the same time, if items are accessing different skills or attainments they would likely show lower levels of inter-correlation.

Psychometric

The term 'psychometric' refers to measurement and the use of standardised instruments to measure some ability or attainment. It is understandable, given the different aspects described above that are essential in the development of a standardised test, that such tests need to be treated with some caution. Sometimes, tests such as these can be misinterpreted.

Psychometric or standardised tests attempt to establish what would be the norm for children of a specific age. Such norm-referenced tests typically produce measures in terms of ranks (e.g. standardised reading scores), but they may fall short of highlighting appropriate intervention strategies because the scores do not provide any information on the child, apart from a score. It says little or nothing of the child's strategies for providing a response, or of the process of thought that was utilised by the child to obtain a response.

Tests that can be accessed by teachers/specialist teachers

The Dyslexia Screening Test

This test looks for difficulties in short-term memory, balance, co-ordination, spelling, speed of processing, reading accuracy, reading fluency and phonological processing.

It is a screening instrument can be used for children between 6.6 and 16.5 years of age, although there is an alternative version developed by the same authors for younger children, the Dyslexia Early Screening Test, and an adult version (Nicolson and Fawcett, 1996). The test consists of the following attainment tests:

- one-minute reading
- two-minute spelling
- one-minute writing

and the following diagnostic tests:

- rapid naming
- bead threading
- postural stability
- phonemic segmentation
- backwards digit span
- nonsense passage reading
- verbal and semantic fluency.

The Dyslexia Screening tests can be accessed by all teachers and are available from the Psychological Corporation.

Cognitive Profiling System for (CoPS™)

(Lucid Creative Ltd, Beverley, Yorkshire, UK)

This consists of activities comprising up to nine games, each with graphic and cartoon characters. As the child plays the games the computer records his or her cognitive skills. These include short-term memory, phonological awareness, auditory and colour discrimination. There is also a test called Lucid Rapid Dyslexia Screening available for children aged four to 15. It comprises three assessment modules, all testing skills that can relate to dyslexia such as phonological awareness. Details are available from www.lucid-research.com

Dyslexia Screener

((Turner and Smith, 2004) Granada Learning, available at: http://www.gl-assessment.co.uk/ (demo) and http://www.gl-assessment.co.uk/dyslexia)

This aims to diagnose pupils aged five to 16 years with dyslexic characteristics through evaluation of:

- non–verbal reasoning
- phonics
- spelling
- visual search
- reading
- verbal reasoning.

As an initial diagnostic tool, it enables you to distinguish between poor reading ability and dyslexia, and gives advice on next steps:

- adaptive testing provides rich and relevant information
- standardised scores enable comparison of pupils' results to the national average

- instant scoring and analysis give immediate feedback
- simple to administer and accessible to use
- suitable for a wide range of pupils
- designed by experts in dyslexia assessment and diagnosis.

Bangor Dyslexia Test

(LDA, Cambridge, www.LDAlearning.com)

This is a commercially available short screening test developed from work conducted at Bangor University (Miles, 1983). The test is divided into the following sections:

- left–right (body parts)
- repeating polysyllabic words
- subtraction
- tables
- months forward/reversed
- digits forward/reversed
- b/d confusion
- familiar incidence.

Special Needs Assessment Profile (SNAP I–IV™)

The Special Needs Assessment Profile (SNAP) (Weedon and Reid, 2003; Weedon, Long and Reid, 2012) is a computer-aided diagnostic assessment and profiling package that makes it possible to track each child's own profile onto an overall matrix providing information on learning, behavioural and other difficulties. From this, clusters and patterns of weaknesses and strengths help to identify the core features of a child's difficulties: visual, dyslexic, dyspraxic, phonological, attention or any other key deficits targeted in SNAP. This can suggest a diagnosis that points the way forward for a teaching programme for that individual child. SNAP includes a behavioural and self-esteem dimension, as well as dimensions focusing on learning, numeracy, movement and literacy. There is a dedicated web site that can be accessed by users containing a number of ideas on teaching to cover difficulties associated with the different SpLDs. The web site is www.SNAPassessment.com

WIAT II UK™ for teachers

Assesses single-word reading, reading comprehension, reading speed and spelling in one assessment. Published by Pearson Assessment: http://www.psychcorp.co.uk/Education/Assessments/Achievement/WIAT-IIUKfor Teachers(WIAT-IIUK-T)/WIAT-IIUKforTeachers(WIAT-IIUK-T).aspx

The age range for this test is four to 85 years. The test offers sub-tests in the three key areas of reading:

- untimed single-word accuracy
- reading comprehension
- reading speed.

Checklists

There are many variations of checklists for identifying dyslexia. Checklists, however, need to be treated with considerable caution. They are not, in any form, a definitive diagnosis of dyslexia and can be of fairly limited value, except, perhaps, for a preliminary screening before a more detailed assessment. Checklists can provide information indicating children's strengths and weaknesses, although this is of limited value; there is no real substitution for a comprehensive educational-based assessment looking at the classroom environment and the curriculum, as well as the learner's strengths and weaknesses. Checklists can be used to monitor progress.

Nursery stage

Houston (2004) has provided extremely useful guidelines based on the practice of Edinburgh City Council. She provides a type of checklist, among the other strategies she recommends. Some of the main components are shown below:

- poor language and pronunciation
- poor rhyming
- immature speech pattern and communication
- poor phonological awareness
- poor concept of time
- poor organisation
- poor listening skills
- poor memory for rhymes, stories, events, instructions
- cannot clap a rhythm or keep a musical beat
- is clumsy, wriggly and accident prone
- is hard to engage, shows little interest in activities
- can be easily distracted
- has poor posture
- poor fine motor skills, including drawing, copying and letter formation
- poor eye tracking and inability to converge from far to near
- poor spatial concepts
- poor body image
- has not established hand dominance
- poor ball skills
- poor balance and co-ordination

- poor letter knowledge
- social skills are very limited or unsuccessful.

Lower primary stage (pupils aged five to eight)

- Find it hard to learn letter–sound relationships
- Confuse letters or words with similar shapes or sounds
- Find it hard to sound out simple words
- Reverse, insert or omit words, letters and numbers
- Have difficulty with spelling very simple regular words
- Muddle the order of letters and words
- Keep losing the place when reading
- Read and do written work very slowly
- Have difficulty pronouncing longer common words
- Have difficulty hearing rhymes and sounds within words
- Have poorly spaced, poorly formed, large faint or small heavily indented writing
- Have difficulty memorising (especially in number work), despite adequate supported in-school practice
- Slow to learn to tell the time
- Slow to learn to tie shoe laces
- Confuse left/right and up/down
- Have difficulty learning the alphabet, months and days in order
- Have delayed or idiosyncratic speech and language development
- Have difficulty carrying out an oral instruction or, more commonly, multiple oral instructions
- Have poor organising ability – losing and forgetting things
- Have poor co-ordination and depth perception – tripping and bumping into things
- Have word-finding difficulties
- Behaviour difficulties, frustration, poor self-image
- Easily distracted – either hyperactive or daydreaming
- Other – please give detail.

It is important to reiterate that class teachers are not expected to be able to diagnose dyslexia, but some general indications are listed below. If several of these are observed frequently in class then this may warrant further investigation.

Children eight years and over

- Still have difficulty with reading
- Read adequately but slowly, making careless errors, and tiring in extended reading situations
- Have considerable spelling difficulties

- Have difficulty copying accurately from the blackboard or a book
- Have failed to accumulate a core of common key words
- Still confuse b/d or was/saw in reading and writing
- Still have difficulty pronouncing longer common words
- Do written work very slowly
- Miss out sounds or syllables in words, spoken and/or written
- Have difficulty memorising number bonds and tables
- Reverse numbers, e.g. 36 or 63
- Still confuse left/right and up/down
- Still have difficulty with the sequence of days, months and the alphabet
- Have poorly formed, poorly spaced immature handwriting
- Have difficulty remembering oral instructions
- Frequently appear confused and process only parts of the lesson
- Have word-finding difficulties
- Good orally, but written work disappointing
- Poor organisation and presentation; forget books and homework
- Behaviour difficulties, frustration, poor self-image
- Easily distracted – either hyperactive or daydreaming
- Clumsy, unpopular in team games, dislikes PE
- Other – please give details.

Standardised tests

Test of Phonological Awareness-Second Edition: PLUS (TOPA-2+™)

(Torgensen and Bryant)

- Ages: five through eight years
- Testing time: kindergarten – 30–45 minutes; early elementary – 15–30 minutes
- Administration: group or individual

This is a norm-referenced measure of phonological awareness for children aged five through eight years. The scale, which can also be administered individually, has demonstrated reliability and the test yields valid results that are reported in terms of percentile ranks and a variety of standard scores.

Comprehensive Test of Phonological Processing (CTOPP-2™)

(Wagner, Torgeson and Rashotte, 1999)

- Ages: five years, zero months through 24 years, 11 months
- Testing time: 30 minutes
- Administration: individual

This test assesses phonological awareness, phonological memory and rapid naming. Persons with deficits in one or more of these kinds of phonological processing abilities may have more difficulty learning to read than those who do not.

Launch into Reading Success (test of phonological awareness)

(Bennett and Ottley)

This is a phonological awareness programme designed just for young children. Reading failure can be prevented at an early stage if identification and intervention with the right programme occur. Launch into Reading Success is a phonological skills training programme designed for use by teachers and other professionals, in schools, and for parents at home. It can provide an effective first step for a child to take in the pursuit of literacy.

Gray Oral Reading Tests, Fifth Edition (GORT-5™)

(Weiderholt and Bryant)

An individually administered test of oral reading ability.

- Ages: six years, zero months through 18 years, 11 months
- Administration time: 20–30 minutes
- User qualification: Level B

This test provides an efficient and objective measure of growth in oral reading and an aid in the diagnosis of oral reading difficulties. Five scores give you information on a student's oral reading skills in terms of:

- rate – the amount of time taken by a student to read a story
- accuracy – the student's ability to pronounce each word in the story correctly
- fluency – the student's rate and accuracy scores combined
- comprehension – the appropriateness of the student's responses to questions about the content of each story read
- overall reading ability – a combination of a student's fluency (i.e. rate and accuracy) and comprehension scores.

Test of Word Reading Efficiency (TOWRE™)

(Torgesen, Wagner and Rashotte)

- Ages: six years, zero months through 24 years, 11 months
- Testing time: 5–10 minutes
- Administration: individual

This is a nationally normed measure of word reading accuracy and fluency.

Word Identification and Spelling Test (WIST™)

(Wilson)

Many teachers who have specialised training use this test. It can pinpoint whether special input would help the student (and can also be done in a group).

Wechsler Individual Achievement Test (WIAT II™ (UK norms and III US and Canada norms only)

Pearson Assessment: www.pearsonassess.com

This is a comprehensive measurement tool useful for achievement skills assessment, learning disability diagnosis and curriculum planning; it is suitable from pre-school children to adults. New norms also allow for the evaluation of and academic planning for college students with disabilities.

The test includes reading and listening comprehension, word reading and pseudo-word reading, spelling and written expression, as well as oral expression. There are also sub-tests on numerical operations and mathematical reasoning.

Phonological Assessment Battery – revised (PhAB-2™)

(Frederickson, Frith and Reason, 1997)

Granada Learning: http://shop.gl-assessment.co.uk/home.php?cat=351

The Phonological Assessment Battery (PhAB) identifies those children aged six years to 14 years, 11 months who need help by providing an individual assessment of the child's phonological skills. It comprises six tests of phonological processing, including:

- alliteration
- naming speed
- rhyme
- spoonerisms
- fluency
- non-word reading test.

This battery of tests:

- provides a clear understanding of a child's level of skill
- helps teachers to prevent potential problems and remedy existing ones
- is ideal for use with children who have English as an additional language
- can be used in conjunction with the Test of Word and Grammatical Awareness to establish a child's all-round meta-linguistic ability.

The manual gives information on test interpretation and programme planning. PhAB is a useful tool with bilingual learners and gives a good measure of how pupils are responding to interventions.

Helen Arkell Spelling Test (HAST-2™)

(Caplan, Bark and McLean)

Helen Arkell Dyslexia Centre: http://www.arkellcentre.org.uk/bookshop/

HAST-2 is a single-word spelling test developed for teachers, specialist teachers and educational psychologists to use with individuals from five years to adult. It can be administered individually or in groups, making it appropriate for use in schools and diagnostic assessments. It contains two parallel forms as well as a longer, combined form. Standardised scores, confidence intervals, percentile ranks and age equivalents are provided. Diagnostic grids have been developed to chart error types and assist with target setting. Support strategies for spelling are offered.

Websites and contacts

Dyslexia: resources

- Crossbow Education, 41 Sawpit Lane, Brocton, Stafford, ST17 0TE
  www.crossboweducation.com
- IANSYT Ltd, The White House, 72 Fen Road, Cambridge, CB4 1UN
  www.iansyst.co.uk and www.dyslexic.com
- Xavier Educational Software Ltd
  www.xavier-educational-software.co.uk
- Texthelp Systems Ltd, Enkalon Business Centre, 25 Randalstown Road, Antrim BT41 4LJ, Northern Ireland. Tel. +44 1849 428 105, Fax. +44 1849 428 574
  Email: info@texthelp.com
  www.texthelp.com
  Text Help® New Zealand, http://www.heurisko.co.nz/texthelp
- Helen Arkell Dyslexia Centre
  http://www.arkellcentre.org.uk
- LDA – Literacy Resources for Special Needs Fax. 0800 783 8648
  www.LDAlearning.com
- Learning Works International Ltd, 9 Barrow Close, Marlborough, Wiltshire, SN8 2BD, UK
  www.learning-works.org.uk
  Provides a range of materials for children to enhance learning. Some excellent materials and activities on memory work. Also publishes an excellent book, *Working with Dyscalculia* by Anne Henderson, Fil Came and Mel Brough (2003).

- The Mystery of the Lost Letters – A tri-lingual, self-help tool for dyslexic learners and their mentors.
  http://www.dyslexia-international.org

Dyslexia: information and support

- Red Rose School, St Annes on Sea, Lancashire, UK. Provides for the educational, emotional and social needs of no more than 48 boys and girls, aged between seven and 16 years. www.redroseschool.co.uk
- The International Dyslexia Association, formerly the Orton Dyslexia Association. Provides resources for professionals and families dealing with individuals with reading disabilities. www.interdys.org
- British Dyslexia Association (BDA). Information and advice on dyslexia for dyslexic people and those who support them. www.bdadyslexia. org.uk
- Learning Disabilities Worldwide. Information on causes, diagnoses, treatment, early signs and warnings. www.LDWorldwide.org
- Dyslexia Association of Ireland. www.dyslexia.ie
- Adult Dyslexia Organisation (ADO). Provides help and assistance to all dyslexic adults. www.futurenet.co.uk/charity/ado/index.html
- Fun Track Learning Center, PO Box 134, Mosman Park, WA 6912 Email: info@funtrack.com.au http://www.funtrack.com.au/
- Helen Arkell Dyslexia Centre http://www.arkellcentre.org.uk
  Runs courses, parent and teacher support, assessments and excellent online bookshop.
- Dyslexia Action. http://www.dyslexiaaction.org.uk. Support, training and assessment centre – has 21 branches in the UK.
- Dysguise Ltd. www.dysguise.com
  Helps people with learning difficulties achieve their full potential in life. Specialises in assessment for dyslexia and other related specific learning difficulties including dyscalculia, dyspraxia and dysgraphia. DysGuise can show how people with these difficulties approach learning. DysGuise also uncovers the positive aspects – this can include visual skills, problem-solving and creativity.
  Team of professional associates across Scotland carry out assessments that help people make the most of their skills and realise their learning potential.
- Dr. Gavin Reid www.drgavinreid.com
  Conducts assessments and seminars in UK, Europe, Middle East, Australia and New Zealand and North America.
- REACH Orton-Gillingham Learning Centre Inc.
  http://www.reachlearningcentre.com 1051 Churchill Crescent, North Vancouver, BC V7P 1P9, Canada is an academic remediation centre that was formed to assist individuals who are struggling to learn to read or spell.

Using the Orton-Gillingham approach to remediating language-based learning difficulties, the staff have all been specifically trained to teach reading, writing and basic language skills to students who have difficulties acquiring these skills.

Other SpLDs

- SNAP Assessment. A tool to inform on 17 SpLDs. SNAP-SpLD is comprehensive, structured and systematic: it maps each child's own mix of problems onto an overall matrix of learning, social and personal difficulties. http://www.snapassessment.com/

Attention deficit disorders

- The National Attention Deficit Disorder Information Service www.addiss.co.uk
- Attention Deficit Disorder Association www.chadd.org and www.add.org
- ADHD behaviour management www.StressFreeADHD.com
- ADHD books – www.adders.org and www.addwarehouse.com
- ADHD diet – www.feingold.org
- Dyscovery Centre – multi-disciplinary assessment centre for dyslexia, dyspraxia, attention deficit disorders and autistic spectrum disorders www.dyscovery.co.uk
- Fintan O'Regan Behaviour Management Training and Consultantcy – http://www.fintanoregan.com

Developmental co-ordination disorders/dyspraxia

- Dyspraxia Foundation www.dyspraxiafoundation.org.uk
- The Dyspraxia Support Group of New Zealand www.dyspraxia.org.nz
- Mindroom (a charity aimed at helping children and adults with learning difficulties) www.mindroom.org

Autistic spectrum disorders; Aspergers syndrome

- National Autistic Society www.nas.org.uk

Speech and language difficulties

- Afasic www.afasic.org.uk
- I CAN www.ican.org.uk
- www.childspeech.net
- www.talkingpoint.org.uk

References

Abikoff, H.B., Jensen, P.S., Arnold, L.I., Hoza, B., Hechtman, I. and Pollack, I. (2002). Observed classroom behavior of children with ADHD: relationship to gender and comorbidity. *Journal of Abnormal Child Psychology*, 30, 349–59.

Adams, J.W., Snowling, M.J., Nehhessy, S.M. and Kind, P. (1999). Problems of behaviour, reading and arithemetic. *British Journal of Educational Psychology*, 69, 571–85.

Adams, K. and Christenson, S. (2000). Trust and the family-school relationship: examination of parent–teacher differences in elementary and secondary grades. *Journal of School Psychology*, 38, 477–97.

Addy, L. M. (2003). *How to Understand and Support Children with Dyspraxia*. Wisbech: Learning Development Aids.

Alexander, R. (2000). *Culture and Pedagogy: International Comparisons in Primary Education*. Oxford: Blackwell.

Al-Sharhan, A. (2012). Efficacy of interventions aimed at reducing behavioural and educational difficulties amongst Kuwaiti students. PhD thesis, University of Surrey, UK.

American Psychiatric Association (APA) (1994). *Diagnostic and Statistical Manual of Mental Disorders (DSM-IV)*. 4th edition. Washington, DC: APA.

American Psychiatric Association (APA) (2000). *Diagnostic and Statistical Manual of Mental Disorders (DSM-IVR)*. 4th revised edition. Washington, DC: APA.

American Psychiatric Association (APA) (2013). *Diagnostic and Statistical Manual of Mental Disorders (DSM-V)*. 5th edn. Arlington, VA: APA.

Ammer, J.J. (1983). A flowchart guide to assist educators in their selection of appropriate assessment instruments. San Francisco, CA (ERIC Document Reproduction Service No. ED 238 208).

Anderson, C. (2011). Developing professional learning for staff working with children with speech, language and communication needs combined with moderate–severe learning difficulties. *British Journal of Special Education*, 38 (1), 9–18.

Anderson, J.A., Kutash, K. and Duchnowski, A.J. (2001). A comparison of the academic progress of students with EBD and students with LD. *Journal of Emotional and Behavioral Disorders*, 9, 106–15.

Ansari, D. and Dhital, B. (2006). Age-related changes in the activation of the intraparietal sulcus during non-symbolic magnitude processing: an event-related fMRI study. *Journal of Cognitive Neuroscience*, 18, 1820–8.

Applegate, A.J., Applegate, M. and Turner, J.D. (2010). Learning disabilities or teaching disabilities? Rethinking literacy failure. *Reading Teacher*, 64 (3), 211–13.

Ardila, A. (2004). There is not any specific brain area for writing: from cave-paintings to computers. *International Journal of Psychology*, 39, 61–7. Available at: http://dx.doi.org/10.1080/00207590344000295

Ashcraft, M.H. and Krause, J.A. (2007). Working memory, math performance, and math anxiety. *Psychonomic Bulletin and Review*, 14, 243–8.

Ashton, C. (2001). Assessment and support in secondary schools: an educational psychologist's view. In L. Peer and G. Reid (eds), *Dyslexia: Successful Inclusion in the Secondary School*. London: David Fulton.

Athey, I. (1982). Reading: the affective domain reconceptualised. *Advances in Reading and Language Research*, 1, 203–17.

Baddeley, A. (1986). Working memory. *Science*, 255, 556–9.

Baer, R.A. and Nietzel, M.T. (1999). Cognitive and behavioural treatment of impulsivity in children: a meta-analytic review of the outcome literature. *Journal of Clinical Child Psychology*, 20, 400–12.

Bandura, A. (1993). Perceived self-efficacy in cognitive development and functioning. *Educational Psychologist*, 28, 117–48.

Barkley, R.A. (2006). *Attention Deficit Hyperactivity Disorder: A Handbook of Diagnosis and Treatment, 3rd Edition*. New York: Guilford.

Barnett, A.L. (2008). Motor assessment in developmental coordination disorder: from identification to intervention. *International Journal of Disability, Development and Education*, 55 (2), 113–29. doi:10.1080/10349120802033436

Barnett, A. and Henderson, S.E. (2005). Assessment of handwriting in children with developmental coordination disorder. In D.A. Sugden and M.E. Chambers (eds), *Children with Developmental Coordination Disorder*. London: Whurr, 168–88.

Bart, O., Hajami, D. and Bar-Haim, Y. (2007). Predicting school adjustment from motor abilities in kindergarten. *Infant and Child Development*, 16 (6), 597–615. Available at: http://onlinelibrary.wiley.com/doi/10.1002/icd.514/abstract

Bartlett, D. and Moody, S. (2000). *Dyslexia in the Workplace*. London: Whurr.

Barton, P.E. (2004). *What Jobs Require: Literacy, Education, and Training, 1940–2004*. Washington, DC: Educational Testing Service.

Baxter, J. and Frederickson, N. (2005). Every Child Matters: can educational psychology contribute to radical reform? *Educational Psychology in Practice*, 21 (2), 87–102.

Beasley, T.M., Long, J.D. and Natali, M. (2001). A confirmatory factor analysis of the mathematics anxiety scale for children. *Measurement and Evaluation in Counseling and Development*, 34, 14–26.

Bell, S. and McLean, B. (2015). Good practice in training specialist teachers and assessors of people with dyslexia. In L. Peer and G. Reid (eds), *Special Educational Needs: A Guide for Inclusive Practice*. 2nd edition. London: Sage.

Bender, W.N. (1997). *Understanding ADHD: A Practical Guide for Teachers and Parents*. Columbus, OH: Merrill.

Berch, D.B. and Mazzocco, M.M.M. (eds), (2007). *Why is Math so Hard for Some Children? The Nature and Origins of Mathematical Learning Difficulties and Disabilities*. Baltimore, MD: Paul H. Brookes.

Berninger, V.W. (2007). *Process Assessment of the Learner (PAL-II) Assessment for Reading and Writing*. San Antonio, TX: Psychological Corporation.

Betts, J.E., Appleton, J.J., Reschly, A.L., Christenson, S.L. and Huebner, E.S. (2010). A study of the factorial invariance of the Student Engagement Instrument (SEI): results from middle and high school students. *School Psychology Quarterly*, 25, 84–93.

Bianco, M. (2005). The effects of disability labels on special education and general education teachers' referrals for gifted programs. *Learning Disability Quarterly*, 28 (4), 285–93.

Bird, R. (2009). *Overcoming Difficulties with Number: Supporting Dyscalculia and Students who Struggle with Maths*. London: Sage.

Bishop, D.V.M. and Snowling, M.J. (2004). Developmental dyslexia and specific language impairment: same or different. *Psychological Bulletin*, 130, 858–86.

Black, P. and Wiliam, D. (1998) Assessment and Classroom Learning, *Assessment in Education*, 5 (1), 7–74.

Bond, C. (2011). Supporting children with motor skills difficulties: an initial evaluation of the Manchester Motor Skills Programme. *Educational Psychology in Practice*, 27 (2), 143–3. doi:10.1080/02667363.2011.567093

Borgelt, C. and Conoley, J.C. (1999). Psychology in the schools: systems intervention case example. In C.R. Reynolds and T.B. Gutkin (eds), *The Handbook of School Psychology*. 3rd edition. New York: Wiley, 1056–76.

Bowers, P.G. and Wolf, M. (1993). Theoretical links among naming speed, precise timing mechanisms and orthographic skill in dyslexia. *Reading and Writing: An Interdisciplinary Journal*, 5, 69–85.

Boyle, M. and Korn-Rothschild, S. (1994). Two dozen-plus ideas that will help special needs kids. *Teaching Pre K-8*, 25 (1), 74–5.

Braden, J.P. (1992). Test reviews: the differential ability scales and special education. *Journal of Psychoeducational Assessment*, 10, 92–8.

Bransford, J.D., Brown, A.L. and Cocking, R.R. (eds) (2000). How people learn; brain, mind, experience and school. Commission on Behavioural and Social Sciences and Education, National Research Council. Washington, DC: National Academy Press.

British Dyslexia Association (BDA) (2005). *The Employer's Guide to Dyslexia*. Sundial: BDA.

British Psychological Society (BPS) (1999). *Dyslexia, Literacy and Psychological Assessment*. Report of a Working Party of the Division of Educational and Child Psychology of the British Psychological Society. Leicester: BPS.

Brown, A.L. and Campione, J.C. (1994). Guided discovery in a community of learners. In K. McGilly (ed.), *Classroom Lessons: Integrating Cognitive Theory and Classroom Practice*. Cambridge MA: MIT Press, 229–70.

Bruininks, R.H. and Bruininks, B.D. (2005). *Bruininks and Oseretsky Test of Motor Proficiency* (BOT-2). 2nd edition. Windsor: NFER-Nelson.

Bryant, B.R. and Bryant, D.P. (2008). Introduction to the special series: mathematics and learning disabilities. *Learning Disability Quarterly*, 31, 3–8.

Bryant, P.E. (1985). The distinction between knowing when to do a sum and knowing how to do it. *Educational Psychology*, 5, 207–15.

Bullis, M. and Yovanoff, P. (2006). Idle hands: community employment experiences of formerly incarcerated youth. *Journal of Emotional and Behavioral Disorders*, 14, 71–85.

Bundy, A.C., Lane, S.J. and Murray, E.A. (2002). *Sensory Integration: Theory and Practice* 2nd edition. Philadelphia, PA: F.A. Davis.

Burden, R.L. (2002) A cognitive approach to dyslexia: learning styles and thinking skills. In G. Reid and J. Wearmouth (eds), *Dyslexia and Literacy*. Chichester: Wiley.

Burden, R.L. (2005). *Dyslexia and Self-concept: Seeking a Dyslexic Identity*. London: Whurr.

Burden, R., and Burdett, J. (2005). Factors associated with successful learning in pupils with dyslexia: a motivational analysis. *British Journal of Special Education*, 32, 100–4.

Burden, R.L. and Burdett, J. (2007). What's in a name? Students with dyslexia: their use of metaphor in making sense of their disability. *British Journal of Special Education*, 34, 77–81.

Butrowsky, I.S. and Willows, D.M. (1980). Cognitive-motivational characteristics of children varying in reading ability: evidence for learned helplessness in poor readers. *Journal of Educational Psychology*, 72, 408–22.

Butterworth, B. (2003). *Dyscalculia Screener*. London: NFER-Nelson.

Butterworth, B. and Laurillard, D. (2010). Low numeracy and dyscalculia: identification and intervention. *ZDM Mathematics Education*, 42, 527–39.

Butterworth, B. and Yeo, D. (2004). *Dyscalculia Guidance: Helping Pupils with Specific Learning Difficulties in Maths*. London: NFER-Nelson.

Cairney, J., Hay, J., Faught, B., Mandigo, J. and Flouris, A. (2005). Developmental coordination disorder, self-efficacy toward physical activity and participation in free play and organized activities: does gender matter? *Adapted Physical Activity Quarterly*, 22 (1), 67–82.

Came, F. and Reid, G. (2008) *Concern, Assess and Provide (CAP) It All!* Wiltshire: Learning Works.

Campbell, J.I.D. (ed.) (2005). *The Handbook of Mathematical Cognition: Developmental Dyscalculia Series*. Hove: Psychology Press.

Cantell, M., Smyth, M.M. and Ahonen, T. (1994). Clumsiness in adolescence: educational, motor and social outcomes of motor delay detected at 5 years. *Adapted Physical Activity Quarterly*, 11, 115–29.

Cantell, M.H., Smyth, M.M. and Ahonen, T.P. (2003). Two distinct pathways for developmental coordination disorder: Persistence and resolution. *Human Movement Science*, 22, 413–31.

Case-Smith, J. (2001). *Occupational Therapy for Children*. St Louis: Mosby.

Caygill, R. and Elley, L. (2001). Evidence about the effects of assessment task format on student achievement. Paper presented at the British Educational Research Association, University of Leeds.

CBI (2008). *Taking Stock: CBI Education and Skills Survey 2008*. London: CBI.

Cermak, S., Gubbay, S. and Larkin, D. (2002). What is developmental coordination disorder? In S. Cermak and D. Larkin (eds), *Developmental Coordination Disorder*. Albany, NY: Delmar, 2–22.

Chan, L.K.S. (1994). Relationship of motivation, strategic learning, and reading achievement in Grades 5, 7, and 9. *Journal of Experimental Education*, 62, 319–39.

Chang, M.K. (1996). *Accommodating Students with Disabilities: A Guide for School Teachers*. Montgomery, AL: National Institute on Disability and Rehabilitation Research (ED/OSERS), Washington, DC (ERIC Document Reproduction Service No. ED 404 826).

Chapman, J. (1988). Learning disabled children's self-concepts. *Review of Educational Research*, 58, 347–71.

Chapman, J.W., Silva, P. and Williams, S. (1984). Academic self-concept: some developmental and emotional correlates in nine year old children. *British Journal of Educational Psychology*, 54, 284–92.

Chard, D.J., Clarke, B., Baker, S., Otterstedt, J., Braun, D. and Katz, R. (2005). Using measures of number sense to screen for difficulties in mathematics: preliminary findings. *Assessment for Effective Intervention*, 30, 3–14.

Chinn, S. (2009). Dyscalculia and learning difficulties in mathematics. In G. Reid (ed.), *The Routledge Companion to Dyslexia*. London: Routledge.

Chinn, S. (ed.) (2014). *Routledge International Handbook: Mathematics Learning Difficulties and Dyscalculia*. Abingdon: Routledge.

Chinn, S.J. and Ashcroft, J.R. (2007). *Mathematics for Dyslexia Including Dyscalculia, 3rd Edition*. London: Wiley.

Chrestensen, C.A. and Baker, C.D. (2000). *Pedagogy, Observation and the Construction of Learning Disabilities*. New Orleans: Routledge (ERIC Document Reproduction Service No. ED 451 672).

Christensen, C.A. (2004). Relationship between orthographic–motor integration and computer use for the production of creative and well-structured text. *British Journal of Educational Psychology*, 74(A), 551–64

Clark, C., Dyson, A., Millward, A. and Skidmore, D. (1997). *New Directions in Special Needs*. London: Cassell.

Clarke, S., Timperley, H. and Hattie, J. (2003). *Unlocking Formative Assessment: Practical Strategies for Enhancing Students' Learning in the Primary and Intermediate Classroom*. Auckland: Hodder Moa Beckett.

Cobb, B., Sample, P.L., Alwell, M. and Johns, N.P. (2006). Cognitive-behavioural interventions, dropout, and youth with disabilities: a systematic review. *Remedial and Special Education*, 27, 259–75.

Coffield, F. (2005). Kinesthetic nonense. *Times Educational Supplement*, 14 January, 28.

Coffield, F., Moseley, D., Hall, E. and Ecclestone, K. (2004). Should we be using learning styles? What the research has to say to practice. Learning and Skills Research Centre. London: Learning and Skills Development Agency. Available at: www.LSRC.ac.uk

Cohen, I. and Goldsmith, M. (2000). *Hands On: How to Use Brain Gym in the Classroom*. 3rd edition. Ventura, CA: Edu-Kinesthetics.

Cohen, G., Kiss, G. and Le Voi, M. (1993). *Memory: Current Issues*. 2nd edition. Buckingham: Open University.

Conderman, G. and Hedin, L. (2011). Cue cards: a self-regulatory strategy for students with learning disabilities. *Intervention in School and Clinic*, 46, 165–73.

Conners, C.K., Epstein, J.N., March, J.S., Angold, A., Wells, K.C., Klaric, J., Swanson, J. et al. (2001). Multimodal treatment of ADHD in the MTA: an alternative outcome analysis. *Journal of the American Academy of Child and Adolescent Psychiatry*, 40, 159–67.

Connolly, A.J. (2007). *KeyMath-3*, Minneapolis: Pearson.

Coopersmith, S.A. (1967). The *Antecedents of Self-esteem*. San Francisco: Freeman.

Council for Learning Disabilities (2011). Comprehensive assessment and evaluation of students with learning disabilities: a paper prepared by the National Joint Committee on Learning Disabilities. *Learning Disability Quarterly*, 34 (1), 3–16.

Critchley, M. and Critchley, E.A. (1978). *Dyslexia Defined*. London: Heinemann.

Crombie, M., Knight, D. and Reid, G. (2004). Dyslexia: early identification and early intervention. In G. Reid and A. Fawcett (eds), *Dyslexia in Context: Research, Policy and Practice*. London: Whurr.

Cullinan, D. and Sabornie, E.J. (2004). Characteristics of emotional disturbance in middle and high school students. *Journal of Emotional and Behavioral Disorders*, 12, 157–67.

Curtis, P. (2008). Education: primary pupils without basic skills highlight Labour's biggest failure, says schools minister. *Guardian*, Thursday, 21 August. Available at: http://www.guardian.co.uk/education/2008/aug/21/primaryschools.earlyyearseducation

DeCastella, K., Byrne, D. and Covington, M. (2013). Unmotivated or motivated to fail? A cross-cultural study of achievement motivation, fear of failure and student disengagement. *Journal of Educational Psychology*, 105, 861–80.

Decker, S.L., Englund, J.A., Carboni, J.A. and Brooks, J.H. (2011). Cognitive and developmental influences in visual–motor integration skills in young children. *Psychological Assessment*, 23 (4), 1010–16. Available at: http://dx.doi.org/10.1037/a0024079

Dehaene, S., Spelke, E. and Pinet, R. (1999). Sources of mathematical thinking: behavioural and brain–imaging evidence. *Science*, 284, 970–3.

Dehaene, S., Piazza, M., Pinel, P. and Cohen, L. (2003). Three parietal circuits for number processing. *Cognitive Neuropsychology*, 20, 487–506.

Denckla, M.B. (1984). Developmental dyspraxia: the clumsy child. In M.D. Levine and P. Satz (eds), *Middle Childhood: Development and Dysfunction*. Baltimore, MD: University Park Press, 245–60.

Denicolo, P. and Pope, M. (2001). *Transformational Professional Practice: Personal Construct Approaches to Education and Research*. London: Whurr.

Dennison, P.E. and Dennison, G.E. (1989). *Brain Gym: Teacher's Edition Revised*. Ventura, CA: Edu-Kinesthetics.

Department for Children, Schools and Families (DCSF) (2009). Sir Jim Rose presents findings of review into dyslexia, 22 June 2009. Press notice 2009/0114. London: DCSF.

Department for Education/Department of Health (DfE/DoH) (2014). *SEN Code of Practice*. London: DfE/DfH.

Department for Education and Skills (DfES) (2001). *The National Numeracy Strategy: Guidance to Support Learners with Dyslexia and Dyscalculia*. London: DfES.

Department for Education and Skills (DfES) (2004). *Behaviour in the Classroom: A Course for Newly Qualified Teachers*. London: DfES.

Disability Rights Advocates (2001). *Do No Harm: High Stakes Testing and Students with Learning Disabilities*. Oakland, CA: LD Access Foundation, Inc. (ERIC Document Reproduction Service No. ED 457 648).

Dockrell, J. and McShane, J. (1993). *Children's Learning Difficulties: A Cognitive Approach*. Oxford: Blackwell.

Dodds, D. and Lumsden, D. (2001) Examining the challenge: preparing for examinations. In L. Peer and G. Reid (eds), *Dyslexia: Successful Inclusion in the Secondary School*. London: David Fulton.

Donlan, C. (1998). Number without language? Studies of children with specific language impairments. In C. Donlan (ed.), *The Development of Mathematical Skills*. Hove: Psychology Press, 255–74.

Dove Ministries for Children (2012). Strengthening fine motor skills. Available at: www.doverehab.com, last accessed 3 July 2013.

Dunford, C., Street, E., O'Connell, H., Kelly, J. and Sibert, J.R. (2004). Are referrals to occupational therapy for developmental coordination disorder appropriate? *Archives of Disease in Childhood*, 89, 143–7.

Dunham, J. (1995). *Developing Effective School Management*. London: Routledge.

Dunn, R., Dunn, K. and Price, G.E. (1975, 1979, 1985, 1987, 1989) *Learning Styles Inventory*. Various editions. Lawrence, KA: Price Systems, Inc.

Durand, M., Hulme, C., Larkin, R. and Snowling, M. (2005). The cognitive foundations of reading and arithmetic skills in 7- to 10-year-olds. *Journal of Experimental Child Psychology*, 91, 113–36.

Dweck, C.S. and Licht, B.G. (1980). Learned Helplessness and Intellectual Achievement. In J. Garber and M.E.P. Seligman (eds), *Human Helplessness: Theory and Applications*. New York: Academic Press.

Dyspraxia Trust (2001). Available from: Dtspraxia Trust, PO Box 30, Hitchin, Herts SG5 1UU.

Edwards, J. (1994). *The Scars of Dyslexia*. London: Cassell.

Elbaum, B. and Vaughn, S. (2001). School-based interventions to enhance the self-concept of students with learning disabilities: a meta-analysis. *The Elementary School Journal*, 101, 303–29.

Elbeheri, G. and Everatt, J. (2009). IQ and dyslexia: from research to practice. In G. Reid, G. Elbeheri, J. Everatt, D. Knight and J. Wearmouth (eds), *The Routledge Companion to Dyslexia*. Abingdon: Routledge, 22–32.

Elbeheri, G., Everatt, J. and Al-Malki, M. (2009). The incidence of dyslexia among young offenders in Kuwait. *Dyslexia*, 15, 86–104.

Elbro, C. and Petersen, D.K. (2004). Long-term effects of phoneme awareness and letter sound training: an intervention study with children at risk for dyslexia. *Journal of Educational Psychology*, 96, 660–70.

Elkins, J. (2002). Learning difficulties/disabilities in literacy. *Australian Journal of Language and Literacy*, 25 (3), 11–18.

Elliott, J.G. and Grigorenko, E.L. (2014). *The Dyslexia Debate*. Cambridge: Cambridge University Press.

Elliott, C.D., Smith, P. and McCulloch, K. (1996). *British Ability Scales*. 2nd edition (*BAS II*). Windsor: NFER-Nelson.

Ericsson, I. (2008). Motor skills, attention and academic achievements: an intervention study in school years 1–3. *British Educational Research Journal*, 34 (5), 301–13. Available at: http://www.tandfonline.com/doi/abs/10.1080/01411920701609299#. VPweiPmsXng

Everatt, J. and Reid, G. (2009). Dyslexia: an overview of recent research. In G. Reid, G. Elbeheri, J. Everatt, J. Wearmouth and D. Knight (eds), *The Routledge Dyslexia Companion*. London: Routledge, Chapter 1.

Everatt, J. and Reid, G. (2010). Motivating children with dyslexia. In J. Fletcher, F. Parkhill and G. Gillon (eds), *Motivating Literacy Learners in Today's World*. Wellington: NZCER Press, 67–78.

Everatt, J., Elbeheri, G. and Brooks, P. (2013). Dyscalculia: research and practice on identification and intervention across languages. In A.J. Holliman (ed.), *The Routledge International Companion to Educational Psychology*. Abingdon: Routledge, 317–26.

Everatt, J., Mahfoudhi, A., Al-Manabri, M. and Elbeheri, G. (2014). Dyscalculia in Arabic speaking children: assessment and intervention practices. In S. Chinn (ed.), *Routledge International Handbook: Mathematics Learning Difficulties and Dyscalculia*. Abingdon: Routledge, 183–92.

Everatt, J., Al-Azmi, Y., Al-Sharhan, A. and Elbeheri, G. (submitted). Emotion and educational achievement in Arabic children.

Everatt, J., Al-Sharhan, A., Al Azmi, Y., Al-Menaye, N. and Elbeheri, G. (2011). Behavioural/attentional problems and literacy learning difficulties in children from non-English language/cultural backgrounds. *Support for Learning*, 26, 127–33.

Farah, L.G., Fayyad, J.A., Eapen, V., Cassir, Y., Salamoun, M.M., Tabet, C.C., Mneimneh, Z.N. and Karam, E.G. (2009). ADHD in the Arab world: a review of epidemiological studies. *Journal of Attentional Disorders*, 13, 211–22.

Faraone, S.V., Biederman, J., Morley, C.P. and Spencer, T.J. (2008). Effects of stimulants on height and weight: a review of the literature. *Journal of the American Academy of Child and Adolescent Psychiatry*, 47, 994–1009.

Farrell, P., Woods, K., Lewis, S., Rooney, S., Squires, G. and O'Conner, M. (2006). *Function and Contribution of Educational Psychologists in Light of the 'Every Child Matters: Change for Children' Agenda*. London: DfES.

Fawcett, A. and Nicolson, R. (1995). Persistent deficits in motor skill for children with dyslexia. *Journal of Motor Behaviour*, 27, 235–40.

Fawcett, A. and Nicolson, R. (2008). Dyslexia and the Cerebellum. In G. Reid, A. Fawcett, F. Manis and L. Siegel (eds), *The Sage Handbook of Dyslexia*. London: Sage.

Fawcett, A. and Reid, G. (2009). Dyslexia and alternative interventions. In G. Reid (ed.), *The Routledge Companion to Dyslexia*. New York: Routledge, 193–202.

Figueroa, R.A. and Newsome, P. (2006). The diagnosis of LD in English language learners: is it nondiscriminatory? *Journal of Learning Disabilities*, 39 (3), 206–14.

Flory, S. (2000). Identifying, assessing and helping dyspraxic children. *Dyslexia*, 6 (3), 205–8.

Fox, A.M. and Lent, B. (1996). Clumsy children: primer on developmental coordination disorder. *Canadian Family Physician*, 42, 1965–71.

Frederickson, N., Frith, U. and Reason, P. (1997). *Phonological Assessment Battery*. Windsor: NFER Nelson.

Friend, M. and Cook, L. (1996). *Interactions: Collaboration Skills for School Professionals*. 2nd edition. White Plains, NY: Longman.

Fuchs, L.S. and Fuchs, D. (2001). Principles for the prevention and intervention of mathematics difficulties. *Learning Disabilities Research and Practice*, 16, 85–95.

Galaburda, A. (2014). Dyslexia and Neuroscience Paper presented at Learning Differences Convention, Sydney, August.

Geary, D.C. (2004). Mathematics and learning disabilities. *Journal of Learning Disabilities*, 37, 4–15.

Geary, D.C. and Widaman, K.F. (1992). Numerical cognition: on the convergence of componential and psychometric models. *Intelligence*, 16, 47–80.

Geary, D.C., Bow-Thomas, C.C. and Yao, Y. (1992). Counting knowledge and skill in cognitive addition: a comparison of normal and mathematically disabled children. *Journal of Experimental Child Psychology*, 54, 372–91.

Gerber, P.J. (1997) Life after school: challenges in the workplace. In P.J. Gerber and D.S. Brown (eds), *Learning Disabilities and Employment*. Austin, TX: Pro-Ed.

Gerber, P.J., Ginsberg, R. and Reiff, H.B. (1992). Identifying alterable patterns in employment success for highly successful adults with learning disabilities. *Journal of Learning Disabilities*, 8, 475–87.

Gersch, I. (1995). Involving the child. *Schools' Special Educational Needs Policies Pack*. London: National Children's Bureau.

Gersch, I. (2001) Listening to children. In J. Wearmouth (ed.), *Special Educational Provision in the Context of Inclusion*. London: Fulton, 228–44.

Gersten, R., Chard, D.J., Jayanthi, M., Baker, S.K., Morphy, P. and Flojo, J. (2009). Mathematics instruction for students with learning disabilities: a meta-analysis of instructional components. *Review of Educational Research*, 79, 1202–42.

Geuze, R.H. and Borger, H. (1993). Children who are clumsy: five years later. *Adapted Physical Activity Quarterly*, 10, 10–21.

Gibbs, J., Appleton, J. and Appleton, R. (2007). Dyspraxia or developmental coordination disorder? Unravelling the enigma. *Archive of Diseases in Childhood*, 92, 534–9.

Gillon, G.T. (2004). *Phonological Awareness: From Research to Practice.* New York: Guilford Press.

Ginsburg, H.P. and Baroody, A.J. (2003). *Test of Early Mathematics Ability.* 3rd edition. Austin, TX: PRO-ED.

Giorcelli, L. R. (1999). Inclusion and other factors affecting teachers' attitudes to literacy programmes for students with special needs. In A.J. Watson and L.R. Giorcelli (eds), *Accepting the Literacy Challenge.* NSW, Australia: Scholastic.

Given, B.K. (1996). The potential of learning styles. In G. Reid (ed.), *Dimensions of Dyslexia. Vol. 2: Literacy, Language and Learning.* Edinburgh: Moray House.

Given, B.K. and Reid, G. (1999). *Learning Styles: A Guide for Teachers and Parents.* St Anne's-on-Sea, Lancashire: Red Rose.

Gjessing, H.J. and Karlsen, B. (1989). *A Longitudinal Study of Dyslexia.* New York: Springer.

Goldberg, R., Higgins, E., Raskind, M. and Herman, K. (2003). Predictors of success in individuals with learning disabilities: a qualitative analysis of a 20 year longitudinal study. *Learning Disabilities Research and Practice,* 18, 222–36.

Goodman, K. (1967). A linguistic study of cues and miscues. *Elementary English,* 42, 639–43.

Goodman, R. (1997). The Strengths and Difficulties Questionnaire: a research note. *Journal of Child Psychology and Psychiatry,* 38, 581–6.

Graham, S. (1990). The role of production factors in learning disabled students' compositions. *Journal of Educational Psychology,* 82 (4), 781–91. Available at: http://dx.doi.org/10.1037/0022-0663.82.4.781

Graham, S. and Harris, K.R. (2006). Preventing writing difficulties: providing additional handwriting and spelling instruction to at-risk children in first grade. *Teaching Exceptional Children,* 38 (5), 64–6.

Gray, C. (2004). Understanding cognitive development: automaticity and the early years [sic] child. *Child Care in Practice,* 10 (1), 39–47. Available at: http://dx.doi.org/10.1080/1357527042000188070

Green, D., Bishop, T., Wilson, B., Crawford, S., Hooper, R., Kaplan, B., *et al.* (2005). Is questionnaire-based screening part of the solution to waiting lists for children with developmental coordination disorder? *British Journal of Occupational Therapy,* 68, 2–10.

Greenbaum, P.E., Dedrick, R.F., Friedman, R.M., Kutash, K., Brown, E.C., Lardierh, S.P. and Pugh, A.M. (1996). National Adolescent and Child Treatment Study (NACTS): outcomes for children with serious emotional and behavioral disturbance. *Journal of Emotional and Behavioral Disorders,* 4, 130–46.

Gregorc, A.F. (1985). *Inside Styles: Beyond the Basics.* Columbia, CT: Gregorc Assoc., Inc.

Grigg, W., Donahue, P. and Dion, G. (2007). The nation's report card: 12th-grade reading and mathematics 200S (NCES 2007-468). US Department of Education, National Center for Education Statistics. Washington, DC: US Government Printing Office.

Grissmer, D., Grimm, K.J., Aiyer, S., Murrah, W.M. and Steele, J.S. (2010). Fine motor skills and early comprehension of the world: two new school readiness indicators. *Developmental Psychology,* 46 (5), 1008–17. Available at: http://dx.doi.org/10.1037/a0020104

Gutkin, T.B. and Ajchenbaum, M. (1984). Teachers' perceptions of control and preferences for consultative services. *Professional Psychology: Research and Practice,* 15, 565–70.

Gutkin, T.B. and Curtis, M.J. (1999). School-based consultation: theory and practice: the art and science of indirect service delivery. In C.R. Reynolds and T.B. Gutkin (eds), *The Handbook of School Psychology*. 3rd edition. New York: Wiley, 598–637.

Hallam, S. (2006). *Music Psychology in Education*. London: Institute of Education, University of London.

Hannaford, C. (1995). *Smart Moves: Why Learning is Not All in Your Head*. Virginia: Great Ocean.

Harter, S. (2012). *Self-perception Profile for Children: Manual and Questionnaires*. Denver, CO: University of Denver.

Haynes, C.W., Ayre, A., Haynes, B. and Mahfoudhi, A. (2009). Reading and reading disabilities in Spanish and Spanish–English contexts. In G. Reid (ed.), *The Routledge Companion to Dyslexia*. London: Routledge.

Hazel, C.E., Vazirabadi, G.E., Albanes, J. and Gallagher, J. (2014). Evidence of convergent and discriminant validity of the Student School Engagement Measure. *Psychological Assessment*, 26, 806–14.

Healy, J. (1992). *How to have Intelligent and Creative Conversations with Your Kids*. New York: Doubleday.

Henderson, A., Came, F. and Brough, M. (2003). *Working with Dyscalculia*. Wiltshire: Learning Works.

Henderson, S.E. and Henderson, L. (2002). Towards an understanding of developmental coordination disorders. The second G. Lawrence Rarick Memorial Lecture. *Adapted Physical Activity Quarterly*, 19, 11–31.

Henderson, S.E. and Sugden, D.A. (2007). *Movement Assessment Battery for Children*. 2nd edition. London: Psychological Corporation.

Hettinger, C. (1982). The impact of reading deficiency on the global self concept of the adolescent. *Journal of Early Adolescence*, 2, 293–300.

Hill, E.L. (2001). The nonspecific nature of specific language impairment: a review of the literature with regard to concomitant motor impairments. *International Journal of Language and Communication Disorders*, 36, 149–71.

Hinshaw, S.P. (1992). Externalizing behavior problems and academic under achievement in childhood and adolescence. *Psychological Bulletin*, 111, 127–55.

Hinshaw, S.P. (1994). *Attention Deficits and Hyperactivity in Children*. Thousand Oaks, CA: Sage.

HMG (1995). Disability Discrimination Act (1995, 2004). London: HMSO.

Houston, M. (2004). *Guidelines for Dyslexia*. Edinburgh: Edinburgh City Council.

Hresko, W., Schlieve, P., Herron, S., Swain, C. and Sherbenau, R. (2003). *Comprehensive Mathematical Abilities Test (CMAT)*. Austin, TX: PRO-ED.

Hubert, B. (2001). *Bal-A-Vis-X: Rhythmic Balance/Auditory/Vision Exercises for Brain and Brain–Body Integration*. Wichita, KS: Bal-A-Vis-X.

Hughes, L. and Cooper, P. (2007). *Understanding and Supporting Children with ADHD: Strategies for Teachers, Parents and Other Professionals*. London: Sage.

Humphrey, N. and Mullins, P.M. (2002). Personal constructs and attribution for academic success and failure in dyslexia. *British Journal of Special Education*, 29, 196–203.

Huntington, D.D. and Bender, W.N. (1993). Adolescents with learning disabilities at risk? Emotional well-being, depression, suicide. *Journal of Learning Disabilities*, 26, 159–66.

Jamieson, C. and Morgan, E. (2008) Managing Dyslexia at University: A Resource for Students, Academic and Support Staff. London: David Fulton.

Jitendra, A.K., Edwards, L.L. and Starosta, K. (2004). Early reading instruction for children with reading difficulties: meeting the needs of diverse learners. *Journal of Learning Disabilities*, 37 (5), 421–40.

Jones, A. and Kindersley, K. (2013) *Dyslexia: Assessing and Reporting. The PATOSS Guide*. London: Hodder.

Jongmans, M. (2005). Early identification of children with developmental coordination disorder. In D. Sugden and M. Chambers (eds), Children with Developmental Coordination Disorder. London: Whurr, 155–67.

Jorm, A.F., Share, D.L., Matthews, R. and Maclean, R. (1986). Behavior problems in specific reading retarded and general reading backward children: a longitudinal study. *Journal of Child Psychology and Psychiatry*, 27 33–43.

Julian, G., and Ware, J. (1998). Specialist teachers for pupils with learning difficulties? A survey of head teachers in schools and units. *British Journal of Special Education*, 25 (1), 28–32.

Junaid, K., Harris, S., Fulmer, K. and Carswell, A. (2000). Teachers' use of the MABC checklist to identify children with motor coordination difficulties. *Pediatric Physical Therapy*, 12, 158–63.

Kadesjo, B. and Gillberg, C. (1999). Developmental coordination disorder in Swedish 7-year-old children. *Journal of the American Academy of Child and Adolescent Psychiatry*, 38 (7), 820–8.

Kaplan, B.J., Dewey, D.M., Crawford, S.G. and Wilson, B.N. (2001). The term comorbidity is of questionable value in reference to developmental disorders: data and theory. *Journal of Learning Disabilities*, 34 (6), 55–65.

Kaplan, B.J., Wilson, B.N., Dewey, D. and Crawford, S.G. (1998). DCD may not be a discrete disorder. *Human Movement Science*, 17, 471–90.

Kaufman, A.S., Lichtenberger, E.O. and Naglieri, J.A. (1999). Intelligence testing in the schools. In C.R. Reynolds and T.B. Gutkin (eds), *The Handbook of School Psychology*. 3rd edition. New York: Wiley, 307–49.

Kaufman, A. and Kaufman, N. (2004). *Kaufman Assessment Battery for Children*. 2nd edition. San Antonio: Pearson Education.

Kern, L., Mantegna, M.E., Vorndran, C., Bailin, D. and Hilt, A. (2001). Choice of task sequence to reduce problem behaviours. *Journal of Positive Behaviour Interventions*, 3, 3–10.

Killick, S. (2005). *Emotional Literacy: At the Heart of the School Ethos*. London: Paul Chapman.

Kirby, A. (1999). *Dyspraxia: The Hidden Handicap*. London: Souvenir Press.

Kirby, A. (2006). *Dyspraxia: Developmental Co-ordination Disorder*. Human Horizon Series. London: Souvenir Press.

Kirby, A., Edwards, L., Sugden, D. and Rosenblum, S. (2010). The development and standardisation of the Adult Developmental Coordination Disorders/Dyspraxia Checklist (ADC). *Research in Developmental Disability*, 31, 131–9.

Kirby, A., Sugden, D., Beveridge, S., Edwards, L. and Edwards, R. (2008). Dyslexia and developmental co-ordination disorder in further and higher education: similarities and differences. Does the 'label' influence the support given? *Dyslexia*, 14 (3), 197–213. doi:10.1002/DYS.367

Kirk, J. and Reid, G. (2003). *Adult Dyslexia Checklist: Criteria and Considerations*. BDA Handbook. Reading: BDA.

Knight, D.F. and Hynd, G.W. (2002). The neurobiology of dyslexi. In G. Reid and J. Wearmouth (eds), *Dyslexia and Literacy: Theory and Practice*. Chichester: Wiley.

Kolb, D.A. (1984). *Learning Styles Inventory Technical Manual*. Boston: Hay Group.

Landerl, K., Fussenegger, B., Moll, K. and Willburger, E. (2009). Dyslexia and dyscalculia: two learning disorders with different cognitive profiles. *Journal of Experimental Child Psychology*, 103, 309–24.

Lane, K.L., Carter, E.W., Pierson, M.R. and Glaeser, B.C. (2006). Academic, social, and behavioral characteristics of high school students with emotional disturbances and learning disabilities. *Journal of Emotional and Behavioral Disorders*, 14, 108–17.

Lane, K.L., Barton-Arwood, S.M., Nelson, J.R. and Wehby, J. (2008). Academic performance of students with emotional and behavioral disorders served in a self-contained setting. *Journal of Behavior Education*, 17, 43–62.

Lauth, G.W., Heubeck, B.G. and Mackowiak, K. (2006). Observation of children with attention-deficit hyperactivity (ADHD) problems in three natural classroom contexts. *British Journal of Educational Psychology*, 76, 385–404.

Lawrence, D. (1996). *Enhancing Self-esteem in the Classroom*. London: Paul Chapman.

Lawrence, G. (1993). *People Types and Tiger Stripes*. 3rd edition. Gainsville, FL: Center for Applications of Psychological Type, Inc.

Leather, C., Hogh, H., Seiss, E. and Everatt, J. (2011). Cognitive function and work success in adults with dyslexia. *Dyslexia*, 17, 327–38.

Lee, Y., Sugai, G. and Horner, R. (1999). Using an instructional intervention to reduce problem and off-task behaviours. *Journal of Positive Behaviour Interventions*, 1, 195–204.

Lemer, C., Dehaene, S., Spelke, E. and Cohen, L. (2003). Approximate quantities and exact number words: dissociable systems. *Neuropsychologia*, 41 (14), 1942–58.

Lewis, C., Hitch, G.J. and Walker, P. (1994). The prevalence of specific arithmetic difficulties and specific reading difficulties in 9- to 10-year-old boys and girls. *Journal of Child Psychology*, 35, 283–92.

Lewis, H.W. (1984). A structured group counseling program for reading disabled elementary students. *School Counselor*, 31, 454–9.

Lindquist, M.M. and Vicky, L.K. (1989). Measurement. In M.M. Lindquist (ed.), *Results from the Fourth Mathematics Assessment of the National Assessment of Educational Progress*. Reston, VA: National Council of Teachers of Mathematics.

Lipton, J.S. and Spelke, E.S. (2003). Origins of number sense: large number discrimination in human infants. *Psychological Science*, 14, 396–401.

Livingstone, R. (1990). Psychiatric comorbidity with reading disability: a clinical study. *Advances in Learning Disabilities*, 6, 143–55.

Lloyd, G. and Norris, C. (1999). Including ADHD? *Disability and Society*, 14, 505–17.

Lockhart, J. and Law, M. (1994). The effectiveness of a multisensory writing programme for improving cursive writing ability in children with sensori-motor difficulties. *Canadian Journal of Occupational Therapy*, 61 (A), 206–14.

Losse, A., Henderson, S.E., Elliman, D., Hall, D., Knight, E. and Jongmans, M. (1991). Clumsiness in children – do they grow out of it? A 10-year follow-up study. *Developmental Medicine and Child Neurology*, 33, 55–68.

Mahfoudhi, A., Elbeheri, G. and Everatt, J. (2009). Reading and dyslexia in Arabic. In G. Reid (ed.), *The Routledge Companion to Dyslexia*. London: Routledge.

Malloy-Miller, T., Polatajko, H. and Anstett, B. (1995). Handwriting error patterns of children with mild motor difficulties. *Canadian Journal of Occupational Therapy*, 62 (5), 258–67.

Maloney, E., Risko, E.F., Ansari, D. and Fugelsang, J.F. (2010). Mathematics anxiety affects counting but not subitizing during visual enumeration. *Cognition*, 114, 721–9.

Manset-Williamson, G. and Nelson, J.M. (2005). Balanced, strategic reading instruction for upper elementary and middle school students with reading disabilities: a comparative study of two approaches. *Learning Disability Quarterly*, 28 (11), 59–72.

Margerison, A. (1996). Self-esteem: its effect on the development and learning of children with EBD. *Support for Learning*, 11, 176–80.

Mari, M., Castiello, U., Marks, D., Marraffa, C. and Prior, M. (2003). The reach-to-grasp movement in children with autism spectrum disorder. *Philosophical Transactions of the Royal Society Series B*, 358, 393–404.

Martin, D., Martin, M. and Carvalho, K. (2008). Reading and learning-disabled children: understanding the problem. *Clearing House*, 81 (3), 113–18.

Martin, N.C., Piek, J.P. and Hay, D. (2006). DCD and ADHD: a genetic study of their shared aetiology. *Human Movement Science*, 25, 110–24.

Maughan, B. (1995). Behavioural development and reading disabilities. In C. Hulme and M. Snowling (eds), *Reading Development and Dyslexia*. London: Whurr.

Mazzocco, M.M.M. and Thompson, R.E. (2005). Kindergarten predictors of math learning disability. *Learning Disabilities Research and Practice*, 20, 142–55.

May-Benson, T., Ingolia, P. and Koomar, J. (2002). Daily living skills and developmental coordination disorder. In S. Cermak and D. Larkin (eds), *Developmental Coordination Disorder*. Albany, NY: Delmar, 140–56.

McCarthy, B. (1987). *The 4MAT System: Teaching to Learning Styles with Right/Left Mode Techniques*. Barrington, IL: Excel, Inc.

McConaughy, S.H., Mattison, R.E. and Peterson, R.L. (1994). Behavioral/emotional problems of children with serious emotional disturbances and learning disabilities. *School Psychology Review*, 23, 81–98.

McInerney, D.M. and Ali, J. (2006). Multidimensional and hierarchical assessment of school motivation: cross-cultural validation. *Educational Psychology: An International Journal of Experimental Educational Psychology*, 26, 717–34.

Macintyre, C. (2009). *Dyspraxia 5–14*. London: David Fulton/NASEN.

McKinney, J.D. (1989). Longitudinal research on the behavioral characteristics of children with learning disabilities. *Journal of Learning Disabilities*, 22, 141–50.

McLean, A. (2004). *The Motivated School*. London: Sage.

McLoughlin, D., Fitzgibbon, G. and Young, V. (1994). *Adult Dyslexia: Assessment, Counselling and Training*. London: Whurr.

McLoughlin, D., Leather, C. and Stringer, P. (2002). *The Adult Dyslexic: Interventions and Outcomes*. London: Whurr.

McMurray, S., Drysdale, J. and Jordan, G. (2009). Motor processing difficulties: guidance for teachers in mainstream classrooms. *Support for Learning*, 24 (3), 119–25.

Medwell, J. and Wray, D. (2008). Handwriting: a forgotten language skill? *Language and Education: An International Journal*, 22 (1), 34–47. Available at: http://wrap.warwick.ac.uk/461/

Michaels, C.R. and Lewandowski, L.J. (1990). Psychological adjustment and family functioning of boys with learning disabilities. *Journal of Learning Disabilities*, 23, 446–50.

Miles, T.R. (1983). *Bangor Dyslexia Test*. Cambridge: Learning Development Aids.

Miles, T.R. (ed.) (2004). *Dyslexia and Stress*. 2nd edition. London: Whurr.

Miles, T.R. and Miles, E. (1992). *Dyslexia and Mathematics*. London: Routledge.

Miles, T.R. and Miles, E. (1999). *Dyslexia a Hundred Years On*. 2nd edition. Buckingham: Open University Press.

Miller, L.T., Missiuna, C.A., Macnab, J.J., Malloy-Miller, T. and Polatajko, H.J. (2001). Clinical description of children with developmental coordination disorder. *Canadian Journal of Occupational Therapy*, 68, 5–15.

Miller, S.P. and Mercer, C.D. (1997). Educational aspects of mathematics disabilities. *Journal of Learning Disabilities*, 30, 47–56.

Missiuna, C. (2003). Children with developmental coordination disorder: at home and in the classroom [booklet]. McMaster University, ON: CanChild [on-line].

Missiuna, C., Rivard, L. and Pollock, N. (2004). They're bright but can't write: developmental coordination disorder in school aged children. *TEACHING Exceptional Children Plus*, 1 (1), art. 3.

Moats, L. (2004). Relevance of neuroscience to effective education for students with reading and other learning disabilities. *Journal of Child Neurology*, 19 (10), 840–5.

Montague, M. and Castro, M. (2004). Attention deficit hyperactivity disorder: issues and concerns. In P. Clough, P. Garner, J.T. Pardeck and F. Yuen (eds), *Handbook of Emotional and Behavioural Difficulties*. London: Sage, 399–416.

Montgomery, D. (2007). *Spelling, Handwriting and Dyslexia*. London and New York: Routledge.

Moody, S. (ed.) (2009). *Dyslexia and Employment: A Guide for Assessors, Trainers and Managers*. Chichester: Wiley.

Mooney, P., Ryan, J.B., Reid, R., Uhing, B.M. and Epstein, M.H. (2005). A review of self-management learning interventions on academic outcomes for students with emotional and behavioral disorders. *Journal of Behavioral Education*, 14, 203–21.

Moser, C. (2000). *Better Basic Skills: Improving Adult Literacy and Numeracy*. London: Department for Education and Employment.

Mosley, J. (1996). *Quality Circle Time in the Primary Classroom*. Cambridge: LDA.

Mruk, C. (1990). *Self-esteem: Research, Theory and Practice*. London: Free Association.

MTA Co-operative Group (1999). A 14-month randomized clinical trial of treatment strategies for attention-deficit/hyperactivity disorder. *Archives of General Psychiatry*, 56, 1073–86.

Murray, M.E. (1978). The relationship between personality adjustment and success in remedial programs for dyslexic children. *Contemporary Educational Psychology*, 3, 330–9.

Nasser, R. (2014). Social motivation in Qatar schools and their relation to school achievement. *Psychological Reports: Relationships and Communications*, 115, 584–606.

National Committee on Learning Disabilities (2008). Adolescent literacy and older students with learning disabilities. *Learning Disability Quarterly*, 31 (4), 211–18.

National Longitudinal Transition Study II (2003). National Center for Special Education Research at the Institute of Education Sciences. Washington, DC: US Department of Education.

Nelson, J.R., Benner, G.J., Lane, K. and Smith, B.W. (2004). An investigation of the academic achievement of K-12 students with emotional and behavioral disorders in public school settings. *Exceptional Children*, 71, 59–73.

Nicol, D. (2009). Assessment for learner self-regulation: enhancing achievement in the first year using learning technologies. *Assessment and Evaluation in Higher Education*, 34 (3), 335–52.

Nicolson, R.I. and Fawcett, A.J. (1996). *The Dyslexia Early Screening Test*. London: Psychological Corporation.

Nicolson, R., Agahi, S., West, T. and Eide, B. (2012). Positive dyslexia: working to our strengths. Symposium presented at IDA Parents Conference, Baltimore, October.

Nunes, T. and Bryant, P. (eds) (1997). *Learning and Teaching Mathematics: An International Perspective*. Hove: Psychology Press.

Oakland, T.D. and Cunningham, J. (1999). The futures of school psychology: conceptual models for its development and examples of their applications. In C.R. Reynolds and T.B. Gutkin (eds), *The Handbook of School Psychology*. 3rd edition. New York: Wiley, 34–54.

Ofiesh, N. and Mather, N. (2012). Resilience and the child with learning disabilities. In S. Goldstein and R.B. Brooks (eds), *Handbook of Resilience in Children*. New York: Springer Science, 329–48.

Oka, E.R. and Paris, S.G. (1987). Patterns of motivation and reading skills in under-achieving children. In S.J. Ceci (ed.), *Handbook of Cognitive, Social and Neurological Aspects of Learning Disabilities, Vol. II*. Hillsdale, NJ: LEA.

Orban, P., Lungu, O. and Doyon, J. (2008). Motor sequence learning and developmental dyslexia. *Annals New York Academy of Sciences*, 1145, 151–72.

Overvelde, A., and Hulstijn, W. (2012). Implicit motor sequence learning in children with learning disabilities: deficits limited to a subgroup with low perceptual organization. *Developmental Neuropsychology*, 37 (7), 579–89. doi:10.1080/87565641.2012.691141

Pagani, L.S., Fitzpatrick, C., Archambault, I. and Janosz, M. (2010). School readiness and later achievement: a French Canadian replication and extension. *Developmental Psychology*, 46 (5), 984–94. Available at: http://dx.doi.org/10.1037/a0018881

Palincsar, A. and Klenk, L. (1992). Fostering literacy learning in supportive contexts. *Journal of Learning Disabilities*, 4, 211–25.

Paul, G., Elam, B. and Verhulst, S.J. (2007). A longitudinal study of students' perceptions of using deep breathing meditation to reduce testing stresses. *Teaching and Learning in Medicine*, 19, 287–92.

Peer, L. and Reid, G. (eds) (2000). *Multilingualism, Literacy and Dyslexia: A Challenge for Educators*. London: David Fulton.

Peer, L. and Reid, G. (eds) (2001). *Dyslexia: Successful Inclusion in the Secondary School*. London: David Fulton.

Pelham, W.E. and Fabiano, G.A. (2008). Evidence-based psychosocial treatments for attention-deficit/hyperactivity disorder. *Journal of Clinical Child and Adolescent Psychology*, 37, 184–214.

Pellegrini, A.D. and Horvatt, M. (1995). A developmental contextual critique of attention deficit hyperactivity disorder (ADHD). *Educational Researcher*, 24, 13–20.

Penso, S. (2002). Pedagogical content knowledge: how do student teachers identify and describe the causes of their pupils' learning difficulties? *Asia-Pacific Journal of Teacher Education*, 30 (1), 25–37. doi:10.1080/13598660120114959

Perie, M., Grigg, M. and Donahue, P. (2005). The nation's report card: reading 2005 (NCES 2006-451). US Department of Education, National Center for Education Statistics. Washington, DC: US Government Printing Office.

Piaget, J. (1970). *The Science of Education and the Psychology of the Child*. New York: Viking Press.

Pianta, R.C. and Caldwell, C. (1990). Stability of externalizing symptoms in five and six year old children and factors related to instability. *Development and Psychopathology*, 2, 247–58.

Piek, J.P. and Edwards, K. (1997). The identification of children with developmental coordination disorder by class and physical education teachers. *British Journal of Educational Psychology*, 67 (Pt 1), 55–67.

Piers, E.V. and Harris, D.B. (2002). *Piers–Harris Children's Self-Concept Scales, Second Edition*. Los Angeles, CA: Western Psychological Services.

Pitcher, T.M., Piek, J.P. and Hay, D.A. (2003). Fine and gross motor ability in males with ADHD. *Developmental Medicine and Child Neurology*, 45, 525–35.

Pollak, D. (ed.) (2009). *Neurodiversity in Higher Education*. Chichester: Wiley.

Portwood, M. (1999). *Developmental Dyspraxia, Identification and Intervention*. London: David Fulton.

Pryce, L. and Gerber, P. (2007). Students with dyslexia in further and higher education: perspectives and perception. In G. Reid, A. Fawcett, F. Manis, L. Siegel (eds), *The Sage Handbook of Dyslexia*. London: Sage.

Pumfrey, P. (2002). Specific developmental dyslexia: 'basics to back' in 2000 and beyond? In J. Wearmouth, J. Soler and G. Reid (eds), *Addressing Difficulties in Literacy Development: Responses at Family, School, Pupil and Teacher Levels*. London: Routledge Falmer.

Rabiner, D. (2013) *Attention Difficulties Update*. Available at: http://www.add.org/ ?page=DiagnosticCriteria

Ramaa, S. (2000). Two decades of research on learning disabilities in India. *Dyslexia*, 6, 268–83.

Ramaa, S. and Gowramma, I.P. (2002). A systematic procedure for identifying and classifying children with dyscalculia among primary school children in India. *Dyslexia*, 8, 67–85.

Ramus, F., Rosen, S., Dakin, S., Day, B.L., Castellote, J.M., White, S. and Frith, U. (2003). Theories of developmental dyslexia: insights from a multiple case study of dyslexic adults. *Brain*, 126, 841–65.

Rasmussen, P. and Gillberg, C. (2000). Natural outcome of ADHD with developmental coordination disorder at age 22 years: a controlled, longitudinal, community-based study. *Journal of the American Academy of Child and Adolescent Psychiatry*, 39, 1424–31.

Reed, T. (2000). The literacy acquisition of Black and Asian 'English-as-an Additional Language' learners. In L. Peer and G. Reid (eds), *Multilingualism, Literacy and Dyslexia*. London: David Fulton.

Reid, G. (1998). An examination of teacher stress within a school organization framework. Unpublished PhD thesis, University of Glasgow, UK.

Reid, G. (2007). *Motivating Learners in the Classroom: Ideas and Strategies*. London: Sage.

Reid, G. (2008). *Motivating Learners in the Classroom*. London: Sage.

Reid, G. (2009). *Dyslexia: A Practitioner's Handbook*. 4th edition. Chichester: Wiley-Blackwell.

Reid, G. (2011) *Dyslexia: A Complete Guide for Parents*. 2nd edition. Chichester: Wiley.

Reid, G. and Green, S. (2009) *Effective Learning: Ideas into Action*. London: Continuum.

Reid, G. and Green, S. (2011) *100+ Ideas for Children with Dyslexia*. London: Continuum.

Reid, G. and Hinton, J. (1999). Teacher work stress and school organisation: a suitable case for inset. *Education Today*, December.

Reid, G. and Kirk, J. (2001) *Dyslexia in Adults: Education and Employment*. Chichester: Wiley.

Reid, G. and Strnadova, I. (2004). The development of teacher and student measures for identifying learning styles. Pilot research study, University of Edinburgh, in collaboration with Charles University, Prague.

Reid, R., Gonzalez, J., Nordness, P.D., Trout, A. and Epstein, M.H. (2004). A meta-analysis of the academic status of students with emotional/ behavioral disturbance. *The Journal of Special Education*, 38, 130–43.

Reynolds, S.L., Johnson, J.D. and Salzman, J.A. (2012). Screening for learning disabilities in adult basic education students. *Journal of Postsecondary Education and Disability*, 25 (2), 179–95.

Rice, M. and Brooks, G. (2004). *Developmental Dyslexia in Adults: A Research Review.* London: NRDC.

Richards, C., Pavri, S., Golez, F., Canges, R. and Murphy, J. (2007). Response to intervention: building the capacity of teachers to serve students with learning difficulties. *Issues in Teacher Education*, 16 (2), 55–64.

Riddick, B. (1996). *Living with Dyslexia: The Social and Emotional Consequences of Specific Learning Difficulties/Disabilities.* London: Routledge.

Riddick, B. (2010). *Living with Dyslexia: The Social and Emotional Consequences of Specific Learning Difficulties/Disabilities.* 2nd edition. London: Routledge.

Riding, R. and Raynor, S. (1998). *Cognitive Styles and Learning Strategies: Understanding Style Difference in Learning and Behaviour.* London: David Fulton.

Ripley, K. (2001). *Inclusion for Children with Dyspraxia/DCD: A Handbook for Teachers.* London: David Fulton.

Ritchey, K.D. (2006). Learning to write: progress-monitoring tools for beginning and at-risk writers. *Teaching Exceptional Children*, 39 (2), 22–6.

Ritchman, N., Stevenson, J. and Graham, P.J. (1982). *Pre-school to School: A Behavioural Study.* London: Academic Press.

Rivard, L.M., Missiuna, C., Hanna, S. and Wishart, L. (2007). Understanding teachers' perceptions of the motor difficulties of children with developmental coordination disorder (DCD). *British Journal of Educational Psychology*, 77 (3), 633–48.

Rose, B., Larkin, D., and Berger, B.G. (1997). Coordination and gender influences on the perceived competence of children. *Adapted Physical Activity Quarterly*, 12, 210–21.

Rose, E. and Larkin, D. (2002). Perceived competence, discrepancy scores, and global self-worth. *Adapted Physical Activity Quarterly*, 19, 127–40.

Rose, J. (2009). *Identifying and Teaching Children and Young People with Dyslexia and Literacy Difficulties.* London: DCSF.

Rosenberg, M. (1989). *Society and the Adolescent Self-Image, Revised edition.* Middletown, CT: Wesleyan University Press. Available through the University of Maryland at: http://www.socy.umd.edu/quick-links/rosenberg-self-esteem-scale

Rosenberg, M.S. and Sindelar, P.T. (1982). Educational assessment using direct, continuous data. In J.T. Neisworth (ed.), *Assessment in Special Education*. Rockville, MD: Aspen.

Rosenthal, J.H. (1973). Self esteem in dyslexic children. *Academic Therapy*, 9, 27–39.

Rourke, B.P. (1989). *Nonverbal Learning Disabilities: The Syndrome and the Model.* New York: Guilford Press.

Rubinsten, O. and Henik, A. (2006). Double dissociation of functions in developmental dyslexia and dyscalculia. *Journal of Educational Psychology*, 98, 854–67.

Rutherford, R.B., Quinn, M.M. and Mathur, S.R. (eds) (2004). *Handbook of Research in Emotional and Behavioural Disorders.* New York: Guilford Press.

Rutter, M. (1995). Relationships between mental disorders in childhood and adulthood. *Acta Psychiatrica Scandinavica*, 91, 73–85.

Sadler, D.R. (2009). Indeterminacy in the use of preset criteria for assessment and grading. *Assessment and Evaluation in Higher Education*, 34 (2), 159–79.

Sadler, D.R. (2010). Beyond feedback: developing student capability in complex appraisal. *Assessment and Evaluation in Higher Education*, 35 (5), 535–50.

Savion-Lemieux, T., Bailey, J.A. and Penhune, V.B. (2009). Developmental contributions to motor sequence learning. *Experimental Brain Research*, 195, 293–306.

Schoemaker, M.M. and Kalverboer, A. (1994). Social and affective problems of children who are clumsy: how early do they begin? *Adapted Physical Activity Quarterly*, 11, 130–40.

Schön, D. (1983) *The Reflective Practitioner: How Professionals Think in Action*. New York: Basic Books.

Schön, D. (1987) *Educating the Reflective Practitioner*. London: Jossey-Bass.

Sela, I., Karni, A. and Maurits, N.M. (2012). Differences in learning volitional (manual) and non-volitional (posture) aspects of a complex motor skill in young adult dyslexic and skilled readers. *Plos ONE*, 7 (9), 1–12. doi:10.1371/journal.pone.0043488

Semrud-Clikeman, M., Bierderman, J., Sprich-Buckminster, S., Lehman, B.K., Faraone, S.V. and Norman, D. (1992). Comorbidity between ADHD and learning disability. *Journal of the American Academy of Child and Adolescent Psychiatry*, 31, 439–48.

Seung-Hee, S. and Meisels, S.J. (2006). The relationship of young children's motor skills to later reading and math achievement. *Merrill-Palmer Quarterly*, 52 (4), 755–78.

Shalev, R.S., Manor, O. and Gross-Tsur, V. (2005). Developmental dyscalculia: a prospective six-year follow-up. *Developmental Medicine and Child Neurology*, 47, 121–5.

Shalev, R.S., Manor, O., Kerem, B., Ayali, M., Bidichi, N., *et al.* (2001). Developmental dyscalculia is a familial learning disability. *Journal of Learning Disabilities*, 34, 59–65.

Siegel, L. (1989). Why we do not need intelligence test scores in the definition and analyses of learning disabilities? *Journal of Learning Disabilities*, 22 (8), 514–18.

Siegel, L. S. (1999). Issues in the definition and diagnosis of learning disabilities: a perspective on Guckenberger v. Boston University. *Journal of Learning Disabilities*, 32, 304–19.

Siegel, L.S. and Lipka, O. (2008). The definition of learning disabilities: who is the individual with learning disabilities? In G. Reid, A. Fawcett, F. Manis and L. Siegel (eds), *The Sage Handbook of Dyslexia*. London: Sage.

Sigurdsson, E., van Os, J. and Fombonne, E. (2002). Are impaired childhood motor skills a risk factor for adolescent anxiety? Results from 1958 UK birth cohort and National Child Development Study. *American Journal of Psychiatry*, 159, 1044–6.

Singleton, C. (Chair) (1999). *Dyslexia in Higher Education: Policy, Provision, and Practice. Report of the National Working Party on Dyslexia in Higher Education*, Hull: University of Hull.

Skinner, R.A. and Piek, J.P. (2001). Psychosocial implications of poor motor coordination in children and adolescents. *Human Movement Science*, 20, 73–94.

Smiley, P.A. and Dweck, C.S. (1994). Individual differences in achievement goals among young children. *Child Development*, 65, 1723–43.

Smith, C., Worsfold, K., Davies, L., Fisher, R. and McPhail, R. (2013). Assessment literacy and student learning: the case for explicitly developing students 'assessment literacy'. *Assessment and Evaluation in Higher Education*, 38 (1), 44–60. doi:10.1080/02602938.2011.598636

Smythe, I. (ed.) (2009). *Employment and Dyslexia Handbook*. Bracknell: BDA.

Smyth, M.M. and Anderson, H.I. (2000). Coping with clumsiness in the school playground: social and physical play in children with coordination impairments. *British Journal of Developmental Psychology*, 18, 389–413.

Snowling, M.J. (2000). *Dyslexia*. 2nd edition. Oxford: Blackwell.

Snowling, M.J. (2012). Editorial: seeking a new characterisation of learning disorders. *Journal of Child Psychology and Psychiatry*, 53 (1), 1–2.

Sorenson, L.G., Forbes, R.W., Bernstein, J.H., Weiler, M.D., Mitchell, W.M. and Waber, D.R. (2003). Psychosocial adjustment over a two-year period in children referred for learning problems: risk, resilience, and adaption. *Learning Disabilities Research and Practice*, 8, 59–65.

St John, S. (2013). Factoring in fine motor: how improving fine motor abilities impacts reading and writing. *Illinois Reading Council Journal*, 41 (4), 16–24.

Stanovich, K.E. (1988). Explaining the differences between the dyslexic and the garden variety poor reader: the phonological-core variable difference model. *Journal of Learning Disabilities*, 21, 590–604.

Stevenson, J., Penningtan, B.F., Gilger, J.W., Defries, J.C. and Gillis, J.J. (1993). Hyperactivity and spelling disability: testing for shared genetic aetiology. *Journal of Child Psychology and Psychiatry*, 34, 1137–52.

Stuck, M. and Gloeckner, N. (2005). Yoga for children in the mirror of the science: working spectrum and practice fields of the training of relaxation with elements of yoga for children. *Early Childhood Development and Care*, 175, 371–7.

Sugden, D.A. (ed.) (2006). *Leeds Consensus Statement: Economic Science Research Council Seminar Series*. Cardiff: Dyscovery Trust.

Sugden, D. and Chambers, M. (eds) (2005). *Children with Developmental Coordination Disorder*. London: Whurr.

Sugden, D.A. and Wright, H.C. (1998). *Motor Coordination Disorders in Children*. Thousand Oaks, CA: Sage.

Sullivan, M. and McGrath, M. (2003). Perinatal morbidity, mild motor delay and later school outcomes. *Developmental Medicine and Child Neurology*, 45, 104–12.

Swanson, E.A. (2008). Observing reading instruction for students with learning disabilities: a synthesis. *Learning Disability Quarterly*, 31 (3), 115–33.

Swanson, H.L. and Malone, S. (1992). Social skills and learning disabilities: a meta-analysis of the literature. *School Psychology Review*, 21, 427–43.

Swanson, J.M., Flockhart, D., Udrea, D., Cantwell, D., Connor, D. and Williams, L. (1995). Clonidine in the treatment of ADHD: questions about safety and efficacy. *Journal of Child and Adolescent Psychopharmacology*, 5, 301–4.

Task Force on Dyslexia (2001). Report. Dublin: Government Publications. Available at: http://www.irlgov.ie/educ/pub.htm

Terras, M.M., Thompson, L.C. and Minnis, H. (2009). Dyslexia and psycho-social functioning: an exploratory study of the role of self-esteem and understanding. *Dyslexia*, 15, 304–27.

The Forensic Echo; Behavioural and Forensic Sciences in the Courts (2000). Dyslexia a disability, but training enough hi-tech employee's discrimination case sputters *The Forensic Echo*, 4 (6), 30 April.

Thomson, M. (2001). *The Psychology of Dyslexia*. London: Whurr.

Torgeson, J.K. (1996). A model of memory from an informational processing perspective: the special case of phonological memory. In G.R. Lyon and N.A. Krasnegor (eds), *Attention, Memory and Executive Function*. Baltimore, MD: Brookes, 157–84.

Torgesen, J.K. (2005). Recent discoveries on remedial interventions for children with dyslexia. In M.J. Snowling and C. Hulme (eds), *The Science of Reading: A Handbook*. Malden, MA: Blackwell.

Torgeson, J.K., Morgan, S.T. and Davis, C. (1992). Effects of two types of phonological training on word learning in kindergarten children. *Journal of Educational Psychology*, 84, 364–70.

Torgeson, J.K., Wagner, R.K. and Rashotte, C.A. (1997). Prevention and remediation of severe reading disabilities: keeping the end in mind. *Scientific Studies of Reading*, 1, 217–34.

Tridas, E.Q. (2007). *From ABC to ADHD: What Parents Should Know About Dyslexia and Attention Problems*. Baltimore, MD: International Dyslexia Association.

Trout, A.L., Nordness, P.D., Pierce, C.D. and Epstein, M.H. (2003). Research on the academic status of children with emotional and behavioral disorders: a review of the literature from 1961 to 2000. *Journal of Emotional and Behavioral Disorders*, 11, 198–210.

Tsang, K., Stagnitti, K. and Lo, S. (2010). Screening children with developmental coordination disorder: the development of the caregiver assessment of movement participation. *Children's Health Care*, 39 (3), 232–48. doi:10.1080/02739615.2010.493772

Tunmer, W.E. and Chapman, J. (1996). A developmental model of dyslexia: can the construct be saved? *Dyslexia*, 2 (3), 179–89.

Turner, M. (1999). *Psychological Assessment of Dyslexia*. London: Whurr.

Turner, M. and Smith, P. (2004). *Dyslexia Screener*. London: Nfer Nelson.

Umbreit, J., Lane, K. and Dejud, C. (2004). Improving classroom behavior by modifying task difficulty: effects of increasing the difficulty of too-easy tasks. *Journal of Positive Behavior Interventions*, 6, 13–20.

US Department of Education (2000). *Learning Disabilities and Spanish-Speaking Adult Populations: The Beginning of a Process*. Washington, DC: Office of Vocational and Adult Education, Division of Adult Education and Literacy.

US Government (2001). Full Funding of the Individuals with Disabilities Education Act, 2001.

Vygotsky, L.S. (1962). *Thought and Language*. Cambridge, MA: MIT Press.

Vygotsky, L.S. (1978). *Mind in Society: The Development of Higher Psychological Processes*. Cambridge MA: Harvard University Press.

Vygotsky, L.S. (1987). *The Collected Works, Vol 1. Problems of General Psychology*. New York: Plenum.

Wagner, D.A. (2000). *EFA 2000 Thematic Study on Literacy and Adult Education: For Presentation at the World Education Forum, Dakar*. Philadelphia: International Literacy Institute.

Wagner, R.K., Torgesen, J.K. and Rashotte, C.A. (1999). *Comprehensive Test of Phonological Processing*. Austin, TX: PRO-Ed.

Walberg, H.J. (1982). Educational productivity: theory, evidence and prospect. *Australian Journal of Education*, 26, 115–22.

Walberg, H.J. (1984). Improving the productivity of America's schools. *Educational Leadership*, 41, 19–30.

Walker, H.M., Ramsey, E. and Gresham, F.M. (2004). *Antisocial Behavior in School: Evidence-based Practices*. 2nd edition. Belmont, CA: Wadsworth.

Wardrop, M. (2014). Personal communication.

Watkinson, E.J., Causgrove Dunn, J., Cavaliere, N., Calzonetti, K., Wilhelm, L. and Dwyer, S. (2001). Engagement in playground activities as a criterion for diagnosing developmental coordination disorder. *Adapted Physical Activity Quarterly*, 18, 18–34.

Wearmouth, J. (2001). Inclusion: changing the variables. In L. Peer and G. Reid (eds), *Dyslexia: Successful Inclusion in the Secondary School*. London: David Fulton.

Wechsler, D. (2005). *Wechsler Individual Achievement Test 2nd Edition (WIAT II)*. London: Psychological Corporation.

Wechsler, D. (2008). *Wechsler Adult Intelligence Scale – Fourth Edition*. San Antonio, TX: Pearson.

Wedell, K. (2000). Interview transcript in *E831 Professional Development for Special Educational Co-ordinators*. Milton Keynes: Open University.

Weedon, C. and Long, R. (2010). *Special Needs Assessment Profile: Behaviour (SNAP-B)*. London: Hodder.

Weedon, C. and Reid, G. (2003, 2005, Version 3 2009). *Special Needs Assessment Profile (SNAP)*. London: Hodder.

Weedon, C., Long, R. and Reid, G. (2012). *SNAP-I™*. London: Hodder.

Weeks, S., Brooks, P. and Everatt, J. (2002). Differences in learning to spell: relationships between cognitive profiles and learning responses to teaching methods. *Educational and Child Psychology*, 19, 47–62.

West, T. (1997) *In the Mind's Eye: Visual Thinkers, Gifted People with Dyslexia and Other Learning Difficulties, Computer Images and the Ironies of Creativity*. New York: Prometheus.

Wiederholt, J.L. and Bryant, B.R. (2001). *Gray Oral Reading Tests – Fourth Edition (GORT-4)*. Austin, TX: Pro-Ed.

Wilkinson, C.Y., Ortiz, A.A., Robertson, P.M. and Kushner, M.I. (2006). English language learners with reading-related LD: linking data from multiple sources to make eligibility determinations. *Journal of Learning Disabilities*, 39 (2), 129–41.

Wilkinson, G.S., and Robertson, G.J. (2006). *Wide Range Achievement Test 4*. Lutz, FL: Psychological Assessment Resources.

Willburger, E., Fussenegger, B., Moll, K., Wood, G. and Landerl, K. (2008). Naming speed in dyslexia and dyscalculia. *Learning and Individual Differences*, 18, 224–36.

Willcutt, E.G. and Pennington, B.F. (2000). Comorbidity of reading disability and attention-deficit/hyperactivity disorder: differences by gender and subtype. *Journal of Learning Disabilities*, 33 (2), 179–91.

Wilson, A.J. and Dehaene, S. (2007). Number sense and developmental dyscalculia. In D. Coch, G. Dawson and K. Fischer (eds), *Human Behavior, Learning and the Developing Brain: Atypical Development*. New York: Guilford Press, 212–38.

Wilson, A.J., Revkin, S.K., Cohen, D., Cohen, L. and Dehaene, S. (2006). An open trial assessment of 'The Number Race', an adaptive computer game for remediation of dyscalculia. *Behavioral and Brain Function*, 30, 2–20.

Wilson, P.H. (2005). Practitioner review: approaches to assessment and treatment of children with DCD: an evaluative review. *Journal of Child Psychology and Psychiatry*, 46, 806–23.

Wilson, P.H. and McKenzie, B.E. (1998). Information processing deficits associated with developmental coordination disorder: a meta-analysis of research findings. *Journal of Child Psychology and Psychiatry*, 39, 829–40.

Wisconsin State Department of Public Instruction, Madison. Div. for Handicapped Children and Pupil Services (1985). *Educational Assessment: A Guide for Teachers of the*

Learning Disabled. Revised edition. Bulletin No. 5232 (Report No. WSDPI–Bull–5232). Madison, WI: Office of Special Education and Rehabilitative Services (ED), Washington, DC (ERIC Document Reproduction Service No. ED 257 225).

Woodcock, R.W. (1998). *Woodcock Reading Mastery Tests: Revised.* Circle Pines, MN: American Guidance Service.

Woodcock, R.W., McGrew, K.S. and Mather, N. (2001). *Woodcock-Johnson III.* Itasca, IL: Riverside.

Woods, K. (2012). The role and perspectives of practitioner educational psychologists. In L. Peer and G. Reid (eds), *Special Educational Needs: A Guide for Inclusive Practice.* London: Sage.

World Health Organization (1992). *The ICD-10 Classification for Mental and Behavioural Disorders: Diagnostic Criteria for Research.* Geneva: WHO.

Wray, D. (1994). *Literacy and Awareness.* London: Hodder & Stoughton.

Wright, J. and Jacobs, B. (2003). Teaching phonological awareness and metacognitive strategies to children with reading difficulties: a comparison of the two instructional methods. *Educational Psychology,* 23 (1), 17–45.

Wright, H. and Sugden, D.E. (1998). School based intervention programme for children with developmental coordination disorder. *European Journal of Physical Education,* 3, 35–50.

Yeo, D. (2003). *Dyslexia, Dyspraxia and Mathematics.* London: Whurr.

Yoshimoto, R. (2005). Gifted dyslexic children: characteristics and curriculum implications. Presentation at the 56th Annual Conference IDA, Denver, 9–12 November.

Young, G. and Browning, J. (2004). Learning disability/dyslexia and employment. In G. Reid and A. Fawcett (eds), *Dyslexia in Context: Research, Policy and Practice.* London: Whurr.

Young, G. (2001). Seven critical needs for successful programs for adults with dyslexia/ LD. Paper presented at the 5th International Conference, BDA, York, April.

Zentall, S.S. (2006). *ADHD and Education: Foundations, Characteristics, Methods, and Collaboration.* Upper Saddle River, NJ: Pearson Merrill Prentice Hall.

Zigmond, N., Vallecorsa, A. and Silverman, R. (1983). *Assessment for Instructional Planning in Special Education.* Englewood Cliffs, NJ: Prentice-Hall.

Zins, J.E. and Ponti, C.R. (1996). The influence of direct training on problem solving on consultee problem clarification skills and attributions. *Remedial and Special Education,* 17, 370–6.

Zoia, S.S., Barnett, A.A., Wilson, P.P. and Hill, E.E. (2006). Developmental coordination disorder: current issues. *Child: Care, Health and Development.* November, 613–18. doi:10.1111/j.1365-2214.2006.00697.x

Index

11 plus examination 103

Abikoff, H.B. 82
achievement, motivation and 109
ADD 6–7 *see also* ADHD
additions 27
ADHD 1, 6–7, 81, 146; co-morbidity
    and 8; learning difficulties and 82–5;
    three presentations of 84–5 *see also*
    behavioural problems
Adult Dyslexia and Skills Development
    Centre 133
Adult Dyslexia for Employment, Practice
    and Training (ADEPT) 127
Ahonen, T.P. 66
Ajchenbaum, M. 101
Al-Azmi, Y. 108
Al-Sharhan, A. 108
American National Assessment of
    Educational Progress 41
Americans with Disabilities Act (1994) 127
Ashton, C. 96–7, 99
assessment: link to intervention 11–13,
    35–6, 37–8; use of term 43–4
assessment framework 36–7, 137–48;
    areas of consideration 145–8; cogni-
    tive measures 138–9; contextualising
    with a view to intervention 141–3;
    problem solving 144–5; processing
    skills 139–41; self-assessment 143–4;
    use of tests 138
Assessment Practicing Certificate 51
assessment process 16–39; considerations
    and strategies for dyslexia 18–19;
    contextualising with view to

intervention 31; diagnostic and
    informal assessment 27–8; five critical
    assumptions 46; formal assessment
    20–7; formative assessment 19–20;
    general points 16–17; information
    processing 35–6; metacognitive
    assessment 32–4; purpose of 17–18;
    reading ability and skills 29–31; skills
    displayed by good readers 34;
    specialist teachers and whole-school
    involvement 29
assisted assessment 32–3
attainments, current level of 10–11
attention deficit disorder *see* ADD
attention deficit hyperactivity disorder
    see ADHD
Attribution Theory 12, 119
autonomous learning 12

Bal-A-Vis-X 71
Bangor Dyslexia Test 154
Barkley, R.A. 7
barriers to learning 9, 28, 111–12;
    anticipating and dealing with 13–14;
    holistic view of 26 tab
Barton, P.E. 42
base line assessment 111
Baxter, J. 95
BDA *Employer's Guide to Dyslexia* 127,
    132, 133
behavioural problems 78–93; assessment
    of 85–7; emotional and behavioural
    disorders (EBD) 80–2; interventions
    87–90; learning difficulties and ADHD
    82–5; presenting difficulties/use of

labels 90–2; relationship with learning problems 78–80
Bell, S. 29, 45
Bender, W.N. 78–9
'big dip' in performance 11
bilateral integration 68–9
Blooms taxonomy 113
Borgelt, C. 102
Braden, J.P. 98
Brain Gym 71
British Dyslexia Association (BDA) 41, 127, 150
Brough, M. 4–5
Brown, A.L. 32
Brown, Gordon 29
Bruininks-Oseretsky Test of Motor Proficiency-2 69
Bryant, B.R. and D.P. 62
Burden, R.L. 108, 110, 124
Butrowsky, I.S. 79, 107
Butterworth, B. 62
Butterworth computerised screener 61, 62

Came, F. 4–5, 29–31, 111, 141
Campione, J.C. 32
Cantell, M. 66
careers advice 134
Carvalho, K. 40
Castro, M. 90
Cermak, S. 67–8
Chambers, M. 71
Chan, L.K.S. 108
Chapman, J. 33
checklists for identifying dyslexia 155–7
Clark, C. 103
clumsy child syndrome see developmental co-ordination disorder
Coffield, F. 122, 123
cognition 35, 36, 139
cognitive behavioural strategies 88
Cognitive Profiling System (CoPS) 153
cognitive skills 9–10
cognitive style 117
Cohen, G. 66
coloured paper 38
co-morbidity 1, 8, 58–9

comprehensive assessment and evaluation 43–4, 46
Comprehensive Mathematical Abilities Test 60
comprehensive schools, establishment of 103
Comprehensive Test of Non-Verbal Ability 131
Comprehensive Test of Phonological Processing 131, 140, 157–8
Concern, Assess, Provide (CAP) It All! 31, 141–2
conduct disorders 81
Conners Scales 87
Conoley, J.C. 102
constructivism 113
consultancy 94, 100–2
control and success 108
Cooper, P. 89
Coopersmith Self-Esteem Inventory 86
creativity 125–6
cultural and linguistic diversity 52
Cunningham, J. 96
curriculum-based assessment 48
curriculum information 37, 146
Curtis, M.J. 100–1
Curtis, P. 40

DCD see developmental co-ordination disorder
decision making 47
decoding/encoding print 18, 138
Dehaene, S. 58, 61
Dennison, P.E. and G.E. 68–9
depression 79, 81
developmental co-ordination disorder (DCD) 65–6, 69–70, 72, 76–7 see also movement
diagnostic and informal assessment 27–8, 50
Diagnostic and Statistical Manual of Mental Disorders 6–7, 49, 65, 83
differences (aspect of assessment) 18, 19, 21
Differential Ability Scale (DAS) 98
differential diagnosis 50
differentiation 13, 38
difficulties/strengths (aspect of assessment) 10, 18

Disabled Students' Allowance (DSA) 128
disclosure of SpLDs to employers 132–3
discrepancies (aspect of assessment) 18, 19, 21, 138
Dunn and Dunn's learning style inventory 118
dynamic tests 32
dyscalculia 1, 4–5 *see also* mathematics learning disability
dysgraphia 1, 3–4
dyslexia 1–2; ADHD and 8; assessment considerations and strategies 18–19; BPS working party report on 94; checklists for identifying 155–7; learning preferences 10; specific characteristics for 17–18
Dyslexia: Assessing and Reporting 112
Dyslexia in Higher Education 127
Dyslexia Screener 153–4
Dyslexia Screening Test 48, 152–3
dyspraxia 2–4, 75 *see also* developmental co-ordination disorder; movement

early intervention, importance of 49–50, 72–3
Educational Act 1944 103
educational psychologists 51, 94–106; consensus and pathways 104–5; consultation 100–2; implications for psychological services and SpLDs 103–4; individual needs 95–6; individual testing v. system based intervention 94–5; problem-based working practices 105; role of 149–50; standardised tests and 99; testing 96–7; working with schools 99–100
Edwards, J. 79
Elbeheri, G. 98, 108
emotional and behavioural disorders (EBD) 80–2; assessment of 85–7
emotional needs *see* motivation; self-esteem
Employment and Dyslexia Handbook 127
empowerment 122; and social model of disability 133
English language learner (ELL) students 52

environmental adaptations 89
environmental experience 9–10
error, systematic and random 46
evaluation 43–4
Everatt, J. 61, 62, 98, 108
explicit teaching 69

Farrell, P. 95
feedback 19–20, 114, 124–5, 131
fine motor skills *see* movement
Fitzgibbon, G. 79, 107
formal assessment 20–7
formative assessment 19–20, 43
Frederickson, N. 95
free writing 37, 146
Fuchs, L.S. and D. 62

General Conceptual Ability Index (GCA) 98
Gerber, P.J. 127
gifted students 125–6
Giorcelli, L.R. 90–1
Given's learning system 118
Goodman, K. 27, 86
Gowramma, I.P. 61
Gray, Colette 74
Gray Oral Reading Test 96, 131, 141, 158
Grissmer, D. 68
Gutkin, T.B. 100–1

handwriting 72, 73–5
Harter's Self-Perception Profile for Children 86–7
Helen Arkell Spelling Test 160
Henderson, A. 4–5
hesitations 28
higher education and the workplace 127–36; careers advice 134; psychological assessment 130–1; stages of support 129–30
Hinton, J. 102
holistic perspective in assessment 9–10
Houston, M. 155
Hughes, L. 89
Humphrey, N. 108
Huntington, D.D. 78–9
hyperactivity 82, 84 *see also* ADHD

impulsivity 6, 82, 84, 86
In the Mind's Eye 13, 147–8
inattention 6, 82, 83–4, 86
inclusion 95, 100, 103
individual testing versus system-based
    intervention 94–5
informal assessment *see* diagnostic and
    informal assessment
informal checklists 21
information: analysis and interpretation 47;
    collection of 46; processing 35–6
input 35
interactive observational style index 22–6,
    118–20
intervention: affect and motivation 115;
    behavioural problems 87–90; contextu-
    alising assessment with view to 31,
    141–3; individual testing versus
    system-based 94–5; link to assessment
    11–13, 35–6, 37–8; numeracy 62–3,
    see also early intervention
Inventory of School Motivation 109
IQ testing 58, 59, 96, 97–9, 139, 149

Jones, A. 112

Kaplan, B.J. 8
Kaufman, A. and M. 97, 98
Kaufman Assessment Battery for Children
    (K-ABC) 98
Kelly's Personal Constuct Theory 110
KeyMath 60
Kindersley, K. 112
Kirk, J. 134
Kiss, G. 66
Kolb's learning style inventories 117–18

labelling 91–2, 112
Landerl, K. 61
Launch into Reading Success 158
Laurillard, D. 62
Lawrence, D. 107
Le Voi, M. 66
learner awareness 13
learning competencies, developing 113
learning experiences 114–15
learning preferences and styles, identifying
    and utilising 13, 117–26; empowerment

122; feedback 124–5; learning process
    124; linking assessment with practice
    121; SpLDs 123–4; style inventories
    117–21; using learning styles 122–3
learnt helplessness 5, 107, 108, 111
Leather, C. 133, 134
Lemer, C. 57
letter formation 72
Lewis, C. 115
Lichtenberger, E.O. 97, 98
Lindquist, M.M. 79
literacy acquisition 9–10
literacy assessment 40–53, 141–2;
    consequences of under-developed
    skills 41–2; cultural and linguistic
    background 52; forms of 48–9;
    guidelines for teachers 50–2;
    importance of assessment for teachers
    43–4; pre-literacy screening 42–3;
    process 44–7; role of in planning for
    learning 49–50
Lloyd, G. 90
locus of control 108
loneliness 81
Lucid Rapid Dyslexia Screening 153

Macintyre, C. 73, 75
Manchester Motor Skills Programme
    (MMSP) 71–2
Margerison, A. 108
Martin, D. and M. 40
mathematics learning disability (MLD)
    54–64; aspects of mathematics learning
    56–7; assessment 59–62; co-morbidity
    and 58–9; features and definitions 54–6;
    intervention 62–3; specific disability
    and sub-types 57–9
maths assessment 147
Maughan, B. 78
Mazzocco, M. 62
McGrath, M. 66
McLean, B. 29, 45
McLoughlin, D. 79, 107, 133, 134
medical model of disability 134, 137
medication-based interventions 87
Medwell, J. 75
metacognitive assessment 12, 32–4
Miles, T.R. 79, 99, 115

miscue analysis 27–8, 37, 141, 146
Moats, L. 40
Montague, M. 90
Montgomery, D. 72
Moody, S. 135–6
Moser Report on 'Adult Literacy' 127
motivation 107–16; and achievement 109; individual perceptions and 109; intervention, affect and 115; self-esteem and 109–11; strategies for maintaining 114
motor skills *see* movement
movement 17, 65–77; assessment of fine motor skills 69–72, 146–7; importance of early intervention 72–3; importance of fine motor skills in learning process 66–7; motor skills and literacy 68–9; relationship between fine movement and literacy 67–8
Movement Assessment Battery for Children-2 69
Mruk, C. 108
Mullins, P.M. 108
multi-sensory learning methods 63, 76

Naglieri, J.A. 97, 98
National Literacy Trust 40
negative emotion 55, 79, 80, 81, 87
Nelson, J.R. 82
non-word recognition tests 37, 145
Norris, C. 90
numeracy 54–64

Oakland, T.D. 96
observational assessment 37, 146
omissions 27
organisation 17, 89–90
orthographic integration 73
Orton-Gillingham approach 5, 125
output 35, 36
overlap and continuum of SpLDs 1, 8–9
over-learning 76, 123

Peer, L. 33
pencil grasp 74, 75
pencil grips 75
Pennington, B.F. 8
phonic approach to maths 5
phonic instruction 10

phonological assessment 20, 37, 146
Phonological Assessment Battery 159–60
phonological awareness 140, 141
phonological memory 140
physical education 75
Piaget, J. 113, 117–18
planning 10–11, 13, 45–6
planning for learning 50, 143
Ponti, C.R. 101
Portwood, M. 2 34
pre-literacy screening 42–3
pre-task discussion 123
pro-active assessment 13–14
problem-based learning approach 105
problem solving 144–5
procedural learning 69
Process Assessment of the Learner 139
processing information 11–13
Professional Association for Teachers of Students with Specific Learning Difficulties (PATOSS) 51, 150
psychological assessment 130–1
psycho-social interventions 87
Pupils Assessment of Learning Styles (PALS) 120–1

questionnaires 34, 109

Ramaa, S. 61
rapid naming 140–1
Raynor, S. 117
reading ability and skills 29–31, 74
reading/listening comprehension test 37, 146
reading trackers 76
reciprocal teaching 32
reflective practitioners 19
Reid, G. 8, 33, 51, 91, 92, 98, 111, 134, 141; assessing reading ability and skills 29–31; learning styles 118–20; organisational approach 102
relaxation 88
repetitions 27, 63, 76
Report of the Task Force on Dyslexia 42–3
reversals 27
rewards 114
Riddick, B. 111–12, 135
Riding, R. 117

Ritchey, K.D. 75
Rosenberg Self-Esteem Scale 86
Rutter, M. 7

'say no to failure' project 111
scanning 68
school action plus 99–100
screening 48–9
screening/baseline assessment 20–1
self-advocacy 135
self-assessment 143–4
self-awareness 107, 108
self-corrections 28
self-efficacy, increasing teachers' 101–2
self-esteem 79–80, 86, 107–16, 135–6;
    barriers to learning 111–12; control
    and success 108; developing learning
    competencies 113; factors accounting
    for low 113; labelling 112; learning
    experiences 114–15; locus of control
    108; motivation and achievement 109;
    and motivational issues 109–11
self-interrogation 34
self-regulated learners 51
self-talk tactics 14, 87
semantic errors 27
SEN Code of Practice 29
sensory assessment 36, 145
Siegel, L. 98, 138
skills displayed by good readers 34
slant boards 75–6
sleep disorder 87
Smyth, M.M. 66, 133
social implications to literacy difficulties 43
social interaction 114
social model of disability 133–4
special educational needs (SEN) 29, 104,
    110
Special Needs Assessment Profile
    (SNAP) 8, 48–9, 110, 154
special schools 95, 96, 100, 103
specialist teachers 29, 150
'specific developmental disorder of
    motor function' *see* developmental
    co-ordination disorder
specific learning difficulties (SpLD):
    increase of students with 41;
    meaning 1; overlap 8–9

speech development 17–18
spelling tests 37, 145–6
static tests 32
Strengths and Difficulties Questionnaire
    (SDQ) 86
Stringer, P. 133, 134
Student Engagement Instrument 109
Student School Engagement Measure 109
substitutions 27
success, control and 108
Sugden, D. 71
suicide 79
Sullivan, M. 66
summary sentences 33
symbolic errors 27
syntactic errors 27
synthesis 47
system-based intervention, individual
    testing versus 94–5
systems consultation 102

tactile modality 10
'Taking Stock' 41
teacher, class/learning support 150
teacher assessment 40–53
technology 133
Test of Early Mathematics Ability 60
Test of Orthographic Competence 145
Test of Phonological Awareness 157
Test of Word Reading Efficiency 158
Test of Written Language 146
tests 138; proper use of 45–6;
    psychometric 96–7, 103, 152; role of
    psychologists and standardised 99;
    standardised 150–2, 157–60
Thompson, R.E. 62, 98
Tunmer, W.E. 33
Turner, M. 98, 100

understanding 11
unexpected underperformance 49
University of Sheffield 128–9
University of Southampton 128
USA, literacy in 41, 42

Vicky, L.K. 79
visual imagery 33
visual perceptual difficulties 75

visual sequencing 68
visual vigilance 68
Vygotsky, L. 113, 124

Wagner, D.A. 43
Warnock Report 103–4
Wearmouth, J. 103
webbing 33
websites and contacts 160–2
Wechsler Adult Intelligence Scale 131, 149
Wechsler Fundamental Adult Skills 131
Wechsler Individual Achievement Test 49, 131, 140, 145, 146, 149, 154–5, 159
Wechsler Individual Intelligence Scale 49
Wechsler Intelligence Scale for Children 97, 98, 138, 139, 149
Weedon, C. 8, 92
weight problems 87
West, T. 147–8
whole-school involvement 29
Wide Range Achievement Test 61
Wide Range Assessment of Memory and Learning 131
Willcutt, E.G. 8

Willows, D.M. 79, 107
Wilson, A.J. 58, 62
Woodcock Johnson Battery of Measures 61
Woodcock Johnson Psycho-Educational Battery 49, 97
Woodcock Reading Mastery Tests 141
Woods, K. 94, 95
Word Identification and Spelling Test 159
word recognition tests 36, 145
workplace 131–6; careers advice 134; disclosure 132–3; self-advocacy 135; self-esteem 135–6; technology 133
Wray, D. 34, 75
Wright, H. 71
writing paper 76
writing skills *see* handwriting

Yoshimoto, R. 125–6
Young, G. 127
Young, V. 79, 107

Zins, J.E. 101